THE HYPOCHONDRIACS

T0058045

THE
HYPOCHONDRIACS

Nine Tormented Lives

BRIAN DILLON

FARRAR, STRAUS AND GIROUX

NEW YORK

To Felicity Dunworth

Farrar, Straus and Giroux
18 West 18th Street, New York 10011

Originally published in 2009 by Penguin Ireland, Great Britain, as *Tormented Hope:
Nine Hypochondriac Lives*
Published in the United States by Faber and Faber, Inc.
First American edition, 2010

Library of Congress Cataloging-in-Publication Data

Dillon, Brian, 1969–
    The hypochondriacs : nine tormented lives / Brian Dillon. — 1st
American ed.
        p ; cm.
    British ed. published under the title: Tormented hope : nine hypochondriac
lives / Brian Dillon. Dublin, Ireland : Penguin Ireland, 2009.
    Includes bibliographical references.
    ISBN: 978-0-86547-946-3 ISBN: 0-86547-946-1
    1. Hypochondria—Biography.   2. Hypochondria—Popular works.
I. Dillon, Brian, 1969– Tormented hope.   II. Title.
    [DNLM: 1. Hypochondriasis—Biography.   2. Famous Persons—
Biography. WM 178 D579h 2010]

RC552.H8D55 2010
616.85'25—dc22

2009040424

www.fsgbooks.com

'My body is that part of the world which my thoughts are able to change.'

Georg Christoph Lichtenberg, *The Waste Books*

Contents

THE HYPOCHONDRIACS

Introduction: A History of Hypochondria

You were well one minute ago, and this minute you are unwell. Your symptoms came on, and with them your fear, in a stray moment of solitude. Perhaps you and your body were alone in the bathroom, with leisure to examine your naked flesh, time enough for your fingers to find a lump where no lump should be, for the unsteamed mirror to reveal a rash or for your hand to pause as you reached for the soap, an obscure twinge dragging at your innards. Or perhaps it happened at night, while you were alone, or as your lover slumbered: on the verge of sleep a sudden sensation as of something shifting inside, a slow waking in the dark as a dull ache intruded on your dreams, or towards dawn a more diffuse feeling that mortality was near. Maybe it was broad daylight, in the midst of the diurnal round – a conversation half-overheard, concerning a colleague's recent diagnosis; a radio interview with the victim of a rare and debilitating disease; a newspaper article, skimmed during the dead time of your daily commute, in which you recognized your own poor diet and sedentary habits.

However the suspicion may have insinuated itself, in the days that follow it seems to sharpen in your mind. Your symptoms appear to point to a specific illness: it is the disease, perhaps, that you have feared all your life, or in recent years; the disease of which a parent died. Your first fears begin to condense into certainties, no less fearful. You feel compelled to research your disease. Unthinking, or thinking too far ahead, you type both your symptoms and the name of the illness of which you are afraid into a search engine, and inevitably there are hundreds of hits. You snatch what time you can to trawl through the relevant websites; if your lifestyle allows, many hours and even whole days can vanish like this. Everything starts to encircle your symptoms. At times, you succeed in distracting yourself: the pain subsides, the blemish or lump seems less massive than it did the day before. But your thoughts lack the lightness or velocity to escape the gravitational pull of your fear.

The alteration is as yet invisible to those around you, but your life has been changed for good. You begin secretly to date everything in relation to the moment you first realized that something was wrong. Your previous existence now looks idyllic and illusive, shadowed in retrospect by what was to come. But although everything has changed it is all, also, quite familiar. You have been here before, felt the same sickening plummet of discovery, the same slow creep of horror as the sinister truth slithered into view. And yet this time, you feel certain, is different. This time, the evidence is irrefutable.

Why then this strange pang of hope as at last, after days, weeks or perhaps months of solitary fretting, you find yourself in a physician's waiting room, rehearsing the story of your symptoms, preparing to expose your body to the uncompromising gaze and implacable verdict of the professional? In the consulting room, your face flushed and your heart racing – the blood-pressure test will be skewed by your anxiety – you watch the doctor heft your file onto the desk, or scroll through your notes on-screen, and you begin, like a penitent in the close precincts of the confessional, to recite your symptoms. The problem, let us say, is with your neck. Or perhaps – because at this point the plot may ramify in countless directions, like a bacterium flourishing beneath a microscope – it is your chest that troubles you, or your abdomen. There may be stiffness of the joints, aches in the muscles, unexplained tingling at the extremities. The guts are very likely to be affected: you might report bouts of indigestion, attacks of wind, discomfort on moving the bowels. It is possible that the skin has erupted, or begun to itch or sting even though no lesion or rash is visible. The heart seems to beat, you report, with alarming force or rapidity; the breath is shallow or painful. Your head hurts all the time, or only intermittently, in different places each time, or in the same place, insistently. Curiously, no matter the symptoms with which you present – and you may or may not have noticed this fact yourself – they seem clustered on the left side of your body. The pain, you admit in answer to the doctor's question, is not severe, nor are you sure that it is getting any worse. But it concerns you, you say, understating now the terror that has brought you here, and you thought it was important to have it checked out.

Time – the time spent being afraid and the time you imagine that you have left – has seemed to contract to this brief interlude: the crucial encounter between doctor and patient. It seems to you now, however, as the physician pauses to consider what you have just described, and glances again at your notes before proceeding to the physical examination, that time has become elastic once more, and stretches around you in the consulting room, filled with uncertainty.

You might reflect, in the interval before the doctor speaks or lays hands on your trembling person, that you have neglected to mention your most striking symptom. It is this: in the days since you first suspected your body of its treachery, you have started to live at the edge of your own life, to withdraw into a state of mind at once alert and somnolent. You listen constantly, in a kind of trance, for communications from your body; it is as if you have become a medium, and your organs a company of fretful ghosts, whispering their messages from the other side. In your daily life, loved ones, friends and colleagues have started to notice that you are hardly there. Occasional, occulted signals come through to them to the effect that you are unwell, but the news, you have remarked, seems hardly to have registered in their minds. It is they who seem to you distracted, unperturbed by the mounting evidence of your ill health. You have long been accustomed to trying to control your body, to neutralize in advance its unpredictable, unruly nature. Now it seems that you have to take charge of other people too: to persuade them, friends and family alike, that there is something amiss. You can feel all certainty slipping away as the face of your doctor, like the face of the last friend or loved one you told of your fear, fails to set itself in an expression of unalloyed assurance. It has seemed to you lately that nobody has been taking you or your symptoms seriously; now it appears that nobody, not even your doctor (who knows you so well), will give you the straight answer you so anxiously need.

*

What does this patient – whom we are about to call a hypochondriac, with all that the word implies about the reality of his or her symptoms and the kind of person who might report them – look like to the physician, or sound like to the family members, friends, employers and colleagues who have been hearing for some time now the same litany of pain or discomfort, the same fears canvassed, the same self-absorption tediously expressed? This is not a question that troubles the hypochondriac in the grip of his or her fear. I did not myself think to ask it in late adolescence or in my twenties, when in the aftermath of my parents' early deaths I became convinced that I would be the next to die, and began to interpret every stray discomfort as a sign of the dread disease that would take me away. (It comes as no surprise now to discover in the literature on hypochondria that a child who grows up in close proximity to illness and death is considerably more likely to develop hypochondriacal tendencies as a young adult.) Nor, still, does the question occur to me on those occasions – they are becoming rarer as I get older, though I suppose middle age must soon bring some worries that will linger – when fatigue or stress or a long period of unproductive work seems to bring on the old fears, and I slip too easily into the habits of thought, apprehension and assurance-seeking described above. It is only later, when the doctor's appointments are over, the dull recital of my symptoms at an end and the diagnosis again a minor one, that I wonder how I must have seemed to those around me. The answer is probably not one that I would really care to hear.

The hypochondriac is well known, anecdotally, to all of us. (This was confirmed each time I mentioned I was writing a book about hypochondria: *we all know at least one*.) As a character type, he or she is pretty disreputable, a malingering drain on one's capacity for patience and empathy, at worst a parasite on scarce healthcare resources. Hypochondriacs are almost always other people: few of us care to admit to the levels of delusion and self-regard that we deprecate in the personality of the hypochondriac. We behave in this regard as if the boundary between sensible vigilance or precaution and pathological preoccupation or fear were perfectly clear, when it is not. The hypochondriac, according to the dominant definitions of a state of mind long known as hypochondriasis and more recently renamed 'health anxiety', is that person who suspects that an organic disease is present in his or her body – occasionally, the suspicion concerns mental illness, or even hypochondria itself – when there is no medical evidence to support that opinion. More than this, the hypochondriac will have established a pattern of such suspicions, almost a career. He or she has in common with the clown (for the hypochondriac is also a figure of fun) the tendency to repeat the same behaviour, to make the same mistakes, in the face of all indications that one ought to desist. The patient, who in time is not merely suspicious but finally convinced that he or she is ill, will not respond to professional reassurance.

*

There are of course many other quirks of the hypochondriac character, some of which may suggest why the patient is so exasperating to the medical profession, while others begin to point to possible origins of the hypochondriacal affliction. (As we shall see, hypochondria is now, and has been for several centuries, a diagnosis in itself.) It seems to the doctor, for example, that the patient

has simply exaggerated certain normal bodily sensations: the beat-
ing of the heart, especially as it obtrudes with one's head on a pil-
low in the quiet of the night; the peristaltic advance of food down
the gullet, the rumblings of the stomach or the movement of gas in
the bowels; perfectly ordinary feelings of giddiness, fatigue or
weakness. The hypochondriac imagines that good health is a neutral condition in which not only does nothing untoward occur
within or on the surface of the body, but nothing happens to the
body at all. (There is also a species of hypochondria that consists in
imagining that one's body is a void, evacuated by disease or supernatural forces.) The patient may have misinterpreted a certain cor-
pus of medical knowledge, official statistics or media conjecture,
thus greatly inflating a tiny risk. He or she might have problems
that are real enough, either physical or psychological, which the
patient cannot or will not address, and has perceived different
symptoms instead. Or it may be, in a tendency that seems calcu-
lated to infuriate medical professionals, that the patient, while
declaring on the one hand an excessive concern with one set of
possible symptoms, adopts a reckless attitude in other respects:
diet, for example, or smoking and drinking habits. Hypochondriacs are no more likely than the rest of the population to look after
themselves, avoid unnecessary risks or even heed a physician's
advice. And in a further twist, it can look to the professional as
though the hypochondriac does not actually seek medical advice or
treatment, or even reassurance that he or she is well, but rather an
unassailable certainty. It may even appear that for the hypochondriac the solidity of a real disease is preferable to the fog of optimism and uncertainty that passes for most of us, most of the time,
as good health.

   The causes of these attitudes and actions are unclear, and this
book does not pretend to answer definitively the question of what
makes a hypochondriac. Among the theories advanced in the last
quarter of a century is that hypochondriasis exists on a continuum

with others of what are known as the anxiety disorders. It has much in common – obsession, withdrawal, repetition, a refusal to accept 'rational' answers to the perceived predicament – with such illnesses as anorexia, body dysmorphic disorder, obsessive-compulsive disorder and generalized anxiety disorder. Hypochondriacs may respond well to a form of psychotherapy, cognitive-behavioural therapy, that seeks to set right erroneous patterns of thought and action rather than address any deeply troubling life narrative or unconscious conflict. Hypochondriasis appears also to ease under a regime of antidepressant medication. According to this way of thinking, it is anxiety itself that is at issue, and the hypochondriac's fear is fundamentally a mistake, an error in his or her apprehension of the body and its relation to the world. The logic seems self-evident: to remove the patient's fear, to allow him or her to function untroubled by doubt, is surely to have cured that person's hypochondria. But this is also prematurely to consign the hypochondriac, and what the hypochondriac knows, or thinks that he or she knows, to the realm of the unwell, when the question that the hypochondriac raises is precisely this: how do we know, any of us, when we are sick and when we are well?

A parade of other questions follows in the wake of this one. How is it possible to know our bodies, in isolation from our experience of our bodies? How can we be sure of such knowledge when the body seems to change from day to day, from hour to hour? What would be a rational attitude towards, or a practical level of alertness to, those changes? Is physical health in fact a matter of knowing our bodies, or of ignoring them and remaining oblivious to the exact processes at work inside us? More hauntingly: how can we reflect upon the prospect of our own deaths, in the way that we surely must as life advances, and at the same time avoid the fear that seizes and cripples the hypochondriac? How far into our daily lives, and into our dealings with each other, ought we to allow the fact or the fear of death to intrude? Are we healthier

people, or better people, or more creative people, for acknowledging it, or for ignoring it?

*

We are not the first to ask such questions. The origins of our modern
notion of hypochondria may be found in two strands of historical
thought and feeling. The first is the universal fear of illness and death.
A number of writers in the sixteenth and seventeenth centuries
examined that fear in a particularly astute fashion, seeing it in relation to religious faith, current medical knowledge and the fearful
capacities of the human imagination. In his essay 'On the Power of
the Imagination', the French aristocrat Michel de Montaigne
describes his own susceptibility to the sight of illness, and the crisis
it caused in his experience of his body:

I am one of those by whom the powerful blows of the imagination are felt
most strongly. Everyone is hit by it, but some are bowled over. It cuts a
deep impression into me: my skill consists in avoiding it not resisting it. I
would rather live among people who are healthy and cheerful: the sight of
another man's suffering produces physical suffering in me, and my own
sensitivity has often misappropriated the feelings of a third party. A persistent cougher tickles my lungs and my throat.

The suggestibility of the mind and body, Montaigne writes, is well
established in history and in his own experience. He has heard, for
example, of a man who was to be hanged and who, although par-
doned at the last minute, expired upon the scaffold, 'struck by his
imagination alone'. He has read of an Italian king who, having
attended a display of bull baiting, dreamed all night of horns on his
head: 'thereupon horns grew on his forehead by the sheer power
of his imagination'. And Montaigne himself, at Vitry in France,
met a man called Germane who until the age of twenty-two had
been a woman named Marie: 'He said that he had been straining to
jump when his male organs suddenly appeared.' Such spontaneous

transformations of the human body, writes Montaigne, are also likely to affect those who tempt fate by feigning to be ill. In his essay 'On Not Pretending to be Ill', he tells admonitory tales of persons rendered actually blind, lame or hunchbacked by their false afflictions. The power of imagination causes disease and is in itself a kind of pathology. But the problem of the imagination cannot simply be solved by adopting a more realistic attitude to one's own body: the body itself, it seems, is capable of ruses and feints, so that we can never be sure that what we see in it, or feel in ourselves, is real.

This theme of the body's duplicity is among the subjects touched on by the poet John Donne in his extraordinary book *Devotions upon Emergent Occasions*, of 1624. Written while Donne was dangerously ill with a 'relapsing fever' (possibly typhus), *Devotions* tracks the disease from its onset, 'the first grudging of the sicknesse', through its crises and remissions, towards the author's eventual recovery. It is in one sense a literally devotional work, punctuated by prayers to the divinity who may well be about to take Donne's life. It is also a gruesomely eloquent account of the patient's mental processes as the disease progresses, of his mind's oscillation between hope and fear. But the poet is not alone in his anxieties: his mental and moral state depends also on his observation of his doctors. Here is Donne, in the sixth of the *Devotions*:

I observe the Phisician, with the same diligence, as hee the *disease*; I see he *feares*, and I feare with him: I overtake him, I overrun him in his feare, and I go the faster, because he makes his pace slow; I feare the more, because he disguises his fear, and I see it with the more sharpnesse, because hee would not have me see it. He knows that his *feare* shall not disorder the practise, and exercise of his *Art*, but he knows that my *fear* may disorder the effect and working of his practise. As the ill affections of the *spleene*, complicate, and mingle themselves with every infirmitie of the body, so doth *feare* insinuat itself in every *action*, or *passion* of the *mind*; and as *wind* in the body will counterfet any disease, and seem the *Stone*, and seem the *Gout*, so *feare* will counterfet any disease of the *Mind*.

Disease, says Donne elsewhere in the *Devotions*, establishes a kingdom in the body, and conceals there its '*secrets of State*, by which it will proceed, and not be bound to declare them'. It is not only the illness, however, that deceives us: the mind, faced with the prospect of illness, will play tricks on itself and on those around us. Nothing in the sick room is what it seems; all is potentially a symbol or allegory for something else.

The second tradition of thinking and writing about illness and fear is born of the term itself: 'hypochondria' is an ancient name for a malady that has as just one of its symptoms the morbid fear of illness and death, but which is also conceived as an organic disease in itself. The seventeenth century had inherited the concept of hypochondriasis from classical physicians and philosophers. The *hypochondrium* – the word is still familiar to contemporary doctors – was the region of the abdomen directly under the ribcage: the Hippocratic writings, for example, refer to a woman 'suffering in her right hypochondrium'. For Diocles of Carystus, writing around 350 BC, hypochondriacal disorders were those of the digestive system. For Plato, in the *Timaeus*, the hypochondrium was 'that part of the soul which desires meats and drinks and the other things of which it has need by reason of the bodily nature' – this the gods 'placed between the midriff and the boundary of the navel . . . and there they bound it like a wild animal which was chained up with man'. In subsequent conceptions of the disorder, hypochondria is associated with the adjacent affliction of melancholia, and exhibits a confusing ambiguity. According to Johannes Crato, writing in the late sixteenth century, 'In this hypochondriacal or flatuous melancholy, the symptoms are so ambiguous that the most well-trained physicians cannot identify the part involved.' The writers of the seventeenth century thus harked back to an antique ailment that took its name from a specific part of the body but seemed to be present in all its organs or members, either intermittently or at once.

The author who best expresses the obscure and vagrant nature of early-modern hypochondria is Robert Burton, whose compendious and digressive (not to say wildly eccentric and entertaining) *Anatomy of Melancholy* was first published in 1621. The book's frontispiece illustrates the several species of melancholic: Solitudo, Inamorato, Superstitiosus, Maniacus and Hypochondriacus. The last type, pictured and personified languishing in fur-lined robes, rests his troubled head upon his left hand – the pose can be seen too in Albrecht Dürer's more famous engraving, *Melencolia I* – and stares vacantly at medicine bottles and apothecary's prescriptions scattered on the floor in front of him. Burton's introductory poem, detailing 'The Argument of the Frontispiece', describes the character thus:

> Hypochondriacus leans on his arm,
> Wind in his side doth him much harm,
> And troubles him full sore, God knows,
> Much pain he hath and many woes.
> About him pots and glasses lie,
> Newly bought from 's apothecary.
> This Saturn's aspects signify,
> You see them portray'd in the sky.

The saturnine hypochondriac, above whom astrological symbols hover, is the subject of a short section in the main body of Burton's book. Between his descriptions of melancholy as it affects the head and melancholy 'abounding in the whole Body', the author lists the 'Symptoms of Windy Hypochondriacal Melancholy', which include:

Sharp belchings, fulsome crudities, heat in the bowels, wind and rumbling in the guts, vehement gripings, pain in the belly and stomach sometimes after meat that is hard of concoction, much watering of the stomach, and

moist spittle, cold sweat . . . cold joints . . . midriff and bowels are pulled
up, the veins about their eyes look red, and swell from vapours and wind
. . . their ears sing now and then, vertigo and giddiness come by fits, turbulent dreams, dryness, leanness . . . grief in the mouth of the stomach, which
maketh the patient think his heart itself acheth.

Curiously, Burton seems to contradict himself on the subject
of fear and sorrow, asserting at first that while common among
hypochondriacs they are not essential to a diagnosis of windy
melancholy, but subsequently claiming that these are the main
precipitating factors. To fear and sorrow may be added, he says,
florid delusions, according to which the patient imagines himself
physically transformed or even invaded by some implausible parasite, such as a serpent or a frog.

   Like others of his century, Burton thought of hypochondria as
primarily a physical disease, but one that included symptoms we
would characterize today as psychological: fear, sorrow and the
conviction that one's body had been altered in some fundamental
way not explicable in terms of the physical symptoms. Thomas
Willis, for example, in *The London Practise of Physick*, published in
1685, combines physical and mental symptoms:

The diseased are wont to complain of a trembling and palpitation of the
heart, with a mighty oppression of the same, also frequent failings of the
spirits, a danger of swooning come upon them, that the diseased always think
death at hand . . . fluctuations of thoughts, inconstancy of mind, a disturbed
fancy, a dread and suspicion of everything . . . an imaginary being affected
with diseases of which they are free and many other distractions of the spirit
. . . wandering pains, also cramps and numbness with a sense of formication
seize likewise all the outward parts: night sweats, flushing of blood.

It was not until the nineteenth century that the imaginative strain in
hypochondria began to dominate, and even then what physicians

and patients intended by the term was a more wide-ranging diagnosis than we might at first recognize in it today. Our own health anxieties are the heirs of both the religious or metaphysical reflections of Montaigne and Donne, and the pathologies described by Burton, or by the seventeenth-century physician Thomas Sydenham, who conceived of hypochondria 'resembling most of the distempers wherewith mankind are afflicted'.

The history of hypochondria – the history, that is, of what was meant by the word and of what we mean by it today – is the history, then, of a 'real' disease which has lost most of its symptoms over the course of several centuries, and also of a prodigious variety of imaginary disease that has come to be recognized once more, in our century, as a pathology in itself, a disorder with identifiable symptoms and some possible cures. The chronology is confusing, the vocabulary ambiguous and palimpsestic, the illness at times as chimerical as the horrors imagined by its victims. But the stakes are clear: to think about hypochondria is to think about the nature of sickness in a fundamental sense, to ask what can legitimately be called a disease and what cannot, to inquire what the proper attitude is to a body that we have learned, since the time of Burton and Donne, to investigate and treat with infinitely greater subtlety, but about which we are perhaps no more eloquent, no happier in our apprehensions of its potential failings and no better equipped to face its eventual extinction. The history of hypochondria is an X-ray of the more solid and familiar history of medicine: it reveals the underlying structure of our hopes and fears about our bodies.

*

This book is not a history of hypochondria, but a history of hypochondriacs. Each of its nine chapters attempts to write the biography of a body, where 'biography' is to be understood in its etymological sense: that is, as a literal writing of life itself (*bios* in the original Greek). I have tried, so far as possible, to stay close to the body in question, be it the actual and ailing body or the imagined, fantastical

body conjured out of delusion or terror. For narrative purposes I
have relied where practicable on letters, diaries, autobiographies,
interviews and the testimony of intimate witnesses to the individual's
ailing life. In certain cases – Charlotte Brontë is the clearest instance,
Andy Warhol another – the subject's work seems to provide as much
insight into his or her case, and beyond, than journals or correspondence. Brontë's hypochondria is displaced, for example, onto the
fictional characters of Lucy Snowe, William Crimsworth and Jane
Eyre; Warhol turns out to know more about fear, fantasy and the
human body in his films than he does in his voluminous diary. For
the most part, however, it is the life that dominates, or rather that
sliver of the life that separates hope and fear. *Bios*, of course, is not
only the private property of an embodied individual. Our physical
being – and with it our ailments, real and imaginary – is invigilated
by several authorities in the course of our lives, among them family,
schools, the medical profession, and the whole complex of opinion
and dogma according to which we comport ourselves, display or conceal our bodies, and submit them to the care and keen attention of
parents, lovers or physicians. Imaginary illness is no less an aspect of
this 'biopolitical' sphere – it too is subject to professional protocols
and public attitudes, so that we can, and must, speak of a culture of
hypochondria. Among the lessons one learns in studying the history
of that culture is that every historical era sees itself as especially or
even uniquely hypochondriacal. In the eighteenth century, hypochondria was thought to derive from an excess of modern luxuries; in
the twenty-first, from too much leisure and easy access to medical
knowledge, or pseudo-knowledge.

   I have chosen the nine hypochondriac lives that follow according
to no exact criteria: for the most part, their stories simply seemed
the most compelling and, in terms of how and what I could write
about them, the most capacious. Sympathy has certainly played a
role: I have not written about anybody with whom I did not feel
that I, or the reader, could identify. (In fact, I rejected one subject,

long planned for inclusion, because I could not find a way to get past the sanitary cordon of his personality, symptoms and behaviour to the core of his experience.) These caveats aside, it seems to me now that the lives in question each exemplify a specific aspect of the hypochondriacal character, or a stage in the centuries-long development of that diagnosis. There are those, like Warhol, who were terrified by disease and by the idea of disease; those, like Glenn Gould, who were more inquisitive about the diseases they feared than merely anxious. Others were clearly sick with a real disease, such as Marcel Proust and his asthma, or suffered real physical symptoms for which there was no ready explanation (Charles Darwin and Florence Nightingale), but these may be counted among the hypochondriacal by virtue of their stage-managing the drama of the sickroom to their own (perhaps unconscious) ends. Still others were simply delusional – Daniel Paul Schreber's hypochondria consisted in gruesome and elaborate beliefs concerning his body's colonization and transformation at the hands of God and his doctors alike. Charlotte Brontë and James Boswell, who self-diagnosed their hypochondria, signalled by the word something closer to what we might today call depression, or a nervous breakdown. All of these categories overlap at times, though Alice James surely languishes apart, the sole example of a curious sort of malingerer: the cheerful, ironic hypochondriac who positively welcomes the onset of an authentic and lethal disease. These, then, are the nine characters; many others, some of whom are mentioned in the pages that follow, could have been written into the story, among them Samuel Johnson, George Eliot, Thomas and Jane Carlyle, Edgar Allan Poe, Charles Dickens, Fyodor Dostoevsky, Emily Dickinson, Howard Hughes, James Joyce and Samuel Beckett.

The reader may note that even the list of rejected hypochondriacs is composed almost solely of writers. While there are no doubt many instances of hypochondriacal monarchs, politicians and tycoons, it is writers and artists who dominate the book, and those not primarily known as literary figures (Darwin, Nightingale, James, Gould, Warhol) were at the same time prodigious writers. In part, it is because they have left us written records of their symptoms, their daily regimens and their apprehensions of the worst that we are able to assert that they were hypochondriacs at all. But the more ambitious, if perilous, conjecture might be that there is in each case an obvious and intimate link between their health anxieties and their creative or intellectual labours. This is both easy to claim and difficult to prove, and one risks a certain cliché regarding the artistic or inventive type. The Romantic notion of the artist as melancholic, neurasthenic or hysterical may no longer have the resonance or persuasiveness it once had, but the image persists and with it the danger of reducing art and innovation to a matter of difference, pathology or even madness. Perhaps we ought better say, with the philosopher Gilles Deleuze, that the artist is he or she who has an especially fine feeling for the bodily proximity of thought, imagination, terror and catastrophe. That is not to say, argues Deleuze, 'that great authors, great artists, are all ill, however sublimely, or that one's looking for a sign of neurosis or psychosis like a secret in their work, the hidden code of their work. They're not ill; on the contrary, they're a rather special kind of doctor.' For the subjects of this book, hypochondria was both an illness and a cure: the catalyst or condition that allowed the artist or thinker to function, that provided in some cases a subject matter, in some an excuse for erratic behaviour, in others the founding condition by which time and space could be set aside for work. Hypochondria, in other words, was a kind of calling, almost a vocation, that structured a life, or the productive portion of a life. At once crippled and cosseted by fear, the hypochondriac suffered in order to work, to write or to discover in solitude.

In this regard, and in many more specific senses that make up the texture of this book, hypochondria has about it something of the tragicomic. The malingerer, the crock, the hopeless case, the legions of the 'worried well': these are characters whom, by definition, it is sometimes hard to take seriously. Hence the rich history, from Molière's *Le Malade imaginaire* to the films and public persona of Woody Allen, of the hypochondriac as comic dupe of medical quackery or anxious existential somatizer. For sure, there are moments of absurdity in the lives to which I have tried to do justice: Darwin's sedulous records of his own flatulence, the agonizingly slow slapstick of Proust's bedridden breakfast routine, Warhol's recourse to crystal healing and cosmetic treatments. But just as I have endeavoured to present the medical lore of each historical period with a seriousness it may no longer seem to deserve, so I have tried to let those absurdities stand as evidence of real pain, authentic anxieties, sincere attempts on the part of these individuals to cure themselves or to coax the world into accepting and accommodating their imaginary ailments. Few of us will escape, in the course of our lives, the same suspicions, the same shock as worrisome symptoms manifest themselves, the same passive (or passive-aggressive) entrusting of ourselves to an expertise that seems to us only marginally more reassuring than the superstitions of the past. Hypochondria makes dupes of us all, because life, or rather death, will have the last laugh. In the physician's waiting room, still unsure whether the symptoms that have lately troubled us are real or imaginary, we might well console ourselves with the knowledge of who has been there before us, and with the lesson, well known to John Donne, with which they came away:

> There is no health. Physicians say that we,
> At best, enjoy but a neutrality,
> And can there be worse sickness than to know
> That we are never well, nor can be so.

1. James Boswell's English Malady

'He is a convalescent whom the last relapse will infallibly destroy.'

Jean-Jacques Rousseau, *Correspondence générale de J.-J. Rousseau*

On Saturday, the 6th of August 1763, James Boswell, who was then two months short of his twenty-third birthday, was received on board the *Prince of Wales* packet-boat at Harwich, on the coast of Essex. The ship was bound for the Dutch port of Helvoetsluys; from there, the young man was to travel north to Leyden, and thence east to the university town of Utrecht where, at the insistence of his father, Lord Auchinleck, he was to study law. Boswell's hopeful mood as he set out – a promised tour of Paris and the German courts lay at the end of his stay in Holland – was shadowed by a sense that this term of study in a less than teeming town was a parental punishment for his recent dissolution in London. His first flight from his native Scotland had been alarming enough, as far as his father was concerned: the eighteen-year-old had quickly converted to Catholicism and at the same time, as if testing the strength of his new piety, acquired a taste for bought sex that he would pursue, for much of his life, with the force of a vocation. Hastily recalled to Scotland by his father, he languished for two years, studying desultorily and dreaming of escape. In the second year, he fathered an illegitimate son whom he never saw.

His second adventure in the capital commenced in November 1762. Lord Auchinleck had grudgingly agreed to his son's returning to London to seek a commission in His Majesty's Foot Guards, a scheme that came to nothing. Instead, as we know from his journals,

Boswell further indulged his physical appetites but also began, under the tutelage of Samuel Johnson, whom he first met in May 1763, to picture for himself a more ordered and serene existence. He determined on a life of study, and of writing, that would keep at bay both carnal chaos and the periodic melancholy that had already threatened him in the months since his arrival in London. He felt, in the days before his departure, that his London life, with its diverting extremes of physical pleasure and intellectual play, but its prospects too for moral improvement, was about to be snatched away. On the first of the month, trying to reconcile himself to his father's plan, he wrote in his journal: 'Resolve now study in earnest. Consider you're not to be so much a student as a traveller. Be a liberal student. Learn to be reserved. Keep your melancholy to yourself, and you'll easily conceal your joy.'

Dining at the Turk's Head with Johnson two days earlier, Boswell had been unable to hide the nostalgia that had seized him even before leaving England, and he was flattered and consoled to discover that his famous friend planned to see him off at Harwich. But seated again at the same establishment on the 3rd of August, suffering a feverish headache and feeling heavy from a bout of insomnia the night before, he was scarcely able to listen as Johnson discoursed at length upon the Convocation of the Church of England. The following day, Boswell's last in London, his mind shrank, agitated, gloomy and dejected, from the prospect of leaving the city, and he had to remind himself, not for the first or the last time, to be manly, steady and dignified, to commit himself to the care of his merciful Creator.

It was in this confused state that he travelled by coach with Johnson to Harwich the next day. They stayed overnight at Colchester, where the elder man, observing a moth burn itself to death as it fluttered about a candle flame, remarked: 'That creature was its own tormenter, and I believe its name was Boswell.' The human subject of this comparison does not record his own response in *The Life of Samuel Johnson*, but moves the scene at once to Harwich, where,

exploring the town, the pair had one of the most celebrated exchanges
in English literature. On leaving the local church, they began to dis-
pute about George Berkeley's philosophical doctrine concerning the
reality of matter, and in particular his positing its non-existence in the
absence of our sensing it. The notion, said Boswell, was impossible to
refute; Johnson replied by suddenly kicking a large stone ('till he
rebounded from it', notes his companion) and announcing: 'I refute
it *thus*.' It was soon time for Boswell to embark, and we may wonder
whether it occurred to him, as the *Prince of Wales* pulled away from
the shore, that his solid friend, on whom he kept his eyes fixed for a
considerable time, had something of the same stone about him as he
strolled the beach, 'rolling his majestic frame in his usual manner',
and whether, as the animated shape on the shoreline shrank and
started to move inland, Boswell questioned the reality of knowledge,
of friendship, of home, or of the strange sensations that had troubled
his mind and body in recent days. At length, the figure on the beach
had vanished, and then too the land itself.

His ship docked in Holland at midday on the 7th of August. After
a day or two at the house of Archibald Stewart, an acquaintance in
Rotterdam, Boswell went to Leyden, where he began to feel 'low-
spirited', and so set out swiftly for Utrecht. It was a journey of nine
hours in a *trek schuit*, an exceedingly slow-moving horse-drawn boat.
Solitude and the sluggish pace of three miles an hour did nothing for
his mood, and he began, he wrote later, to brood over his own dismal
imaginations. His father, in one of the moments of crushing pedantry
that characterize his communications with his son, had asked him to
observe closely the agricultural habits of the Dutch, but it is doubtful
whether, as his covered craft pushed between the pastures of central
Holland, Boswell paid much attention to the species and number of
the livestock he passed, or to the crops awaiting harvest. He may not
even have noticed, as the sun sank towards a Saturday evening, the
tower of Utrecht's medieval cathedral rising to meet him. On arriving in the cathedral square, however, he would have been struck at

once by its curious aspect: the tower was connected to the cathedral proper only by a pile of overgrown rubble, bony and pale in the fading light. The nave had collapsed during a storm in August 1674, and almost a century later the debris had still not been cleared away. Boswell faced the prospect of lodging next door to a ruin – his hotel, the Nouveau Château d'Anvers, stood across the square from the amputated campanile. A deep melancholy, he writes, now fell upon him. He was shown to a bedroom on an upper floor and left to dine there alone among its cheerless old furnishings. On each hour, the thirty-five bells of an elaborate carillon, housed in the octagonal lantern of the cathedral tower and timed by adjustments to a vast metal drum below, tolled out the same dreary psalm. As the clangorous tune subsided again, Boswell, in his solitude, thought himself old, miserable and abandoned, and he 'groaned with the idea of living all winter in so shocking a place'.

He woke the next day in an even more pitiful state. Alone, knowing nobody and with nothing to occupy him until the academic term started, he sank into even deeper despair, and sincerely believed that he was going mad. Eventually, he ran out into the streets around the louring wreckage of the cathedral. He groaned aloud as he turned from the square, cried out as he crossed the city's turbid canals and wept openly in the faces of passing strangers. He seems to have written nothing in the days to come and we have to rely on the letters he wrote in the following weeks to reconstruct his agony, a suffering with which he had been intermittently familiar since the age of seventeen – though on reflection he thought he might date its onset to an illness at the age of twelve – and which he already knew by the names of melancholy and hypochondria. The first is the term he uses, in a letter of the 16th August to his friend William Temple, to describe a wretchedness that, he says, nobody who has not suffered it can fully comprehend. 'I have been melancholy', he writes, 'to the most shocking and most tormenting degree.' After two days in this condition, in a city that seemed to

embody his state of mind, he resolved to quit Utrecht, and returned
to Rotterdam. Staying again with Stewart, he confided his collapse
to the young merchant, whom he hardly knew. Stewart contrived
schemes to distract and amuse his dismal fellow Scot, but none of
them worked. Boswell was gripped by a conviction that his father
would learn of his affliction and impute it, once more, to his son's
innate idleness and dissipation. The thought made him waver, even
in writing to Temple, a trusted friend, between declarations of his
utter failure (as scholar, gentleman and son) and frantic efforts to
pass the episode off as a distemper that time would heal. He almost
convinced himself of this, asking Temple to 'wait patiently to see
what time will produce', before falling once again, in the last sentence of the letter, into abjection: 'O dear! I am very ill.'

*

'Good God! What distracted horrors did I now endure!' wrote
Boswell of the ensuing weeks of chaos and irresolution. He could not
decide which European city might be his best hope of solace. He
thought of going to Berlin, Geneva or Paris. Most of all, he thought
about London, and his former happiness there – conveniently forgetting the countless journal entries that record his battle, during the
previous year, against hypochondriacal or melancholic symptoms. In
the end, he decided on a tour of Dutch cities in the company of John
Morgan, an American who had graduated recently from the medical
faculty at Edinburgh. They travelled north, to Gouda, Amsterdam
and Haarlem, but when their rough circuit of the country took them
back to Utrecht, the city still seemed so terrible to Boswell that he
could not stay, and they returned to Rotterdam.

Before setting out on the tour, Boswell had written to a friend,
George Dempster, whom he knew to be in Paris, hoping that they
might meet soon, in Brussels. He now discovered that Dempster, on
receipt of his letter, had left immediately for Brussels and, finding no
sign of his friend, remained there patiently for five days. Two letters
were waiting for Boswell on his return, in which Dempster, more in

exasperation than in anger, describes him as a 'mass of sensibility', asks him to think of his time in Holland as 'the dark watery passage which leads to an enchanted and a brilliant grotto' and advises that journal-keeping and 'debauching a Dutch girl' might be the likeliest remedies for his malaise. In fact, Boswell was by now feeling rather better, which improvement he attributed, as he set out from Rotterdam to Utrecht on the 5th of September, to reading Johnson's essays and tak-ing regular exercise. As he readied himself to return to the scene of his collapse, he appears to have known that his problems were temporal and textual, his illness a matter of irregular habits of body and mind, and its cure close at hand in the form of his books and his own diaries. His hypochondria, as he learned to call it, was bound up, in short, with the time he spent, or did not spend, reading and writing.

In late September, in a letter to John Johnston, a friend from his time at the University of Edinburgh, Boswell described again the catastrophic events of early August. As if unsure of his ability to flesh out in words the full horror of his suffering, he asked his friend to 'pause here a little to figure for yourself what I endured'. In truth, his prose pictures were vivid enough. But Boswell, whose self-portrait in letters and diaries is his first consciously literary project, was already in the habit of stepping back from his sentences to gauge their effect, and of casting his own examined life in a number of genres at once. The vast bulk of what he wrote about himself in Hol-land has been lost. His London journal affords a remarkably detailed report of the previous year of his life: his search for a profession, his adventures in the city's brothels and the beginnings of his friendship with Dr Johnson. There remains no such record of his time in Hol-land. Boswell kept up his journal-writing, but on leaving Utrecht in June 1764 he entrusted all his papers to a friend, the Reverend Robert Brown, requesting that the whole cache be sent on to him in Scotland. It seems that Brown passed the parcel to a young army officer, who took it as far as London; but when the papers arrived at Auchinleck, the Dutch journal was missing. What we lack, in consequence, are Boswell's nocturnal thoughts, set down at length at the end of the day. What we have instead, alongside his letters, are his morning memoranda: notes that typically open with a review of the previous day's events and go on to outline a plan of study, a physical regime or a set of social engagements for the day ahead. He was generally less at ease with himself first thing in the morning, less likely to forgive the lapses of the day before, more apt to look on the day to come as a chance to redeem or cure himself.

Boswell's writing habits constitute the real drama of his months in Utrecht, the nexus where his hopes, his fears and his hypochondria are subtly convolved. From the moment of his return to Utrecht, his morning memoranda recount a struggle between his unruly body and the rigorous abstraction of time. Once again, he was housed in full view of the half-ruined cathedral, at an inn called the Cour de l'Empereur, where he engaged a servant and sent for a tailor to come and measure him for 'a Leyden suit of green and silver'. His thoughts then turned to how best to fill his time in the fortnight or so before lectures began. (Boswell had only to cross the square to attend them: the law faculty occupied rooms around the cathedral's cloister.) Temple had written, advising him to spend six hours a day reading; Stewart wrote too, inquiring whether he was still tormented by 'the *dreadful bell*' and recommending another regime – on waking, he was to thrust his head out of the window and open his mouth wide to the morning air, then proceed to dance and caper about the room for twenty-five minutes. After devouring three pints of porridge and milk, he must turn to his law books; by way of recreation, he might later allow himself to read the *Spectator* or Johnson's journal the *Rambler*. Boswell had meanwhile begun to draw up the first of many timetables for himself. From mid September, the tone of his memoranda is both pedantic and urgent:

FRIDAY 16 SEPTEMBER . . . Latin till breakfast, something till eleven, then dress and at twelve French, then walk and dine. Afternoon, journal

&c. But next week you go to lectures, which will employ two hours and one in writing notes, about which you need not be exact. Mem. worthy father. Guard against liking billiards. They are blackguard, and you'll have high character with Count Nassau &c., if you don't play. Be easy and natural, though a little proud. Write out full mem. that this is your winter to get rid of spleen and become a man.

A mania for planning, and for rewriting his plans, overcomes Boswell at this point; his plans even contain, as here, reminders to copy out further plans. No spare hour is left unaccounted for – 'something till eleven', he writes, as if to say '*anything*' – and no aspect of his daily life escapes prescription or censure. On the 18th, a Sunday, he tells himself to be shaved and dressed at half past eight (the memoranda were generally written as soon as he awoke), to go to church after breakfast and then return to his rooms and attend to his journal. 'Keep up to plan,' he tells himself. Time and again, however, as the autumn mornings darken, he finds that he has to recall his sluggish mind to his journal, to his plan of study, or to the very memoranda in which he is setting out his schedule. Boswell was trying, and failing, to keep up with himself.

In fact, his plans had been falling apart from the outset. His body, for a start, seemed to revolt against the rigours of the diurnal round. His digestive system – ever a source of obsession for writers of his century – was either overtaxed, leaving him feeling heavy and lethargic, or underworked. 'Never want dinner,' he wrote: 'you will hurt your health.' Early in October he would address the subject from the other end: 'from this day follow Mr. Locke's prescription of going to stool every day regularly after breakfast. It will do your health good, and it is highly necessary to take care of your health.' (Here is Locke, in Section 24 of *Some Thoughts Concerning Education*: 'if a man, after his first eating in the morning, would presently solicit nature, and try whether he could strain himself to obtain a stool, he might in time, by a constant application, bring it to be habitual.') Irregularity of all sorts was precisely the problem. No matter how carefully he laid his plans in the morning – assuming, that is, that he woke early enough, and with sufficient energy to write them down – his life was a series of lapses. Billiards and bad diet were only the beginning; the more fundamental problem was his failure to find a moral and intellectual framework. With his spirits, as he thought, rallying after his melancholy fit, even a good mood could be dangerous: 'Your happiness is not produced by dissipation and gaiety, and so may vanish suddenly. It is wrought out by philosophy and pious resolutions of doing your duty as a man, with fortitude. Never forget this strong period of your life.'

*

'The mind of most men will grow uneasy without some actual plan,' wrote Boswell to Temple at the end of September. His schemes now began to proliferate, as if he hoped that a profusion of plans would keep his mind so fixed on the future that present pleasures, or pains, could not distract him from his course. He seemed to think that he could parse his life, like a sentence or an equation, before living it, that his every thought and action composed a prospectus for the man he might become. The tense he lived in was the future perfect: what will have been.

His days began with a prose sketch of what he hoped to achieve by nightfall, accompanied, almost always, by an acknowledgement that the previous day's plan had come to nothing: '*from this time* let plan proceed: seven to eight, Ovid; eight to nine, French version; ten to eleven, Tacitus; three to four, French; four to five, Greek; six to seven, civil law; seven to eight, Scots; eight to ten, Voltaire. Then journals, letters, and other books.' Occasionally, things seemed to go well – 'you go on charmingly. Be steady and firm' – and he could allow himself some small relaxation of his routine. Six hours a day, he reflected, were sufficient to read the legal texts and literary works that he had set himself, and to bring his journal up to date. He might allow himself three hours off for amusement in the evenings. But for the most part he found himself falling behind in his studies, so that his memoranda make for a curious reading experience: anxious and repetitive, their content almost unchanging but the tone increasingly harried and staccato. As he felt his self-control slipping, his sentences became shorter and their mood strictly imperative: 'after church, journal all evening, to bring it up once clear. Then you'll be quite regular. Never desist an hour from plan . . . This morning read from breakfast till college, Van Eck, so as to bring him up . . . Be temperate and rise at seven each morning . . . Take constant exercise . . . Bring up journal clear, and after this clear it every three days.'

His rage for routine reached its apogee about the middle of the month. The memorandum for the morning of the 15th is not unusual: Boswell instructs himself again to bring his journal up to date, to 'attain tranquillity' and try to appear less giddy in company than he had the night before at a dinner hosted by Count Nassau. (That dinner, in the entry for Friday the 14th, is itself the subject of some fraught and detailed forethought: he plans to appear 'quite the man of fashion' in scarlet and gold, white silk stockings and handsome pumps, brandishing an elegant toothpick case, a present from an unnamed lady.) But the references to his plan have begun to be capitalized; it seems that some more definitive document has superseded daily revisions to his regime. The manuscript in question is headed 'Inviolable Plan / to be read over frequently'. It begins with a brief description of his present predicament: though determined to make himself a man, worthy of the title of Laird of Auchinleck, he has had his resolutions undone by 'a fit of the spleen'. He believed he had 'a real distemper. On your first coming to Utrecht you yielded to that idea. You endured severe torment. You was pitiful and wretched. You was in danger of utter ruin.' And yet: 'this severe shock has proved of the highest advantage'. Idleness, he has come to realize, is his 'sole disease'; resolution and diligence have already seen it off to some extent. He has begun to take command of himself; piety, hard work and vigilance have started to shape his

character. He determines now to continue in this dignified fashion;
he acknowledges that trifles, fancies and antipathies may still distract
him, but trusts that temperance will see him through.

The Inviolable Plan is a document of a young man's ambition to
reflect upon himself; it is not, however, evidence of much real self-
knowledge. Boswell was far from the paragon of self-preservation
he imagines, no matter how often he might have read over the Plan.
But the document demonstrates eloquently the terms in which he
and his century conceived of self-control, and what they meant by
its undoing. His great fear was that he would 'dissolve'. This metaphor – it was something more than a metaphor as far as the medical
and moral imagination of the eighteenth century was concerned –
appeared to organize all his thoughts. He dreaded his becoming
formless, friable or liquid, a character without distinct lines, a soul
without design, a body without borders. 'Indulge not whims, but
form into a man,' he wrote, equating maturity, masculinity and
steadfastness with physical integrity and inviolability. The temptation to idleness or excess pleasure appeared, in his mind, to breach
the defences of his being, as though he were himself a kind of Holland: a fragile land, temporarily reclaimed. The future, he hoped,
was a territory drained of luxury and distraction, solidly diked
against a sea of seductions. As the year came to a close, he felt that
he might have built sufficient defences against his former peevishness and languor – you felt gloom, he notes of an evening spent
reading Tacitus and writing his journal, but you bore it, and are
ever resolved to bear it. Travelling to Leyden, and thence to The
Hague a few days before Christmas, he withstood the nine hours in
a cold and gloomy *trek schuit* with a new fortitude. Harden, he tells
himself at the end of 1763. Be firm.

*

Boswell's illness is an affliction at once of the body and the imagination. The Plan, the memorandum and the timetable are meant to
effect a rapprochement between body and mind that will ensure

their unity of function, like the parts of a geared machine. But Boswell cannot get the ratios right: the amounts of time spent working, sleeping or amusing himself are never in their proper proportion. He must constantly adjust one to affect the others. On the 9th of December he had to admonish himself for a physical indulgence that, if he allowed it to continue, would undermine his character: 'Have a care. You are not quite right at present. Your health is not perfect. That disorder of the stomach distresses you. Be more regular to go to bed. Eat a light dinner; drink less wine and a good deal of water to give a clear digestion . . . Lay your hand upon your heart. Pause. Withstand pleasure or you will be dissolved.'

At a late stage in his Dutch disease, Boswell makes, in a letter to Temple, his now customary link between melancholy and writing – his mind is a wax tablet on which the wax has melted in 'the furnace of sorrow', and all his principles run together in one 'dead mass'. His mind is also, however, 'a collection of springs'; all these springs have become unhinged, and the machine has thus been destroyed. A year earlier, in London, in a brief period of cheerfulness, he imagined the action of his psyche as at last regular and exact: 'I move like very clockwork.' After a night of music and dancing, he felt 'like an air-pump which receives and ejects ideas with wonderful facility'. Twenty-five years later, in a series of essays written for the *London Magazine* in the persona of 'The Hypochondriack', he would revisit the analogy: 'as the main-spring actuates the wheels and other component parts of a watch, so the soul actuates the faculties of the mind; and as the main-spring of a watch may either be broken all-together, or hurt in different degrees, we may justly talk from analogy in the same terms of the soul.' Throughout his life, Boswell deployed a terminology that varied with medical fashion. At the end of his first term at Utrecht, in the course of a few of his daily memoranda, he calls himself by most of the available titles: he is splenetic, nervous and melancholy. He is not yet, at least in terms of his self-diagnosis, hypochondriacal, but in 1777, by which time the word had become his favoured self-description, he would look back on this period of his youth as merely one in a series of hypochondriac fits: 'I call myself the Hypochondriack from former sufferings.'

What did Boswell and his contemporaries mean by the word 'hypochondria'? Like the related disorders of spleen, nerves, melancholia and hysteria, hypochondria often seems so varied and diffuse a diagnosis as to be quite useless. Such is the abundance of its symptoms that countless readers of the numerous texts devoted to the disease in this period must have recognized themselves there. Bernard de Mandeville, in *A Treatise of the Hypochondriack and Hysterick Passions* (1711), averred that the disorder – known as 'hypo' in men and 'vapours' in women – might make itself known in the form of heartburn, a flushing of the face, excessive belching and flatulence, constipation, headaches, vertigo, insomnia and nightmares. The patient, he writes, is beset by doubts, fears, suspicions and a crippling irresolution; everything offends him, and a trifle puts him in a passion. Mandeville admits that the disease is so various in its signifiers that he has seen no two cases quite alike. This observation does not lead him to question the reality of the affliction, but he points out that the patient is peculiarly sensitive to slights of any sort and in particular to doubts regarding the veracity of his loud complaints. As for the causes of hypochondria, Mandeville proposes a combination of physical and emotional factors. Hypochondria is brought on by venery and excessive use of the brain. The hypochondriac has typically been beset by 'immoderate Grief, Cares, Troubles, and Disappointments'. Bearing in mind, however, the abdominal seat of much of his discomfort, he might also (and here we may picture Boswell alone in his student lodgings, poring over Johnson and his journal) have carelessly indulged himself by 'leaning the Stomach and Praecordia against large Books, Desks and Tables'.

In 1725, in his *Treatise of the Spleen and Vapours: or, Hypochondriacal and Hysterical Affections*, Richard Blackmore effects the key advance of the century in the understanding of hypochondria. He begins more or less in agreement with Mandeville about the hypochondriac symptomatology – the sufferer is prone to pains, aches, vertigo, dizziness, dullness, drowsiness or insomnia, to 'tumultuous, sad and monstrous Dreams', to dramatic 'Belchings and loud Eructations'. The illness is also known as 'the English spleen', for 'the Natives of this Island were especially prone'. Blackmore's real insight, however, comes in his assertion that hypochondria involves 'a tender and delicate Constitution of the Nervous System, and an inordinate Fineness and Activity of their [that is, the patients'] inmates'. The body suffers spasms and contractions as a result of 'unwelcome News, sad Accidents, sudden Outcry, or the very opening of a Door'; the nervous system is thus vexed, its connections 'broken or ruffled'. In *A New System of the Spleen, Vapours and Hypochondriack Melancholy*, of 1729, Nicholas Robinson concurs; after outlining the now familiar variety of symptoms – yawning, paleness, loss of appetite, dizziness, lowness of spirits, 'impertinent or groundless Fears' – he declares that the disease originates in a slackening of the nerve fibres. These are made up, he writes, of minute *machinulae* which can be jolted out of their proper distance from each other, giving rise (if they are stretched too far apart) to spleen, vapours, melancholy and hypochondria or (if they have been shunted too close together) to fits and paroxysms.

Precisely how these writers conceive of the nature and function of the nerves is a matter of some confusion; the exact substance of the fibres remains obscure, and so the images used to describe them vary widely. George Cheyne, whose *The English Malady*, published in 1733, was the main influence on conceptions of hypochondria at work later in the century, believed that the whole body was made of fibres, of which the nerves were simply one sort. Diverse substances were knitted together to form a single fabric, a machine built of an infinite number and variety of channels, pipes and conduits. The nerves, as 'sensible' (that is, sensitive) fibres, Cheyne writes, are apt to become 'elastic' or 'destructile', depending on the stresses placed on them. As the body's most susceptible filaments, they require an exact and constant tension, a 'just Mediocrity'. Hypochondria disrupts this happy mean between tension and elasticity. Cheyne, like his predecessors, recites a small catalogue of symptoms – noise in the bowels or ears, restlessness, fidgeting, peevishness, discontent, inconstancy, lethargy, watchfulness – but is in truth more exercised by the origins of hypochondria. This is where his title comes into play: contemporary England (here he is echoing Blackmore) seems especially enfeebled in this regard. Why should this be so? The answer lies in the perennial eighteenth-century theme of the dangers of luxury and excess. 'Since our Wealth has increas'd', he writes, 'and our Navigation has been extended, we have ransack'd all the Parts of the *Globe* to bring together its whole Stock of Materials for *Riot*, *Luxury*, and to provoke *Excess*. The Tables of the Rich and Great (and indeed of all Ranks who can afford it) are furnish'd with Provisions of Delicacy, Number, and Plenty, sufficient to provoke, and even gorge, the most large and voluptuous Appetite. The whole *Controversy* among us, seems to lie in out-doing one another in such Kinds of Profusion.' Cities, especially London, sink under all this aberrant plenty; they are filled with bad air and the furniture of modern idleness: theatre seats, card tables, sprung coaches and sedan chairs. Their bodies' sluices, gutters and culverts dammed up by excess and inactivity, the English have suffered an increase in the nervous distempers that the subtitle of Cheyne's book enumerates: 'spleen, vapours, lowness of spirits, hypochondriacal and hysterical distempers, &c.'

Cheyne's is the theory of hypochondria with which Boswell was most familiar. When he considered his low mood, he acknowledged that it was brought on by inactivity. When he thought of the heaviness that afflicted his limbs and brought his digestion to a leaden halt, he knew that it was occasioned by excess at table. And when he reflected on his moral incontinence, he blamed the attractive bustle of city life. He identified fully as a hypochondriac, imagined himself an example of Cheyne's glum breed. But at the same time – and especially under the influence of Johnson, whose own struggle with melancholia Boswell took as his model – he believed he could cure himself of his modern malady by force of will alone. He believed, at his most optimistic, that he could think, plan and write his way out of it. He did not at such moments suspect that his obsession with his own illness, and his convoluted methods for freeing himself from it, were also symptoms of an intractable disorder. Boswell's efforts to control his hypochondria were in themselves classic signs of hypochondria as it was imagined by Cheyne, but expressions too of a prodigious concern with one's own well-being that has not ceased to be known by the same name.

*

Throughout his stay in Utrecht, Boswell tried hard to improve his French: it would benefit him more in the long run than learning Dutch, and was anyway the natural language of the refined society on the margins of which he now found himself. At times the miniature essays he composed in French move beyond the confines of his daily life, while at others they are no more than extensions of his journal or memoranda. Between the 12th and 14th of October, he composed a short text that drifts unexpectedly from whimsical reflections towards a rather telling reminiscence. He begins: 'I like exceedingly to wash my feet in warm water. It gives me a kind of tranquillity.' Even better, he surmises, is a warm bath, a solace to the whole body, such as the Romans perfected. Of course, he notes, such an agreeable immersion is dangerous, and a young man ought to guard against effeminacy by accustoming himself to cold baths, for vigour and liveliness.

Still, the dream of warm, watery ease leads him to recall a formative moment when, as a boy, he stole a little luxury in the austere aftermath of his first attack of hypochondria. The crisis, when he was twelve, was occasioned, he believed, by the loss of his first tutor, John Dun, and his replacement by Joseph Fergusson, a severe individual of 'no taste – no delicacy'. Boswell developed a heavy cold, then a digestive disorder; the best doctors in Scotland were summoned from the University of Edinburgh, and diagnosed a nervous complaint. He was sent to Moffat, in the Lowlands, to be treated with the resort's sulphurous waters. 'I was put into a horrible tub,' he recalls in 1763, 'a scanty covering was thrown over me, and in that state I was obliged to remain for half an hour. I had as my supervisor a barbarian of a Presbyterian preacher, who called out from time to time in a harsh voice, "Take care, you rogue! If we see the least disobedience to our orders, we shall proceed to instant punishment." And that was why I kept quiet, though I was extremely bored.' In his memory, the treatment is also an opportunity to be alone with his thoughts and to enjoy the idle comfort of his body; in spite of his constant haranguing by Fergusson, he discovers in his bath, beneath his scanty covering, a solitude that is delicious and also isolating. From this moment on, he thinks his salvation and his ruin alike will come from sitting huddled away from the world.

His second hypochondriac episode occurred five years later. In his journal he admits: 'the truth is with regard to me, about the age of seventeen I had a very severe illness. I became very melancholy. I imagined that I was never to get rid of it. I gave myself up as devoted to misery. I entertained a most gloomy and odd way of thinking. I was much hurt at being good for nothing in life.' The torment had begun in the summer of 1757, when he was greatly affected by his first exposure to metaphysics and to theological writings on the nature and possibility of free will. Once more he was sent to Moffat. Under the influence of an 'old Pythagorean' he became a vegetarian and cultivated his misanthropy. He resolved 'to suffer everything as a martyr to humanity. I looked upon the whole race with horror.' His journal is full of references to his feeling uneasy, anxious, deflated: 'this afternoon I became very low-spirited. I sat in close. I hated all things. I almost hated London. O miserable absurdity!' He was especially susceptible to the effects of place upon his mood. In May 1763, he visited Oxford for a few days, dined with friends and was shown around the colleges. He set out with a noble conception of the university, but on arriving found his mind possessed by a horror of the very notion of a college, which he now pictured as a place of confinement and gloom. 'Nothing but cloud hung upon me,' he wrote.

On his return to London, he found he was repulsed even by the city he loved, and a few days later, as if to confirm his new loathing, was drawn, though he knew it would make him suffer, to the most dismal spectacle the city could afford. At the gallows at Tyburn, he watched the execution of Paul Lewis, a 24-year-old clergyman's son, sentenced for robbery. 'There was a most prodigious crowd of spectators,' he recalled. 'I was most terribly shocked, and thrown into a very deep melancholy.'

*

Samuel Johnson was not unacquainted with the illness of which his young friend complained in the first year of his establishing himself in London. After leaving Oxford in his early twenties, Johnson suffered a protracted period of anxiety, lassitude and low spirits. The symptoms plagued him periodically for the rest of his days. A passage in one of several biographies that attempted to compete with Boswell's, Arthur Murphy's *An Essay on the Life and Genius of Samuel Johnson, LL.D.* (1792), sketches the nature of Johnson's lifelong suffering:

Indolence was the time of danger: it was then that his spirits, not employed abroad, turned with inward hostility against himself. His reflections on his own life and conduct were always severe; and, wishing to be immaculate, he destroyed his own peace by unnecessary scruples. He tells us that, when he surveyed his past life, he discovered nothing but a barren waste of time, with some disorders of body, and disturbances of mind, very near to madness. His life, he says, from his earliest youth, was wasted in a morning bed; and his reigning sin was a general sluggishness, to which he was always inclined, and, in part of his life, almost compelled, by morbid melancholy and weariness of mind. This was his constitutional malady, derived, perhaps, from his father, who was, at times, overcast with a gloom that bordered on insanity.

What bound the two together in their bouts of melancholy, in other words, was a belief in their own laziness (and a propensity to write about it at length, thus rather belying their own self-descriptions). They shared an interest in the problem of rising in the morning; the *Life* records a bizarre conversation in which Johnson recounts to Boswell the case of Mrs Elizabeth Carter, who contrived an alarm involving a candle, string and a heavy weight that would crash to the floor and wake her in the mornings. Surely, says Boswell, it is possible to bring the human body to a state where rising from bed will no longer be painful. He imagines a mechanism by which he might be raised to a semi-recumbent posture: a system of pulleys attached to a hinged bed. In fact, he had first envisaged this contraption in the final months of his time in Utrecht, when indolence plagued him again. He concluded regretfully that such a system, working against his body's natural inclination to the horizontal, would itself cause him great pain.

Johnson, however, was constantly on guard against the idea that his, or his friend's, languor was innate. Nor would Johnson countenance the notion, derived from Cheyne, that the hypochondriac distemper was a sign of social distinction, nor that it was as common as Boswell, having read *The English Malady*, was apt to believe. He counselled repeatedly that diligence and will were the best counters to melancholy. In the *Life*, Boswell recalls one such piece of advice, given him by Johnson as they travelled to Oxford. Boswell was naturally wary of revisiting the city that had caused him so much pain some years earlier, but Johnson assured him that such destructive thoughts were best allayed by forcing one's mind to some absorbing activity: '"Sir," said he, "take a course of chemistry, or a course of rope-dancing, or a course of anything."' Boswell, typically, appreciated the advice but had already undercut it in his own mind: 'I *thought* of a course of concubinage, but was afraid to mention it.'

Johnson's example is a constant presence in the fragmented account that remains of Boswell's time in Holland. Returning to Utrecht after first fleeing from the city in revulsion, Boswell carries the *Rambler* with him: a reminder of the value of his friend's advice and of the restorative power of writing. In his most fractured and panicked memoranda, he commands himself to think of Johnson and apply himself more avidly to the lessons in his essays. Strangely, the two wrote to each other seldom during the winter of 1763 and 1764. Boswell's first two letters to Johnson, in which he related in full the nature of his breakdown, have not survived; we know their broad content only from Johnson's reply, of the 8th of December. The first letter, he says, 'gave me an account so hopeless of the state of your mind, that it hardly admitted or deserved an answer; by the second I was much better pleased; and the pleasure will still be increased by such a narrative of the progress of your studies, as may evince the continuance of an equal and rational application of your mind to some useful enquiry'. For the most part, Johnson, though sympathetic to his friend's sufferings, thought he indulged them too readily, that he was too willing to believe himself possessed of a sensibility that others lacked, that Boswell dramatized his nervous symptoms to make himself seem more intense, elevated and pro-found. That he was, in short, a hypochondriac in the modern sense.

*

Boswell thought that his obsession with time – with plans, projects and prospectuses – was a way to control his hypochondria, to shock himself from his lethargy and assuage his fears. But perhaps it is more accurate to conclude that hypochondria was itself a way of organizing his time. He half imagined that his calendars and private syllabi would rouse him from his slumbers, and half knew that each time the system would fall back exhausted. He had not considered that his schemes and his symptoms were part of the same psychic structure, nor that (however debilitating) it was an intensely useful one. Boswell's fraught, compulsive, hypochondriac relation to time was in fact what made him a writer.

In 1777, he began to write the essays that appeared under the pen-name 'The Hypochondriack'. He published seventy in all; the last – 'On Concluding' – appeared in August 1783. Their topics, as befitted a literary form he inherited from his heroes Joseph Addison and Johnson, were a mix of perennial moral themes and controversies of the day: he wrote on marriage, prudence, hospitality, war, a recently invented refrigerating device, savages, conscience, similarities among authors, censure, reserve and diversion. Several times he addressed the subject of drink. He wrote about death, and his own morbid thoughts: 'A Hypochondriack fancies himself at different times suffering death in all the various ways in which it has been observed; and thus he dies many times before his death. I myself have been frequently terrified, and dismally afflicted in this way; nor can I yet secure my mind against it at gloomy seasons of dejection.' In an essay on the subject of fear, he advised his readers against meditating too closely on death. (This against venerable philosophical wisdom: Montaigne, for example, thought a clear apprehension of one's coming demise a necessary accompaniment to a good and happy life.)

He started the series with an essay on the related topics of hypochondria and the literary form of the essay itself. The two were clearly related. His purpose, he wrote, was 'to divert Hypochondriacks of every degree, from dwelling on their uneasiness, by presenting them such essays on various subjects as I can furnish from my own intellectual store'. The periodical essay – short, concise, reflective, not pretending to a thorough treatment of its subject, but with the potential for digression and dilation as well as pith and insight – was the hypochondriac's ideal literary genre. The author could console himself – as he began, inevitably, to doubt his powers – with the thought that the essay would soon be complete, and serial composition would become an organizing principle for his labours and for his life. That was the theory; there remained the question of how to begin. Nothing, he writes later, characterizes a hypochondriac more accurately than an inability to get started. In a later essay, again on the theme of hypochondria, he finds that he has to coax himself into writing about the subject: 'to do it, however, and that *now*, in this very paper, I am resolved; whether I shall do it well or ill; for I believe that firmly to reject all pleas of temporary inability, is the best way to acquire that best of all habits – a promptitude in execution.'

Among the last in the Hypochondriack's meditations is an essay on diaries, in which Boswell reflects once more on the relationship between writing and time. Johnson had counselled that he should bring his diary up to date while the impression of events was fresh, 'for it will not be the same a week afterwards'. But this, it seems, is a torment to one afflicted with hypochondria; it has occurred to Boswell that he ought not to live more than he can actually record, that he must not overtax his own documentary powers, 'and I have regretted that there is no innovation for getting an immediate and exact transcription of the mind, like that instrument by which a copy of a letter is at once taken off'. The fantasy is remarkable for its similarity to the desire he failed to fulfil twenty years earlier: the idea of somehow coinciding with himself in time, at last catching up with his own ambitions and imagination, rather than lagging behind as he has done all his life. In the final lines of the essay 'On Diaries', nearing the end of the series, and thus approaching the dissolution of the character of The Hypochondriack, he pictures for the reader just this moment of punctual intersection with himself, of perfect discipline and decorum, alone in his room. 'The Diary of this day', he writes in conclusion, 'will be little more than that "I sat quietly at home, and wrote The Hypochondriack, No. LXVI. on Diaries."'

*

Boswell returned to Utrecht on Tuesday, the 17th of January 1764, feeling happy and comfortable. He had passed the intervening weeks at The Hague and at Rotterdam, where he stayed again with Archibald

Stewart. Having concluded the old year with the tentative hope that he had definitively overcome his hypochondria, he began the new year feeling gloomy, splenetic and idle. On the 2nd of January he complained of his laxity yet again, regretting his continued attraction to cards and billiards: 'you are now a little jaded with all this idle, unnatural, sickly dissipation. Be firm on guard these three days, so as to depart sound. Never be moved with trifles. Be manly and silent.' On the 12th he noted another deviation at the card table, and was forced to upbraid himself once more: 'make a firm resolution, a *promise*, never to play but when necessary, as 'tis low and unworthy'. On the eve of his departure for Utrecht, he felt his mood fluctuate almost hourly. He dined, he thought, too heartily, but had at least the presence of mind to keep his distress to himself; even Stewart, his confidant on his first arrival in Holland, was not aware of it. Silence, he wrote the next day, was his great refuge. His appetite for intimacy was, he thought, as destructive as his lust for food, drink, whoring and gaming: having remained *retenu* throughout the day, he hoped to take his leave the next day 'full of spirits as after trial'.

For some time, he had been in love with two women at once: Catherina Elizabeth van Geelvinck – she appears in his letters and memoranda as 'La Veuve' – and Isabella van Tuyll, whom Boswell knew as Zélide. (With the latter, on leaving Utrecht, he would carry on a long correspondence that came to nothing in the way of romance, but in the course of which they each admitted to suffering from hypochondria.) La Veuve was twenty-five years old; she had been widowed six years earlier and had a son of six or seven. 'One does not like a widow,' wrote Boswell to Temple, asking to be talked out of his fascination with her. This fascination for La Veuve was by turns light and gallant and obsessive, almost morbid. On the 8th of February he declared his love for La Veuve, and he wrote up the interview the following morning. She was playfully suspicious of his intentions, asking if he was sincere, if he had principles, or faults. To the last question he answered that he sometimes suffered from bad humour,

but the attacks did not last long. In his morning memoranda, however, he conflated his desire – or rather his constant imaginative
indulging of his desire – with his hypochondria. Later in the month,
after a long dialogue in the course of which she had assured him that
she would never fall in love, he found himself planning to spy on her:

Then think: this is spleen – expel it. You're miserable with it. 'Tis not, then,
generous, and it may grow frivolous. Recover clear, firm tone, nor allow
fretful passions to have habit. You are fortunate your mistress is your friend
and confidant, and you can from time to time talk to her. But she'd tire of a
whiner. Come, be manly; resolve, and be worthy of her, and see if you could
be a sensible husband. Expel sloth. Speak no more of her . . .

That night, the 20th of February, his stomach was 'disordered';
he does not say whether his discomfort was another consequence of
overindulgence, or the result of the anxious hours since morning
that he had spent wavering between desire and indifference. It was
still dark when he rose the following day, exhausted, the image of
La Veuve having hovered over him all night like one of the ghosts of
which he had been so afraid as a boy at Auchinleck, and set out into
the square. He had by now become used to the sight of the slim
dark tower skirted below by fallen masonry, and had even learned
to ignore the hourly clamour of the carillon; but this morning, as he
hurried from the silent square, he shuddered a little, then braced
himself against the cold with a quick swig from the bottle he had
thrust under his coat on the way out. It was a walk of some twenty
minutes to St Catherine's Gate, to the west; the city was alive and
brightening by the time he passed through the ornate gatehouse and
stood on the bridge over the old canal. Long, low canal boats were
jostling at the quay to his right; above them stood a small wooden
sentry box. He approached, and engaged the sleepy German cara-
bineer within with a surprising request. Before long, Boswell was
huddled in the box, sharing his gin with the genial guard. A carriage

approached, and rattled slowly across the central wooden section of the bridge. Boswell was entranced: 'She looked angelic, and that glimpse was ravishing . . . You stood on ramparts and watched her disappear. You was quite torn with love.' He went immediately to his morning fencing lesson. (His fencing master, he records, was an agile 'old carle' of ninety-four, as healthy and spry as a man of thirty.) The exercise did not invigorate him: all day he was dreary, silent, gloomy, altogether 'very bad'. At night he was 'listless and distressed and obliged to go drawling to bed. This day study hard; get firm tone; go on. Mademoiselle will be your friend.'

*

When he sat down on the 9th of March to write the day's memorandum, he had put his two loves out of his mind for the present. The previous day, he had received news that his son, Charles, not yet a year-and-a-half old, had died. 'Yesterday you rose well,' he wrote, somehow keeping to his habitual testing of his temperament before the day began; 'after breakfast you received a letter from Johnston with accounts of the death of the poor little child. Alas, what is the world? You was distressed and sunk.' Boswell had never seen the child, who was born shortly after he left Edinburgh in November 1762. His mother was a servant-girl, Peggy Doig; Boswell had arranged for the boy to be cared for by a foster-mother, had sent money to support him, and received reports from Johnston, who visited him regularly. His son's death threw him into disarray once more. He woke in the mornings, he wrote, in eight minds; he found he could not get out of bed; he was assailed by the 'black foe', melancholy; he thought he was dying, and felt himself 'melted with tender distress'. His thoughts began once more to fly between extremes: he wrote to his father, admitting his grief, and a page later announced that he was cured. He admonished himself in writing for his descent into despair, trying to convince himself that the pain was bearable, then succumbed again: 'there's no more of it! 'Tis all over.'

On the 23rd of March, he wrote to Temple: 'this is an affliction of uncommon nature; for although I never saw him, believe me, I am not a little distressed. I mourn for an idea. I mourn for one with respect to whom I had formed many agreeable plans which must now be dashed from my mind.' In an effort to distract himself, he drew up another plan. He would translate John Erskine's *Principles of the Law of Scotland* into Latin, and he began to work the scheme into his daily memoranda: 'fix law hours, and wrote a page [of] Erskine as regular as ten lines; also journal, so much each morning . . . This day, several pages of Erskine and some journal. Resolve: be busy and recover mind.' Two months later, his resolution wavering, he began to baulk at the 500 hours he estimated the task would occupy, and announced that the plan was not 'an absolutely necessary one'. The translation remained unfinished. Once more, however, writing had allowed him to parcel out his hours; as long as he was busy his hypochondria might be kept at bay. And as before, Boswell's meticulous record of his progress, or lack of it, started to look like a symptom in itself.

He left Utrecht early in May, and travelled to The Hague. En route, on the 5th, he visited Jerome David Gaubius, a celebrated physician and professor of medicine at Leyden. In his memorandum of the following morning, he records that Gaubius told him he would be cured of his hypochondria by the age of thirty; he does not say whether the prediction consoled him with the vision of a contented middle age or if the years of misery ahead weighed heavily upon him as he reached The Hague. Leaving Utrecht had done nothing to regulate his mood. On the 17th, tormented by the thought of spending another four months in Holland, and increasingly unsure if he was up to the task of translating Erskine, he went to bed early so that he could rise at six. But he slept for ten hours and, having got up, went back to bed mid-morning. 'O fie!' he wrote in his memorandum. Feeling 'dismal', he resolved to 'go to Amsterdam and try Dutch girl Friday, and see what moderate Venus will do'. A week later he consulted Johannes David Hahn, a professor at Utrecht and Leyden:

'You told him case. He pronounced gravely: bad nerves, acrimoni-
ous juices, lax solids. Sweeten, fortify, amuse. No metaphysics,
plain common sense. No claps. Women are necessary when one has
been accustomed, or retention will influence the brain. Nicely dis-
puted.' A third doctor – Tissot, 'a true original, a shrewd, lively
little fellow of sixty' – countered a couple of days later that 'a hypochondriac should not be cured by medicines, but by a regular
employment of all the hours of the four and twenty.' Boswell could
not discern whether he had been too hard or too easy on himself in
the months since his arrival in Holland. In the end, it had been his
propensity for plans that had made him ill: the weight of expectation
had crippled him, and his efforts to live up to his own, his father's
and his friends' hopes had made him redouble the dose of a medicine, an unaccustomed discipline, that turned out to be poisonous to
his system. His Plan may have been Inviolable, but he was himself
dissolved by his own efforts to remain steadfast and manly.

*

In *The Conflict of the Faculties* (1798), Immanuel Kant – whose regular habits were such that his neighbours in Königsberg were said to
set their clocks by his daily walks – admitted that he had a natural
disposition to hypochondria. It was caused, he said, by his flat and
narrow chest, which left little room for the movement of his heart
and lungs. In his youth the malady had almost made him tire of life.
He had since, however, quite mastered his hypochondria by sheer
force of will, diverting his attention from the oppression in his chest
by reflecting that, if he were genuinely ill, there was nothing that
could be done. (The philosopher also counsels that one can cure
oneself of the unhealthy habit of eating in the evenings by dining
heartily at midday, banish pathological emotions by merely avoiding thinking and walking at the same time, and improve one's general health by breathing only through the nose.) Hypochondria,
writes Kant, consists in 'the weakness of abandoning oneself
despondently to general morbid feelings that have no definite object

(and so making no attempt to master them by reason)'. His definition of the disease already looks forward to our modern sense of the word – the hypochondriac engages in 'fainthearted brooding about the ills that could befall one' – but is bound up, as for Boswell, with a failure to properly manage one's time. Oddly, Kant claims that the hypochondriac cannot end his own suffering by will alone, but also contends that a rational man simply 'vetoes' hypochondria from the outset. Whatever the chronology of this mental battle, its optimistic upshot is that the patient, having rid himself of his morbid thoughts, 'goes on, despite the claim of his inner feeling, to his agenda for the day . . . and turns his attention to the business at hand'.

But what if the business at hand – the quotidian sequence of tasks to be carried out, letters, journals and essays to be written, books to be read and translated – is precisely the place where hypochondria takes hold? What if the patient, his heart sunk by the thought of solitude and study, seeks to cure himself by more solitude and further study? What if that thing he insists on calling his hypochondria is really no more and no less than an obsession with self-regulation? This was Boswell's disease: a morbid self-consciousness regarding the place of his body in time, a far too keen awareness of the split between body and mind, an excruciating sense of just how far the one lagged behind the other. But is this endless anatomizing of the daily round of plans and disasters, schemes and crises, not also a way of getting things done? The Hypochondriack's seventy essays, the eleven months of daily memoranda that Boswell wrote in Holland, the 500 pages of quarto manuscript that made up his lost Dutch journal: all of this industry occurs despite – which is also to say, because of – Boswell's enduring misery. Hypochondria is a way of giving oneself, time and again, a fresh start. It is a structuring principle masquerading as chaos, resolve disguised as fear, a way of appearing on the stage of your own life as if in the costume of a new character, in a scene you have scripted yourself.

Towards the end of March, around the time that he first conceived the idea of a translation of Erskine, Boswell had gone out into the farmland around Utrecht in the early afternoon. Looking back at the bell-tower rising above the city, he drew his sword, which glittered in the sun, and fell to his knees. Perhaps his youthful struggles at Moffat, during the second of his hypochondriac fits, with the concepts of fate and free will came back to him as he knelt in the flat field at the edge of the city. If fate had decreed him incurably melancholy, he declared to the spring air, then he would accept the burden; but if, as he believed, he possessed free will, then he swore, with God as his witness, to bear his disease but 'not own it'. Returning to the cathedral square, he dined and then mounted the tower. He must have felt, as he began his ascent of the 364-foot structure, that he was at last facing down the grim view that had so distressed him on his first arrival in Utrecht. A narrow and winding stone staircase led to the apartments of the belfry-man and his family; they lived only a few yards from the hourly cacophony that had threatened Boswell's sanity eight months earlier. From there, a still narrower and steeper set of steps, spiralling into a darkness lit intermittently by the late afternoon light as it sneaked through tiny windows, took him to the top of the tower. In 1815, a traveller, Charles Campbell, wrote of the upper reaches of the tower: 'when you seem to be so weary as to be incapable of another step, half the horizon suddenly bursts upon the view, and all your complaints are overborne by expressions of admiration . . . A circle of probably more than sixty miles diameter strains the sight from this tremendous steeple.' As Boswell emerged dizzily into the light, and spied in the distance the spot where, earlier that day, he had flourished his sword in his own private drama and sworn to withstand his affliction, he felt himself to have risen above his late sorrow at the death of his son, above his struggles with time, study and the temptation to a dissolute life, above his father's dismal expectations of his character – even, in the end, as he surveyed the scene of his recent torments, above his own hypochondriacal nature.

2. Charlotte Brontë: A Little Nervous Subject

'Temperament for the most part nervous. Brain large, the anterior
and superior parts remarkably salient . . . She is occasionally
inclined to take a gloomier view of things than perhaps the
facts of the case justify.'

J. P. Browne, 'Phrenological Estimate of the Talents and
Dispositions of a Lady'

On the 21st of April 1835, Charlotte Brontë turned nineteen. The
same day, she received a letter from Margaret Wooler, principal of
Roe Head girls' school, where she had been a student three years
earlier. The regime at Roe Head had been tolerant and the conditions in which the girls lived relatively comfortable; the school is
not to be confused with the Clergy Daughters' School, the institution at Cowan Bridge in Lancashire where, in 1825, Charlotte's
sisters Maria and Elizabeth contracted typhoid. (They died, respectively, in May and June of that year; readers of *Jane Eyre* will know
that school as Lowood, and recall the outbreak of disease that killed
Jane's friend Helen Burns and spread 'gloom and fear within its
walls; while its rooms and passages steamed with hospital smells,
the drug and the pastille striving vainly to overcome the effluvia of
mortality'.) Charlotte, however, had been unhappy at Roe Head,
tamping down her desire to write in favour of a dedication to the
light of learning that brought its own rewards but left her convinced
that her future role consisted in suppressing her true self in the
name of duty. In the three subsequent years at home in Haworth,

Yorkshire, she had been free to explore, alongside her surviving sisters Emily and Anne, and especially in the company of her brother Branwell (whose dissolution was not yet apparent), the various fantastical and romantic realms that the siblings had invented to fill the grey days at the edge of the moor. Miss Wooler's letter, written in sincere appreciation of Charlotte's prior accomplishments at the school, and offering her a position as a teacher there, signalled the end of her freedom. There was no question, in light of the family's financial circumstances, of her turning down the offer.

Charlotte and Emily (who was to be a pupil at the school) set out for Roe Head on the 29th of July, the day before Emily's seventeenth birthday. The younger sister did not last long there. Liberty, wrote Charlotte years later, 'was the breath of Emily's nostrils'; unaccustomed to the discipline and enclosure of a school, she 'fell rapidly into a decline', as one of her sister's biographers puts it. Emily was recalled home, and Anne sent in her place, adding to the sense of dislocation that Charlotte had already begun to feel. She had embarked on a life of drudgery: her waking hours were taken up by teaching and the correcting of her pupils' work. She had little time to indulge her imagination, still less to write down the results of her reflections and inventions. In the brief moments of solitude that she stole, she was seized by her imagination in a morbid fashion to which she was unused. On the 11th of August she described, on a sheet of letter paper she had brought from home, the onset of one of these attacks. She had been instructing three of her pupils in grammar when, the classroom falling silent, she was suddenly assailed by the thought that she might spend the best part of her life feigning patience in the face of her pupils' obtuseness. Turning to the window, she looked out at the sweet August morning and, lifting the sash, listened to the uncertain sound of a dying wind from the south. The wealth of fictional life that she and her siblings had amassed at Haworth was suddenly clear to her, and its loss painfully present. 'Then came on me rushing impetuously all the mighty phantasm that we had conjured from nothing to a system strong as some religious creed,' she wrote. 'I felt as if I could have written gloriously – I longed to write . . . if I had had time to indulge it I felt that the vague sensations of that moment would have settled down into some narrative better at least than anything I ever produced before. But just then a Dolt came up with a lesson. I thought I should have vomited.'

Three years passed in this fashion. Charlotte found herself, in those brief periods when she could give herself over to her interior visions, conjuring scenes, characters and whole narratives out of the gloom that surrounded her. She was tormented by memories of the stories that she and Branwell had composed at home, and distressed to discover that he had killed off one of the central characters in their fictional kingdom of Angria. It was around this time too that she wrote to the Poet Laureate, Robert Southey, declaring her desire to devote herself entirely to literature. Her letter has not survived. Southey's dismissive reply arrived two and a half months later. Her daydreams, counselled the poet, were likely to induce a distempered state of mind, unfitting her for the demands of ordinary life. He meant, specifically, the life of a woman: 'literature cannot be the business of a woman's life, and it ought not to be. The more she is engaged in her proper duties, the less leisure will she have for it, even as an accomplishment and a recreation.' Charlotte did not need to be told how little free time a woman of her standing had available; but she replied civilly, apologizing for her overheated language and thanking him for his advice. She received in turn a second letter, in which Southey recommended that his young correspondent 'take care of over-excitement, and endeavour to keep a quiet mind'.

Years later, writing to Margaret Wooler, Charlotte would diagnose her unquiet mind: at Roe Head – and in particular at Dewsbury Moor, where the school had relocated in the summer of 1837 – she had suffered, she said, from 'hypochondria – a most dreadful doom':

I can never forget the concentrated anguish of certain insufferable
moments, and the heavy gloom of many long hours, besides the preternatural horrors which seemed to clothe existence and nature and which
made life a continual waking nightmare . . . When I was at Dewsbury
Moor I could have been no better company to you than a stalking ghost,
and I remember I felt my incapacity to *impart* pleasure fully as much as my
powerlessness to receive it.

It is one of four writings in which she refers to hypochondria; the
others are all novels. Quite what she meant by the term is unclear
from the context of her letter. The symptoms she mentions are all,
as we would put it today, psychological, and we can only conjecture that she might have had in mind a definition of the disorder
with which she may have become familiar at Haworth. The Brontës'
family library contained a medical manual, Thomas John Graham's
Modern Domestic Medicine, published in 1826. (Readers of *Villette*
[1852], a novel in which the subject of hypochondria is broached
explicitly on more than one occasion, will perhaps recall the character of John Graham Bretton, who, having vanished from the narrative early on, appears later, mysteriously, as 'Dr. John'.) Graham
maps the mental and emotional landscape of the illness thus:

Sometimes the hypochondriac is tormented with a visionary or exaggerated sense of pain, or some concealed disease; a whimsical dislike of
particular persons, places or things; groundless apprehensions of personal danger or poverty; a general listlessness and disgust; or an irk-
someness and weariness of life; in other instances, the disease is strikingly
accompanied with peevishness and general malevolence; they are soon
tired with all things; discontented; disquieted . . . often tempted to
make away with themselves; they cannot die, they will not live; they
complain, weep, lament, and think they lead a miserable life: never was
anyone so bad.

We cannot say for certain that Charlotte Brontë was well acquainted with this passage, but her fictional references to the subject all point towards a collection of psychological symptoms that the novelist seems to have assumed was self-evident: the illness encompasses a kind of depression, and an apprehension of the worst. On the one occasion that hypochondria is mentioned in *Jane Eyre*, it is to the morbid sense of an impending danger that Brontë has Rochester allude on the night before he and Jane are due to be married. 'I wish this present hour would never end,' says Jane, 'who knows with what fate the next may come charged?' Her cheeks, remarks Rochester, are flushed, her eyes glittering in the light of the fire she has just stirred. 'This is hypochondria, Jane,' he counters; 'you have been over-excited, or over-fatigued.' She tells him that she had lain awake for some time the night before, listening to a rising gale that seemed to muffle another sound, low and mournful, coming from within the house. On falling asleep, she dreamed of a dark, windy night, a winding, unknown road and a shivering child that wailed in her arms. She saw Thornfield Hall ruined and overgrown, climbed one of its crumbling walls and, as she fell from a narrow ledge, woke to find an unknown woman, spectral and vampiric, standing before the mirror in her room. In time, the 'vision of woe', as Rochester hastily dismisses it, will resolve itself for Jane and the reader alike: the wedding will be abandoned, the nocturnal visitor revealed as Rochester's first wife, the house burned to the ground and its owner blinded. For now, having made his diagnosis, he urges her to dream instead of 'happy love and blissful union'. Her hypochondria, he concludes, has made of her a 'little nervous subject'. In this brief fireside exchange between Rochester and Jane, the psychiatric terminology of the day is raked over, and its light extends a little into the darkness that the novelist knew.

*

By the time that Brontë began to use it, the term 'hypochondria' had come to denote such a dizzying perplex of symptoms and causes that it is almost impossible to picture clearly just what it conjured up for the average physician and his worried patient. A review of the medical literature of the period reveals a concept (or perhaps only a word) that seems to have spread, in the minds of doctors and lay public alike, with all the vigour of an opportunistic infection or (a less anachronistic metaphor) a toxic miasma. Hypochondria was variously discovered agitating the brain, jangling the nerves or, as traditionally, following the Greeks, troubling the viscera. It might manifest itself in physical symptoms, as an alteration in affect or emotion, or in the form of delusions; the hypochondriac could be subject to chronic pain and discomfort, brought low by an intractable melancholy, or think himself horribly transformed – turned to glass, for example. Doctor and patient found it difficult to distinguish the symptoms in question from those of several similar afflictions. Hypochondria was obscurely related to such disorders of mind and body as hysteria, melancholia and neurosis, and any one of these might be judged an accessory to the sufferer's hypochondriasis, or – depending upon the medical authority consulted – be discounted as an unrelated impostor of hypochondria proper. The temptation, for the contemporary reader of the medical treatises in question – and of the literary turns to that body of knowledge, a few of which will feature in the present chapter – is to assume that 'hypochondria' did not exist at all, that its depredations upon the mind and body may be subsumed under the rubric of one or other subsequent diagnosis: depression, schizophrenia, the anxiety disorders. This would be a premature judgement.

In the eighteenth century, hypochondria remained in part a form of physical suffering, though the precise location of the complaint moved from the hypochondrium – the organs of the lower abdomen – to the overall complexion of the body. ('Complexion' meant not only the surface manifestation of the underlying state of the body, but the whole make-up, texture, knitting together of the members, bones, tissues and conduits.) The nervous hypothesis canvassed by George Cheyne in 1733 was expanded upon throughout the century. Robert Whytt, in his *Observations on the Nature, Causes and Cure of Those Diseases Which Are Commonly Called Nervous, Hypochondriac, or Hysteric* (1764), proposed an analysis of illnesses specifically caused by an 'uncommon delicacy' or 'unnatural sensibility' of the fibres in question. He admits that the idea of nervous disease has become so prevalent that physicians are apt to call 'nervous' all those illnesses whose nature and causes otherwise elude them. He will treat only of a '*peculiar* sense' of the term. But Whytt's effort at delimiting the subject is complicated by his assertion of the prodigious variety of even his '*peculiar* sense'. The colours of the chameleon, he writes, are not more numerous than the variations of this inconstant and protean disease: 'those morbid symptoms which have been commonly called *nervous*, are so many, so various, and so irregular, that it would be extremely hard, either rightly to describe, or fully to enumerate them.'

Whytt attempts an account nonetheless. His list of 'the most common and remarkable' symptoms includes: heartburn; wind in the stomach and intestines; low spirits; anxiety; timidity; flushes and chills; muscular pains and convulsions; flying pains in the head; flatulence; belching; costiveness; palpitations; fainting; breathing difficulties and a sense of imminent suffocation; yawning and sighing; hiccups; fits of weeping or laughter; giddiness; disturbances of sight, sound or smell; drowsiness; insomnia, 'attended with an uneasiness which is not to be described'; nightmares; sadness, despair and peevishness; elation; confused or vagrant thoughts; strange fancies and, as though such torments were not enough to occupy the patients' minds, 'persuasions of their labouring under diseases of which they are quite free; and imagining their complaints to be as dangerous as they find them troublesome'. The hypochondriac, it seems, is deluded, and suffers from an inordinate sensitivity, but he is not,

Whytt insists, insane. (Hypochondria is thus to be distinguished from melancholia; the difference between the two troubles many of the treatises on either subject.) Rather, he is prey to a 'great delicacy and sensibility of the whole nervous system', combined with specific weaknesses elsewhere in the body. Given that his physical symptoms also 'imitate the symptoms of almost all other diseases', it is no surprise that the patient appears generally over-sensitized, fearful, 'nervous' in the ordinary modern sense of the word.

The nervous origin of hypochondriac symptoms was further elaborated upon by William Cullen, whose fame rests mostly on his having coined the term 'neurosis'. In his *First Lines of the Practice of Physic* (1777), Cullen divided diseases into four classes, of which nervous disorder or neurosis was one, itself in turn divided into four orders: Comata (deprivations of voluntary motion), Adynamiae (deprivations of involuntary motions, whether vital or natural), Spasmodic Affections (irregular motions of the muscles) and Vesaniae (disorders of the intellectual functions). Hypochondria belonged to the second category; Cullen was careful to differentiate hypochondriasis from both hysteria and melancholia. 'Hypochondria' was primarily a 'spasmodic' disease of the muscles; 'hypochondriasis', while close to hypochondria in the sense that both types of patient exhibited 'mistaken judgment' and 'false imagination', was largely restricted to delusions regarding the state of the individual's health. Still, Cullen's description of one set of symptoms of 'Hypochondriasis, or the Hypochondriac Affection, Commonly Called Vapours, or Low Spirits' is surely sufficiently vague as to overlap confusingly with adjacent forms of lassitude or anxiety:

In certain persons there is a state of mind distinguished by a concurrence of the following circumstances: A languor, listlessness, or want of resolution and activity with regard to all undertakings; a disposition to seriousness, sadness and timidity; as to all future events, an apprehension of the worst or most unhappy state of them; and therefore, often upon slight grounds, an apprehension of great evil. Such persons are particularly attentive to the state of their own health, to even the smallest change of feeling in their bodies; and from any unusual feeling, perhaps of the slightest kind, they apprehend great danger, and even death itself. In respect to all these feelings and apprehensions, there is commonly the most obstinate belief and persuasion.

To the lay mind, we may assume, this profusion of empirical detail and brave conjecture was a rich fund of fact and metaphor from which to draw when faced with an enigmatic or diffuse set of symptoms. Hypochondria, to put it too simply, became fashionable. It became one of those terms – 'melancholia' had been the dominant example in the seventeenth century, as 'hysteria' would become for the late nineteenth – which, if not exactly catch-alls for slippery cases, tend to spread their descriptive nets much further than the writers who first defined them could have imagined. In the first half of the nineteenth century, the hypochondriac may have been prey to all of the physical symptoms that the authorities of the eighteenth had outlined; but he was also a patient plagued by a less well-defined unease. Where a writer like George Cheyne, with his concept of the 'English malady', had allowed the definition to spread to a general sense of cultural or societal distemper, hypochondria in this period seems more intimately an illness of the isolated person. The nineteenth-century hypochondriac suffers alone, even as his society's understanding of the disease becomes more generalized, more easily, even carelessly, applied. It is possible to call oneself, or somebody else, a hypochondriac and not worry unduly about defining or elaborating that diagnosis; its origins, symptoms and aetiology are both obvious and oddly unclear. At the same time, hypochondria starts to signify more precisely, though not yet exclusively, an imaginary illness or tenacious fear of such. Still, we should pause again to remind ourselves that there was real suffering involved; hypochondria, as we shall see, was a name that could be given to several sorts of advanced torment, including loneliness, grief, terror of mortality and the pain of unrequited love. In its most dramatic and richly imagined forms, it seems even to have defined a late version of the Gothic imagination and a vision of the creative temperament stymied, isolated or in exile.

The medical portrait of the haggard hypochondriac is remarkably similar to that advanced in 1839 by Edgar Allan Poe. 'The Fall of the House of Usher' is usually read as a tale of familial decadence or dissolution: there are suggestions of incest, of a long-incubated horror at the heart of the Usher dynasty, embodied both in the wracked body and mind of Roderick Usher and in the decaying mansion in which the narrator discovers him. But it is also a study of Usher's 'hypochondria': a malaise that makes him inordinately sensitive to all manner of real and imagined torments. Hypochondria, Poe's story suggests, is a physical and mental affliction, but also a form of heightened sensibility, a kind of allergy to the physical world, and a disease of the imagination that has grotesque and fatal consequences.

The narrator, at the start of the tale, appears strangely sensitive to the atmosphere and substance of the house to which Usher, a friend of his boyhood, has summoned him. Reflected in the black water of a stagnant tarn or pool, surrounded by blasted trees and rank vegetation, the building, with its vacant windows, regards him like a ravaged face. Its owner's visage is no less alarming: he is cadaverously pale, his eyes have a 'miraculous lustre', his voice is alternately leaden and vivacious, his tremulous gestures betray an extreme agitation. He suffers, he says, from a nervous complaint that has made him morbidly susceptible to almost all sensation: 'the most insipid food was alone endurable; he could wear only garments of certain texture; the odours of all flowers were oppressive; his eyes were tortured by even a faint light; and there were but peculiar sounds, and these from stringed instruments, which did not inspire him with horror.' He is convinced too of the sentience of all vegetable things: the trees about the house, the fungi that grow on its walls. The very atmosphere that hangs around Usher Hall seems to him to be alive and sensate. This disease, concludes the narrator, is 'hypochondria'.

In part, Poe applies the terminology of contemporary medicine ironically. Usher's sister Madeline, who seems to expire on the night of the narrator's arrival, suffers from an enigmatic disorder that conflates several diagnoses: 'The disease of the lady Madeline had long baffled the skill of her physicians. A settled apathy, a gradual wasting away of the person, and frequent although transient affections of a partially cataleptical character . . .' Perhaps the three references to hypochondria in the tale are to be taken no more literally, and ought not to point to Poe's belief in a precisely defined disorder. But the demise of Roderick Usher (and his sister, who has meanwhile crawled, bloodied and mad, from her tomb) is without doubt the result of an excess of sensitivity: towards his own physical sensations, to solitude and fear, and to the oppressive character of the house that eventually tears itself to pieces behind the fleeing narrator.

*

On Tuesday, the 8th of February 1842, after weeks of preparation, Charlotte, Emily and their father Patrick Brontë set off from Yorkshire to London in the company of their friends Mary and Joe Taylor, who were to escort them to Brussels. Their train left the station in Leeds at nine o'clock in the morning and reached Euston Square at about eight in the evening. The Ostend packet that would take them to Belgium was scheduled to leave early the next morning, but the Brontës had decided to rest and see something of London before embarking on the next leg of their journey, so were booked on the second crossing of the week, on Saturday. The party made its way to the Chapter Coffee House in Paternoster Row, where Patrick Brontë had once stayed as a young curate thirty years before. In its time, the establishment had welcomed such guests as Johnson, Goldsmith and Chatterton, but its reputation had dwindled and it was now a modest staging post for travelling clergymen and university students. From the windows of the inn, the next morning, Charlotte and Emily could see the dome of St Paul's cathedral; its bells seemed to summon them into the streets. They spent the next three days exploring the city's galleries and museums, and Charlotte relished, as they walked about London, what she called the peculiar, chopped-up speech of its inhabitants. On the Saturday morning, before dawn, the Brontës and their travelling companions took a carriage to the Steamship Company's wharf at London Bridge and boarded the packet. The ship reached the open sea a few hours later; it would take fourteen in all to reach Ostend. In *Villette*, Charlotte has Lucy Snowe, her narrator, recall the same journey: 'I was not sick till long after we passed Margate, and deep was the pleasure I drank in with the sea-breeze; divine the delight I drew from the heaving channel waves, from the sea-birds on their ridges, from the white sails on their dark distance, from the quiet, yet beclouded sky, overhanging all.'

'All was beautiful, all was more than picturesque,' wrote Charlotte later of the journey, in an old-fashioned diligence, through flat, wet farmland from Ostend to Brussels. The five travellers reached the city after dark on Sunday evening, and made their way to the Hôtel d'Hollande, not far from the diligence terminus on the Rue de la Madeleine. Charlotte and Emily were enrolled at the Pensionnat Heger, where they were to study French so as to be able to return to England and start their own school. The Pensionnat was situated at 32 Rue d'Isabelle, at the bottom of a steep flight of stone steps that led to the Royal Park. On the other side of the park was the royal palace; below the school were the narrower, busier streets of the city's commercial district, and not far away the cathedral of St Michel and St Gudule, to which, in time, overcome by solitude and obscure desires, Charlotte would find herself drawn. For now, it was the school itself that impressed her: a large white building that boasted, she noted as a porter opened the huge door, marble paving in its hallway and imitation marble upon the walls.

Through a glass door at the end of the passageway, she glimpsed a walled garden: the model of the garden where Lucy Snowe, in *Villette*, who at times mirrors Charlotte's movements precisely, would feel herself under surveillance, and into which she would creep at night to bury a packet of letters that she insisted were not love letters. The two young women were welcomed to Rue d'Isabelle by Claire Zoë Heger, who now ushered them into an imposing salon just off the hall.

Madame Heger was thirty-eight years old; her husband, Constantin Roman Heger, thirty-three. She ran the pensionnat, having inherited it from an aunt; he taught at an adjoining school for boys. M. Heger, however, was an intermittent presence in the corridors and courtyard of his wife's establishment: a dark and stocky figure whom the sisters glimpsed at first only at meals and as he made his way about the school, ever alert to the behaviour and progress of the pupils. Within weeks, he had begun to take a keen interest in the new arrivals from England: impressed by their talents – and perhaps also by their aloofness from the much younger pupils around them – he proposed a course of study considerably more advanced than the rote learning of French grammar and vocabulary to which they were at first exposed. Mrs Gaskell, Charlotte's first biographer, recounts his plan to acquaint them with 'the most celebrated French authors' by having them imitate in their own compositions the styles of the classics. Emily, especially, was at first resistant to this aping method, though Charlotte, despite her initial reservations, wrote later that it felt natural to her to submit to an obviously superior intellect.

Despite the influence of such an intellectually inspiring teacher, Charlotte and Emily found it difficult to adjust to life in Brussels. Aged twenty-five and twenty-three respectively, they shared their lessons and their dormitory with fifteen-year-olds. They seem to have taken immediately against the majority of their fellow pupils, thinking them morally corrupt, stupid and deceitful. The native character, wrote Charlotte, was 'singularly cold, selfish, animal and inferior'. They felt the type of politeness practised by the Belgian girls to be no more than a form of dissimulation, a trait they linked to the country's Catholicism. An anti-papal streak runs through many of Charlotte's letters and all of her novels: the Catholic faith was nothing more to her than a form of idolatry, and it expressed itself, she thought, in a poisonous mixture of false piety and sensual indulgence. She and Emily refused to attend the pious lecture that M. Heger, a zealous member of the Society of St Vincent de Paul who gave over much of his time to the education of the city's poor, delivered to the assembled pupils each evening. On Sundays they attended Anglican services in the Chapel Royal, 800 yards uphill from the pensionnat, and were there befriended by an English family. The Jenkinses recorded their impressions of Charlotte, an eloquent conversationalist who nonetheless had not yet overcome the effects of her seclusion at Haworth: she had the habit, recounts a biographer, of 'gradually wheeling round on her chair, so as almost to conceal her face from the person to whom she was speaking'.

After eight months, the stay in Brussels was cut short. Early in September, news came from home that a close friend of Branwell's, William Weightman, had died of cholera. Later in the month, their friend Martha Taylor, Mary's sister, was taken ill with what appeared to be dysentery; she was diagnosed with cholera around the middle of October and died the night before Charlotte reached her bedside. Worse was to follow: later that month, a letter came to inform the sisters that their aunt Elizabeth Branwell was ill and not expected to live. Before they could leave for home, a second letter arrived, telling of her death on the 29th of October. Early the following year, while Charlotte was still in mourning at Haworth and the family was contending with the emotional and financial collapse of Branwell Brontë, M. Heger wrote from Brussels to commend Patrick Brontë on his daughters' progress at the pensionnat, and to express regret at losing his 'two dear pupils'. He asked their father to let them return to the school, where, he wrote, they would swiftly complete their studies and acquire, he was sure, 'that assurance, that aplomb, so necessary to a teacher'. Furthermore, he was willing, should Mr Brontë approve his plan, to offer at least one of them a position 'according with her taste, and that pleasant independence so difficult for a young person to find'. Charlotte, it was decided, should return, Emily remaining at Haworth in expectation of the three surviving sisters setting up, in time, thanks to their aunt's legacy, a 'flourishing seminary' of their own.

*

Three years later, in a letter to Ellen Nussey, a fellow pupil at Roe Head, Charlotte wrote: 'I returned to Brussels after Aunt's death against my conscience – prompted by what then seemed an irresistible impulse – I was punished for my selfish folly by a total withdrawal of happiness and peace of mind.' She had left behind, as she saw it, a family in disarray, solely in order to further her own intellectual ambitions. As her biographer Rebecca Fraser notes, this self-admonition is easily taken as evidence of her attraction to Constantin Heger. But the case is more complicated: Charlotte at no point articulates an adulterous desire for him; the emotions she was to feel in the coming months can in no way be reduced to the pain of an unrequited or unconsummated love. Her suffering, the hypochondria that once again assailed her, was rather a combination of her feelings for M. Heger, her loneliness, and her unexpressed or unfulfilled ambitions as a writer. She confided these latter to her teacher; though he acknowledged her talent, he also, like Southey, could not countenance the neglect of wifely duty that a literary career would entail. She ought instead, he counselled, to build on her educational progress so far, and look forward (or, as Charlotte saw it, resign herself) to the life of a teacher. In secret, she outlined on the cover of her German exercise book the plot of a magazine story she planned to write, the narrative of 'certain remarkable occurrences' that she listed in turn: '1st, reverses of fortune; 2nd, new arrival; 3rd, loss of relatives; 4th, crosses in the affections; 5th, going abroad and returning; 6th . . .' The sixth was blank. It was to be filled, perhaps, in the weeks to come; or maybe it would remain empty, like the days that now seemed to stretch intolerably before her. Constantin Heger – whether or not at the insistence of his wife, we shall never know – had begun to grow colder towards his intense and wilful student. Charlotte had started to suspect that Mme Heger had spies among the staff, and complained to Emily that M. Heger had abandoned her:

M. Heger is wondrously influenced by Madame, and I should not wonder if he disapproves very much of my unamiable want of sociability. He has already given me a brief lecture on universal *bienveillance*, and perceiving that I don't improve in consequence, I fancy he has taken to considering me as a person to be let alone – left to the error of her ways; and consequently he has in great measure withdrawn the light of his countenance, and I get on from day to day in a Robinson Crusoe-like condition – very lonely.

*

Charlotte Brontë fictionalized her time in Brussels twice: first in *The Professor*, then in *Villette*. *The Professor* tells the story of one William Crimsworth, an orphan who, on leaving Eton, scorns the plans his family benefactors have for his entry into the clergy and marriage to one of his cousins. Instead, he seeks out his estranged brother, Edward, a northern mill owner, and is engaged by him as a lowly clerk. He quickly discovers that he has no stomach for this sort of servitude, and resolves to put his education to better use as a schoolteacher in Brussels. At a school for boys on the Rue d'Isabelle, he is engaged to teach English by a M. Pelet, and soon after also by Mademoiselle Reuter, proprietor of a girls' school next door. Like Charlotte, he finds the business of teaching to be exhausting and tedious, and his pupils wanting in intellect and application. Like her, too, he is appalled by what he sees as the corruption and sensuality of his female students; a product, he does not doubt, of their Catholicism. But one student, an older Anglo-Swiss girl, shows a degree of intellectual and moral soundness that surprises, and eventually seduces, him. William Crimsworth, it is clear, is an amalgam of M. Heger and the young Charlotte herself.

The Professor is in part an example, and perhaps to some degree a parody, of the literature of self-advancement that was so popular in the middle of the nineteenth century. Crimsworth is in every respect a self-made man: he turns his back on a life of unearned privilege in order to make his own economic and moral (in this genre, they are essentially the same thing) way in the world. He is also one of the least sympathetic protagonists in nineteenth-century fiction: his indifference towards, or outright scorn for, all those he meets in the course of his self-fashioning – apart, that is, from the implausible paragon, Frances, whom he eventually marries – is undoubtedly what made the novel unpublishable in Charlotte's lifetime. But the oddest thing about Crimsworth is his insistent, almost morbid, fascination with physiognomy. No character speaks on the page without the hero's first having pored over his or her physical failings. His pupils are variously slovenly and unwashed, gaunt, brutal-looking, given to shameless leering in his presence, exhibiting ill-temper on the forehead, vicious propensities in the eye, envy and deceit about the mouth. The voguish pseudo-science of phrenology, too, provides the means to describe and judge each character's face: mutiny and hate are graven on the forehead of a certain student, sagacity and sense in the open countenance of Mademoiselle Reuter. The book is permeated by the notion that character, in its psychological and moral senses, is inseparable from bodily being. Everybody is readable in this way, except, it seems, the dissimulator Crimsworth, who successfully shams forbearance until it no longer suits him to do so.

It would no doubt be too crude to conjecture that Crimsworth's eventual (strangely brief) mental collapse, and his subsequent self-diagnosis as a hypochondriac, are simply the consequences of his suppression of his true emotions throughout the novel. But there is

something abrupt and even implausible about the way Brontë introduces the subject. Crimsworth returns to his lodgings after Frances,
to his delight, has agreed to marry him. Still thrilled by the interview
with his beloved, he goes to bed hungry and wakes, he says, feeling
like Job when a spirit passed before his face; a voice seems to say: '*In
the midst of life we are in death.*' 'That sound,' Crimsworth recalls,
'and the sensation of chill anguish accompanying it, many would
have regarded as supernatural; but I recognized it at once as the
effect of reaction. Man is ever clogged with his mortality, and it
was my mortal nature which now faltered and plained; my nerves
which jarred and gave a false sound, because the soul, of late rushing headlong to an aim, had overstrained the body's comparative
weakness. A horror of great darkness fell upon me; I felt my chamber invaded by one I had known formerly, but had thought for ever
departed. I was temporarily a prey to hypochondria.' He had been
acquainted with the illness once before: 'she', as he personifies the
disease, had been the secret tormentor of his parentless boyhood,
harrying him with thoughts of his own death. 'Why did hypochondria accost me now?' he asks. There is no answer: within a paragraph, he has repulsed the disease 'as one would a dreaded and
ghastly concubine coming to embitter a husband's heart towards his
young bride'. (The image is highly suggestive, in the light of
Brontë's probable guilt at her infatuation with M. Heger.) The
hypochondriac fit lasts only eight days; he says nothing to anybody
of what he has suffered, and is soon at Frances's side again: freed, as
he puts it, from the tyranny of his demon.

*

Late in the summer of 1843, the Pensionnat Heger was closed for
the summer vacation, and its boarders sent home. Charlotte was
more alone than ever. On the 1st of September, tormented by
thoughts and emotions that she would later characterize as hypochondriacal, and having got into the habit, as she wrote to Emily, of
wandering the boulevards of Brussels alone for hours on end, she

struck out towards the cemetery where Martha Taylor had been buried a year earlier. She walked far beyond it onto a hill from which nothing was to be seen but fields, as far as the horizon. It was evening when she entered the city again. Fearing to return to the school where no welcome awaited her, she threaded once more the streets about the Rue d'Isabelle. Perhaps her weary steps were quickened now by the solitary's need to appear purposeful and independent in public, or perhaps, as is suggested by the place to which at length they took her, she no longer gave any thought to appearance. Above her, the bell of the cathedral of St Michel and St Gudule had begun to sound and, finding herself before its massive gates, Charlotte decided to go in.

She does not describe in any great detail the scene that greeted her, nor express to Emily, as one might expect, any repugnance for the pious vulgarity of the decor. The cathedral, then as now, was dominated by baroque statuary, which had replaced the original ornamentation, ripped out in the course of the Reformation in 1579. From the entrance of the nave to the altar, a procession of apostles, most shown holding the instruments of their martyrdom, looked down on her from soaring columns. An oak pulpit of astonishing complexity towered even above these statues. At its base, Adam and Eve laboured to support the pulpit itself; between them was the tail of the serpent, which coiled about the whole edifice till it reached the canopy or sounding board above; and there, standing on a crescent moon, the Blessed Virgin and the infant Jesus pierced the snake's head with a golden cross. From every inch of the pulpit, there sprouted oak leaves and branches, an eagle raised its wings from the top of the left-hand staircase, and above the heads of the original sinners in Eden a dark oaken skeleton clung to the gilt drapery, grinning horribly at the congregation below. The fearsome aesthetic of the pulpit was continued in the oak confessionals that shone in the faint light: penitent angels with lowered heads clutched darkly gleaming skulls, while the human sinners on either

side were enclosed by twisted pillars and overlooked by angels'
heads. It was towards one of these deeply shadowed structures that
Charlotte now found herself drawn. 'An odd whim came into my
head,' she wrote. 'I felt as if I did not care what I did, provided it
was not absolutely wrong, and that it served to vary my life and
yield a moment's interest. I took a fancy to change myself into a
Catholic and go and make a real confession to see what it was like.
Knowing me as you do, you will think this odd, but when people
are by themselves they have singular fancies.'

Charlotte's letter hardly plumbs the depth of her depression,
nor fully expresses the violence of the grief that must have brought
her to countenance the strange interview that followed in the confessional. We have to turn to the pages of *Villette*, the novel that
most dramatically recounts her crisis, to understand the interior
mystery of her hypochondria. The novel's narrator, Lucy Snowe, is
a self-described hypochondriac. When we first meet her, an orphan
shuttled between various guardians and employers, she assures her
readers that she is a character of little consequence. 'I, Lucy Snowe,'
she tells us, 'plead guiltless of that curse, an overheated and discur-
sive imagination.' She is only an observer of life, a modest and
colourless creature. Crossing the English Channel, like Charlotte,
she falls into a reverie and seems to see the continent of Europe
stretched before her in the sunshine, its pastures, woods and streams
'grand with imperial promise'. But she quickly checks herself –
'cancel the whole of that, if you please, reader' – and disavows her
own artistic vision. It is only the onset of seasickness, she concludes;
and daydreams, in any case, are delusions of the demon.

Lucy, like her creator, is abandoned at the pensionnat during the
summer vacation. Though she has not yet admitted it to the reader,
she is in love with Paul Emanuel, the schoolmaster who in many
respects resembles Constantin Heger. He is not married, and runs
the pensionnat with Madame Beck, who keeps such a close watch on
Lucy that she feels herself to be under constant surveillance in the

classroom, in the grounds of the school, in her own apartment. Even her furniture, she suspects, has been raided by the vigilant schoolmistress, who is intent on uncovering the true character of her reticent employee. Left alone, she finds that her spirits, already lowered by Mme Beck's treatment of her, now sink into indifference and resignation. Unlike Charlotte, she is not totally alone during the vacation: she has been left in charge of a pupil whom Brontë calls 'the crétin'. This hapless girl is silent, innocent and, in her behaviour, 'aimlessly malevolent'; her care requires unnamed physical ministrations that Lucy can hardly bear. (It is perhaps not too fanciful to suggest that the sullen and thoughtlessly suffering girl is a manifestation of Lucy's own predicament, much in the way that in *Jane Eyre* Rochester's mad wife stands for certain unruly desires of Jane's.) It is only when she is at last relieved of this duty by an aunt of the girl's that Lucy ventures from the pensionnat, into the streets, then out of the city, following Charlotte's solitary excursion till she too ends up entering a Catholic church – though it is not, in the novel, the same cathedral – and contemplating an uncharacteristic confession.

Like the novelist, Lucy expresses a conventional horror at Catholic rites and institutions; her confession too is an act of desperation, though not, she assures the reader, of madness. She has left behind the awful stillness of the dormitory; the empty white beds looked to her like spectres, their coronals each a death's head, huge and sunbleached. Now, in the pervading gloom of the church, purpled by the light from the stained glass, she scrutinizes the face of the elderly priest within the confessional and concludes from his physiognomy, so unlike that of the 'grovelling' native clergy, that he is a Frenchman, and possibly a kind one at that. Unsure of the formula for confession, she blurts out: 'Mon père, je suis Protestante.' The priest asks why she has come to him. Lucy outlines her recent suffering: 'I had been living for some weeks quite alone; I had been ill; I had a pressure of affliction on my mind of which it would hardly any longer

endure the weight.' Her confessor responds by blaming her symptoms on her Protestantism, urging her to seek solace in the true faith,
and offering his counsel if she will agree to come to him the following
morning. Lucy has no such intention: 'Did I, do you suppose, reader,
contemplate venturing again within that worthy priest's reach? As
soon should I have thought of walking into a Babylonish furnace.'
Her resistance to his faith is actually beside the point: his kindness
has already released her from the grasp of her morbid thoughts. But
on leaving the church, still weak, she wanders again through the
ancient, picturesque streets until, caught up in a hailstorm, she aims
herself through the darkness, hoping to sink down on the steps of a
great building. Instead, she seems to pitch headlong down an abyss,
and falls unconscious on the stone.

Throughout *Villette*, Lucy Snowe oscillates between periods of
almost preternatural alertness – to her surroundings, to real or perceived slights from her employers, to the alien culture in which she
finds herself – and sudden swoons into weakness, delirium or unconsciousness. Just as the novel appears to begin three times, each time
teasing the reader with a new narrative thread, so its heroine is as if
reborn after each physical or emotional crisis. In the case of her collapse on leaving the confessional, she wakes to find that she is in the
care of the Bretton family, who have not been seen since the opening
of the novel: the Dr John whom Lucy has met in Brussels is now
revealed to be Graham Bretton, son of Lucy's godmother, grown up
and already recognized by Lucy, who has kept the information from
the reader. Graham, on hearing of her 'low spirits', concludes that
she is beyond his abilities to treat: 'Medicine can give nobody good
spirits. My art halts at the threshold of hypochondria: she just looks
in, sees a chamber of torture, but can neither say nor do much.' But
Lucy recovers from her hypochondriacal attacks and learns something from them. Her breakdowns are the necessary conditions for
her making her way in the world; what she calls her hypochondria is
a way of retreating into herself, the better to emerge transformed

socially, professionally or romantically, though still claiming to be
alone, a mere watcher of the life around her. Time and again, Lucy
tells us that she is nobody, when in fact she is engaged in a protracted
experiment concerning the problem of being somebody, and has a
habit of keeping from us the nature of her discoveries.

Illness is for Lucy one such trial of her self-in-progress: it tests
the limits of who she is and what she can endure. Her physical
symptoms are bound up with her psychological state: her pulse
races, she feels an intense nervousness or rising panic. At one point
she acquiesces in a pretence regarding her health that is meant to
quieten her nerves but succeeds only in awakening strange new
sensations in her. Following a fraught exchange with Mme Beck,
who objects strongly to Lucy's involvement with Paul Emanuel,
she retires to her room. Early the next morning, going out into the
courtyard, she catches sight of her reflection: her lips and cheeks
are white, her eyes glassy, the lids purple and swollen. The whole
school knows the source of her distress, but under Mme Beck's
direction all, including Lucy herself, go along with the fiction that
she is suffering from an especially vicious headache. She is put to
bed the following night with a strong opiate, and is soon asleep. But
Mme Beck has miscalculated the dose (Lucy is unsure whether she
has been given too much or too little) and her patient is soon awake
again, possessed by a curious excitement: 'I became alive to new
thought – to reverie peculiar in colouring. A gathering call ran
among the faculties, their bugles sang, their trumpets rang an
untimely summons. Imagination was roused from her rest, and she
came forth impetuous and venturous. With scorn she looked on
Matter, her mate.' There follows a bizarre chapter in which Lucy
appears to rise from her bed and set out into the night. The town of
Villette, the novel's stand-in for Brussels, is alive with light and
noise; a fete is in progress, and seemingly all of Lucy's acquaintances
in the city are to be seen in the park, bathed in a weird glow: 'in
a land of enchantment, a garden most gorgeous, a plain sprinkled

with coloured meteors, a forest with sparks of purple and ruby and golden fire gemming the foliage; a region, not of trees and shadow, but of strangest architectural wealth – of altar and temple, of pyramid, obelisk, and sphynx; incredible to say, the wonders and the symbols of Egypt teemed throughout the park of Villette.' It is as if, at the moment that her hypochondriacal feelings overcome her, Lucy is subject, literally, to visions: illness and unhappiness, once they have reached a certain point of crisis, allow her to indulge the imagination that she elsewhere denies she possesses.

The most explicit reference to Lucy's hypochondria – or at least to her identification with the symptoms of the disease in another – comes, however, much earlier in the novel. Not long after her collapse during the long vacation, Lucy is persuaded, despite her natural resistance to such spectacles, to attend a concert at the hall of a local musical society. Having assured the reader several times already that she lacks all social graces and has no imagination, Lucy now finds herself wearing a new pink dress (bought by her godmother, in whose care she has been convalescing), and is soon ushered into the concert hall: a garishly lit, heavily draped and gilt room that dazzles her and 'seem[s] the work of eastern genii'. In her wonderment she observes the entrance of the royal family:

Well do I recall that King – a man of fifty, a little bowed, a little grey: there was no face in all that assembly which resembled his. I had never read, never been told anything of his nature or his habits; and at first the strong hieroglyphics graven with an iron stylet on his brow, round his eyes, beside his mouth, puzzled and baffled instinct. Ere long, however, if I did not *know*, at least I *felt*, the meaning of those characters written without hand. There sat a silent sufferer – a nervous, melancholy man. Those eyes had looked on the visits of a certain ghost – had long awaited the comings and goings of that strangest spectre, Hypochondria. Perhaps he saw her now on that stage, over against him, amidst all that brilliant throng. Hypochondria has that wont, to rise in the midst of thousands – dark as

Doom, pale as Malady, and well nigh strong as Death. Her comrade and victim thinks to be happy one moment – 'Not so,' says she; 'I come.' And she freezes the blood in his heart, and beclouds the light in his eye.

What are we to make of this description, at once intensely concentrated on the King's physiognomy and somewhat vague as to the exact map of woe that is to be read there? As we know from *Jane Eyre*, Brontë had an abiding interest in physiognomy and phrenology, and employed facial description as an index of character to a degree that is unusual even for Victorian fiction, which is rich with such detail. But whereas in the novels of Dickens, for example, the face and body denote a moral complexion that will be demonstrated by the character's behaviour, in Brontë they point instead to some less easily expressible interior: the face both hides and reveals (but only reveals to the sensitive gaze) the drama within. The King is assailed by 'that darkest foe of humanity – constitutional melancholy', but his suffering remains hidden from his subjects. Only Lucy is able to read the signs: 'Full mournful and significant was that spectacle! Not the less so because, both for the aristocracy and the honest bourgeoisie of Labassecour, its peculiarity seemed to be wholly invisible: I could not discover that one soul present was either struck or touched.' She identifies not only with the King's melancholic aspect, but with his hiding his real self from those around him. Hypochondria, for Lucy, is a matter of feeling oneself exiled from the mass of humanity, solitary in the midst of the crowd. This is what she has in common with her creator: an imagination that can only be expressed as morbidity.

*

Early in the summer of 1851, while the weather was wet, dark and close, Charlotte Brontë began to complain of 'rampant and violent' headaches that invariably ended with 'excessive sickness'. 'Pleasant moments I have,' she wrote, 'but it is usually a pleasure I am obliged to repel and check, which cannot benefit the future, but only add to its solitude, which is no more to be relied on than the sunshine of one summer's day. I pass many portions of the night in extreme sadness.' A peaceful stay at Mrs Gaskell's house went some way to alleviating her symptoms, but soon after leaving she was ill again, and tormented by the 'blank intervals' during which she could not write. By the new year she was unable 'to stoop over a desk without bringing on pain and oppression in the chest'; she could not sleep, and feared that her illness was consumption, which had killed Anne and Emily. Her physician, Dr Ruddock, prescribed pills for an 'inertness of the liver'; they contained mercury, which caused her to salivate constantly and made her mouth sore, her teeth loose and her tongue swollen. In spring, the winds, she said, depressed her nervous system, and she wrote to Mrs Gaskell that, if she had to live this part of her life over again, her 'prayer must necessarily be "Let this cup pass from me"'. In May, following Ruddock's advice, she travelled north-east to Filey, and visited Anne's grave at Scarborough. Her headaches continued, joined now by an insistent pain in her side. But slowly her spirits began to lift. She walked by the sea, and even swam in 'a peculiar bathing contraption'. Upon returning to her manuscript, however, she found the writing no less arduous: 'Submission, courage, exertion when practicable, these seem to be the weapons with which we must fight life's long battle.' It was only with extreme effort, constantly 'disgusted with myself and my delays', that she finished the novel in October. The process had been accompanied throughout by constant anxiety about her health, and an array of ailments that now began to abate.

Charlotte Brontë's hypochondria, that mix of illness, fear and depression, was in a sense, like Boswell's, a way of organizing her time, or at least planning an ideal regimen according to which she could write at last, thus escaping the sense of distracting responsibility that had first troubled her at Roe Head. While time, for Boswell, seemed to be endlessly elastic, his days filled with fruitless reverie and dissipation from which he had to rein himself in, Brontë fantasized a kind of temporal luxury, an escape from the exigencies of familial or social duty. (She found the demands of her increasing fame scarcely tolerable, and while in the first stages of writing *Villette* upbraided Thackeray for having spread the news, at a lecture of his she attended in London, that the author of *Jane Eyre* was in the room.) To her publisher George Smith, she conjured up the perfect conditions for writing the story of Lucy Snowe. She ought to be immured, she said, in a 'Chamber in the Wall':

There the prophet might be received and lodged, subject to a system kind (perhaps) yet firm; roused each morning at six punctually, by contrivance of that virtuous self-acting couch which casts from it its too fondly clinging inmate . . . served with a slight breakfast then with the exception of a crust at one, no further gastronomic interruption till 7 p.m., at which time the greatest and most industrious of modern authors should be summoned by the most spirited and vigilant of modern publishers to a meal, comfortable and comforting – in short, a good dinner . . . of which they should partake together in the finest spirit of geniality and fraternity – part at half-past nine and at that salutary hour withdraw to recreating repose. Grand would be the result of such a system pursued for six months.

Perhaps Lucy's protectiveness of her own privacy has its origin in this fantasy. (It is unclear if she discovered the 'self-acting couch' in the pages of Boswell.) It is not only that she resembles the author in terms of her social reticence; she also feels the intimacy of her room, her books and papers to have been exposed by the vigilant regime of the pensionnat. It is only by falling ill that she can find for herself the right kind of solitude, in which to invent her future self.

3. On the Expression of Emotion: Charles Darwin

'The voluntary part of his brain seemed to have too easy and too free an access to his involuntary part. Therein, I believe, lies the source of all his ills.'

Sir Arthur Keith, *Darwin Revalued*

The room that was Charles Darwin's study faces north-east onto the back garden of Down House in Kent, and directly overlooks a tortured mulberry tree that his children often climbed as he worked. A closer inspection of the tree today shows it to have been deeply rent along its trunk; whether by disease, decay or the tenacious scraping of childish heels, it is impossible to say. The tree rests the largest of its twisted limbs on a slender wooden crutch-like pole. Its gaping, desiccated torso appears to have been half filled at some point, by way of repair, with a rough sort of concrete, this in turn imperfectly disguised by pitch or tar. The study itself seems, in the course of its museification, to have been metaphorically slicked over with some impenetrable medium, behind which the atmosphere itself has solidified, such is the air-locked mood that greets the visitor at first. Darwin's books are safely vitrined on the right-hand wall as one enters, while to the left a red rope ensures that the visitor can only gape in unknowing awe at the volumes, manuscripts and instruments that carefully litter the table in the centre of the room, and must squint to make out the features, in three prints above the fireplace, of the botanist Joseph Hooker, the geologist Charles Lyell and Darwin's grandfather, Josiah Wedgwood. The room, and the biographical moment it affects to preserve, might as well have been placed under a bell jar, such as sits gleaming and empty among Darwin's papers.

Certain details, however, threaten to crack the hard surface of historical reconstruction, letting us touch, for an instant, the texture of the life and labour that the study once contained. Darwin was not in the habit of writing at the Pembroke table in the centre of the room, nor at the smaller, revolving 'drum' table that currently sits, its various curiosities and chemical bottles well lit, between the window and the bookshelves. Instead, his papers and pens sat on a portable, cloth-covered board that at present, faded to a pale crimson, edges just off the far end of the table. The board sat in turn on the arms of a high-backed eighteenth-century chair of austere mock-classical design. In a room filled with mysterious receptacles and strange animal and mineral specimens, this chair is the most curious object. It sits upon four cast-iron legs of about a foot in length, apparently cannibalized from an old bedstead, at the end of which are four small wheels, by which Darwin manoeuvred himself about his study while seated. The resulting contraption looks so unwieldy, and so peculiarly tailored to its owner's desire to be mobile, upright and elevated, that it conjures a sitter of notable, if not neurotic, fastidiousness in the matter of his own physical comfort.

In the far left corner of the study, according to the museum's audio guide, a screened-off area contains Darwin's personal privy; a shallow metal bath and a number of water jugs have been arranged so as to suggest his ablutions, but not to hint at anything more private than that. Darwin, says the calm and cultivated voice, was frequently unwell, and was here able to minister to his various ailments without being diverted for long from his research or writing. Here too, we are told, he submitted himself to the hydrotherapy or water cure to which he habitually had recourse for many years. The study, in other words, asks us to picture not only a mind at work but a body, labouring, suffering and at rest. It was a body, so the room hints, that caused its owner considerable care, a body that needed to be hedged about, in its daily existence, with countless small accommodations and luxuries, to be by turns protected, invigorated, salved and occasionally exercised. Darwin's body, it seems, was against him, and everything he achieved he coaxed from a constitution under constant attack from a dizzying number of symptoms. He lived, as one is only obscurely aware while touring his home, on the verge of invalidism for most of his productive adult life. Perhaps in the end the somewhat numbed, tentative and prophylactic air that prevails at Down House has its origin in this history: Charles Darwin did not live wholly in the world whose view of itself he altered for ever.

*

Darwin's earliest memory concerned the sudden onset of physical pain. He described the incident in an 'autobiographical fragment' that he wrote (with his customarily careless attitude to spelling, grammar and punctuation) in 1838:

My earliest recollection, the date of which I can approximately tell, and which must have been before I was four years old, was when sitting on [his sister] Carolines knee in the dining room, whilst she was cutting an orange for me, a cow run by the window, which made me jump; so that I received a bad cut of which I bear the scar to this day. Of this scene I recollect the place where I sat & the cause of the fright, but not the cut itself.

In his youth, he evinced a distressing and — so far as his intended medical career was concerned — ruinous susceptibility to the physical suffering of others. As a student at Edinburgh he was present, he later recalled, at 'two very bad operations', carried out, of course, without anaesthetic; he could not bear the sight (nor, perhaps, the screams) and had to leave the theatre. His father advised him instead to become a clergyman, and he spent three years as a pre-divinity student at Cambridge. There, in January 1829, he reported to his cousin William Darwin Fox that his lips had 'lately taken to be bad'. Two years later, to his sister Susan, he complained that his hands were 'not quite well'. In neither case do we have any clear sense of the nature of his affliction, but he seems to have taken the ailments badly, reporting for instance that the state of his lips had reduced him to a 'sort of hybernation'.

In his second year at Edinburgh, Darwin had joined the Plinian Society, a student group that introduced him to the new naturalism of Jean-Baptiste Lamarck and the emerging concept of evolution. In 1831, the botany professor John Stevens Henslow proposed him as naturalist on a planned voyage of HMS *Beagle* to chart the coasts of Patagonia and Tierra del Fuego. His father at first objected, but relented under pressure from Josiah Wedgwood. Throughout the late autumn and into winter the ship awaited suitable weather, and Darwin became increasingly agitated: he feared that seasickness would incapacitate him, and that his father or the ship's captain would learn of the palpitations he had begun to suffer on his arrival at Plymouth. (The captain, Robert FitzRoy, an adherent of the physiognomic theories of Johann Kaspar Lavater, had already contemplated turning the young man away on account of the unsuitable shape of his nose.) Once the *Beagle* set sail, late in December, Darwin's worst fears concerning his tendency to seasickness were realized. The means by which he tried to treat himself during the next five years included a diet of biscuits and raisins; a hot mixture of sago, wine and spices; peppermint; hops; carbonate of soda; laudanum; and lavender water. The 'only sure thing' that would counter his nausea, however, was to lie still, preferably in a hammock, and he eventually hit upon a routine by which he could work for about an hour, 'take the horizontal' for a time, and then resume his labours.

Otherwise, his illnesses aboard the *Beagle* were predictable, if on at least one occasion also cause for concern at home. In April 1832, in a Brazilian forest, he began to feel feverish and nauseated, but

claimed to have cured himself within a day or so by eating cinna-
mon and drinking port wine. In October of the following year he
appears to have suffered heatstroke, and spent three days under the
care of 'a goodnatured old woman' whose favoured treatments
included pressing orange leaves or split beans to the patient's tem-
ples. (Darwin noted other curious symmetrical treatments among
the Brazilians: the local remedy for a broken limb was to kill and
cut open two puppies and bind them each side of the arm or leg.) In
September 1834, while visiting a Chilean gold mine, he became ill
after drinking some local wine; his stomach was greatly affected
and it was a month before he felt well again.

'I find the noodle and the stomach are antagonistic powers,'
wrote Darwin to Caroline in May 1838. Having returned from his
voyage in October 1836, he had worked hard at writing up his geo-
logical and zoological observations, and in that time gained almost
sixteen pounds in weight. A year later, however, he had begun to
suffer once more from 'uncomfortable' and 'violent' palpitations of
the heart, from headaches, gastric upsets and a generalized feeling of
physical disturbance. (We may note here that this latter symptom –
the sense, quite apart from any specific ailments to which the patient may point, *that something is wrong* – has a long history among
hypochondriacs.) Late in 1838, he became engaged to his cousin
Emma Wedgwood. Their correspondence includes many references
to Darwin's ill health, and Emma wrote solicitously: 'If you knew
how I long to be with you when you are not well! You must not
think that I expect a holiday husband to be always making himself
agreeable to me & if that is all the "work" that I shall have it will not
be much for me to bear whatever it may be for you. So don't be ill
any more my dear Charley till I can be with you to nurse you and
save you from bothers.' In the week leading up to their wedding in
January 1839, a fierce headache threatened to postpone the event.

Later that year, Darwin reported himself 'languid and uncomfortable'. His years of more or less solid invalidism had begun in

earnest, though neither the letters nor the evidence of his having consulted certain doctors (his father included) will quite cohere into an accurate map of his symptoms. Here follows instead a selection of his complaints and his optimistic assertions concerning his treatment. Attending a service at King's College in 1839, he and Emma found the church unheated and almost empty: Darwin was immediately unwell. Early the following year, Emma described him as existing in a constant state of distressing languor. He hoped to be 'set . . . going again' by Dr Henry Holland, but the treatment — its exact nature is unknown — did not work. His father, however, seems to have had more luck: a few months later, Darwin noted that his periodic vomiting had apparently been cured thanks to the (again obscure) ministrations of Dr Robert Waring Darwin. 'At present I only want vigour,' he wrote, and this was a recurring self-description: he felt himself at various times 'dull', 'old', 'spiritless' and 'stupid'. In letters to Joseph Hooker, he despaired of ever writing anything of scientific worth, and described episodes of excessive excitement, violent shivering, gastric pangs and yet more vomiting. Hooker, who was not reticent on the topic of his own ill health, recalled visiting his friend, for several days at a time, in the mid 1840s. At eight o'clock in the morning, the two men would converse for about half an hour on the subject of Darwin's research. 'The morning interviews', wrote Hooker, 'were followed by his taking a complete rest, for they always exhausted him, often producing a buzzing noise in the head, and sometimes what he called "stars in the eyes", the latter too often the prelude of an attack of violent eczema in the head during which he was hardly recognizable. These attacks were followed by a period of what with him was the nearest approach to health, and always to activity.' As a rule, Darwin would apparently recover by midday, and he and Hooker could then carry on their conversation well into the afternoon.

By the time the family moved to Down House in 1842 – Darwin had recently completed his *Structure and Distribution of Coral Reefs,*

the first of three volumes on the geology of South America – Emma
must have grown accustomed to her husband's ill health. Indeed,
the indulgent tone of her letters around this time seems to express
a kind of relish for attending to his many needs. Four years earlier
she had written that 'nothing could make me so happy as to feel that
I could be of any use or comfort to my own dear Charley when he
is not well.' In 1840 she confided to an aunt: 'It is a great happiness
to me that when Charles is most unwell he continues just as sociable
as ever, and is not like the rest of the Darwins, who will not say
how they really are; but he always tells me how he feels and never
wants to be alone, but continues just as warmly affectionate as ever,
so that I feel I am a comfort to him.' A skein of conjugal and domestic ties, intimacies that might knot themselves into resentment,
seems already woven through this last statement. Perhaps another
woman would have felt that a husband who *always* told her how he
felt and *never* wanted to be alone was not exactly an ideal companion; but sickness, from Emma Darwin's point of view, seems to
have given her a more affable, even-tempered husband, and this
assertion of Darwin's continued good humour in the face of his ailments runs also through the memoirs of his children.

*

In a short text that describes his 'residence at Down from Sep. 14
1842 to the present time 1876', Darwin writes: 'My chief enjoy-
ment and sole employment throughout life has been scientific work;
and the excitement from such work makes me for the time forget,
or drives quite away, my daily discomfort.' But he could also write:
'Even ill-health, though it has annihilated several years of my life,
has saved me from the distractions of society and amusement.' Darwin's hypochondria consists in a protracted discovery of the uses of
being unwell. His most explicit statements about the subject have
to do with illness and his domestic life; the two seem to have been
superimposed in his mind like a specimen and the slide on which it
may be examined under the microscope. Except that it is not clear

in this case which was the transparent support and which the object under scrutiny: we cannot say whether Darwin was a patient first and a husband second, or vice versa. His attitudes to both marriage and illness were ambiguous. 'I hope', he wrote to Huxley in 1854, 'that your marriage will not make you idle: happiness, I fear, is not good for work.' Perhaps, he once conjectured, a scientist ought not to be married at all, 'for then there would be nothing in this wide world worth caring for & a man might (whether he would is another question) work away like a Trojan'. Darwin's disquiet in this regard seems to encompass something more than the traditional frustration felt by the ambitious patriarch faced with the reality of 'the pram in the hall' (as the critic Cyril Connolly famously put it). He is, rather, unsettled in a larger sense by the absconding present, by the suspicion that life is antithetical to labour.

Like all rigorous regimes and routines to which we submit ourselves (or to which we only wish we could force ourselves), Darwin's daily timetable was both a way of ensuring that he attended to the tasks at hand – which is to say, both family life and his research – and a way of neutralizing them in advance, of making sure that he did not have to give himself over entirely to their rigours, pleasures or challenges. He was in this sense, one might say, the anti-Boswell. Where Boswell built hopeful bulwarks of work and study against the venal overrunning of his person and personality, only to have them breached immediately by sloth and temptation, Darwin seems to have worried that his being would dissolve if he let himself succumb to the unpredictable experiment of sustained labour. But if the work could be mapped in advance, recited in his head like a theorem, then he could conceivably stave off this undoing, and still achieve the goals he set for himself. The same was true of family life: an indulgent father and affectionate husband, he nonetheless for many years parcelled out his presence and attention in the most meticulous fashion. Physical illness was the method by which Darwin negotiated with chronology. The extent to which sickness could be said to impose, as it always does, a certain timetable, and the degree to which the patient himself took charge of his own time management, could no longer be distinguished. In this sense, it scarcely matters whether he was really unwell or not; the effect was the same: an organized and only dully painful life, punctuated by periods of greater suffering that in themselves became the pretext to submit for a time to an alternative, and no less rigorous, nor useful, regime.

Darwin's son Francis has left us a detailed account of the daily routine that his father followed for many years. He breakfasted alone at a quarter to eight, and began work promptly at eight o'clock. After an hour and a half – he considered this his most productive time of the day – he went into the drawing room for the post, hoping always that there was not much in the way of professional correspondence, and lay on the sofa while family letters were read aloud to him, until half past ten, at which time he returned to work till twelve or a quarter past. He was often at that point heard to exclaim: '*I've* done a good day's work', and would then generally strike out from the house in the direction of his greenhouse, where he briefly examined his experimental plants or looked at germinating seeds. Not far from the greenhouse was the entrance to a small patch of woodland, through which Darwin had had cut a roughly circular path about a mile long, the 'Sand-walk'. After one turn of the woods, he went indoors for lunch. Afterwards he lay again on the sofa in the drawing room, and read a newspaper; then, till three, he wrote letters, the board resting on the arms of his peculiar high chair. There followed a novel-and-smoking interlude in his bedroom, and at four o'clock he left the house once more for a half-hour walk. On returning, he worked in his study till half past five, did nothing for half an hour, and retired again to his room, where one of his children often read to him.

Darwin dined at half past seven, with the rest of the family; as his son records, he often ate no more than an egg or a small piece of meat. After dinner he played two games of backgammon with

Emma, becoming, so his son recalled, regularly animated at his own bad luck. He then read a scientific volume – that is, read it to himself – before returning from his study to the drawing room to listen to Emma play the piano. He went to bed, generally exhausted, at half past ten, but frequently lay awake for hours, unable to dismiss some scientific question or other from his thoughts. Francis Darwin recalled:

It was a sure sign that he was not well when he was idle at any times other than his regular resting hours; for, as long as he remained moderately well, there was no break in the regularity of his life. Weekdays and Sundays passed by alike, each with their stated intervals of work and rest. It is almost impossible, except for those who watched his daily life, to realise how essential to his well-being was the regular routine that I have sketched: and with what pain and difficulty anything beyond it was attempted. Any public appearance, even of the most modest kind, was an effort to him. In 1871 he went to the little village church for the wedding of his elder daughter, but he could hardly bear the fatigue of being present through the short service. The same may be said of the few other occasions on which he was present at similar ceremonies.

With the strict rationing of his time went, in other words, a careful doling out of his presence in public. 'During the first part of our residence,' Charles Darwin wrote, referring to the move to Down in 1842, 'we went a little into society, and received a few friends here; but my health almost always suffered from the excitement, violent shivering and vomiting attacks being thus brought on. I have therefore been compelled for many years to give up all dinner-parties; and this has been somewhat of a deprivation for me, as such parties always put me into high spirits. From the same cause I have been able to invite here very few scientific acquaintances.' Illness was as much a means of ordering the space in which he moved as it was a way of controlling time. It matters not a jot in this regard whether he was really ill (though that question, as we shall see, has exercised biographers, medical historians, scientific admirers and detractors alike since shortly after his death). Darwin's experience was of suffering, and it was that experience that allowed him to organize his life in ways that were as beneficial as they were perhaps also destructive. It meant that he could retreat from the world, and even from the profession of scientist. London, he wrote, 'so generally knocks me up, that I am able to do scarcely anything' – the better to pursue his scientific inquiries.

In the *Diary of Health* that he kept from the 1st of July 1849 to the 16th of January 1855, filling sixty-four foolscap sheets, he summarized his complaints and the various cures canvassed. His most frequent symptom was 'flatulence', abbreviated in the pages of the *Diary* to 'flat', 'ft', 'fits of ft', or 'fits', so that contemporary visitors to Down House, pausing to peer at the few pages on display, come away with the impression that Darwin suffered from fits of, perhaps, an epileptic nature. In fact, by 'flatulence' he and his time meant something more diffuse than we might signify by the word today – though it certainly referred to noxious eructations and trapped wind, it also pointed to all kinds of painful gastric and abdominal symptoms, dry coughs and frequent respiration. Darwin's flatulence, according to his meticulous record-keeping, was variously 'slight', 'moderate', 'considerable', 'baddish', 'sharp' and 'excessive', with countless gradations in between. It was frequently accompanied by nausea, retching and vomiting, and left him feeling 'oppressed', 'fatigued' and 'heavy'. Boils, too, were subject to careful examination and precise description: each eruption occasioned a small narrative or drama concerning its onset, development, eventual size and finally whether it subsided or 'broke'. All of this was accompanied at regular intervals by fear, shivering and sinking sensations. Such symptoms do not seem to have seriously affected his work schedule, though they frequently stopped him from travelling to attend professional meetings and family gatherings.

Quite what was wrong with Darwin has been a matter of considerable conjecture since his death. Briefly, the pretenders to the title of Darwin's main affliction may be divided into physical and psychological diseases, with a place set aside, perhaps, for the more literal-minded of anti-evolutionists, for whom his illness was not so much an emanation of his guilt at unseating the divine as an actual godly punishment for having formulated the theory in the first place. The earliest suggestions were less fanciful: an obituary of 1882, in the *British Medical Journal*, asserted that Darwin had suffered all his life from 'a condition of the nervous system reacting upon the digestive organs which necessitated the greatest care'. The voyage of the *Beagle* was thought by many biographers of his own century to have been the obvious culprit in Darwin's early life: either his seasickness had permanently undermined his constitution – quite how this occurred was left unclear – or the episode of Chilean fever in 1834 had, as Thomas Huxley put it, 'left its mark'. Dr William W. Johnston, in an article published in 1901 entitled 'The Ill Health of Charles Darwin: Its Nature and Its Relation to His Work', proposed that Darwin was suffering from 'chronic neurasthenia of a severe grade', a diagnosis that was almost, in its late Victorian application, as capacious and vague as that of hypochondria had been during Darwin's lifetime. In 1903, a Dr George M. Gould, in his book *Biographic Clinics: The Origin of the Ill-health of De Quincey, Carlyle, Darwin, Huxley, and Browning*, averred that a 'refractive anomaly of the eyes' had caused Darwin ocular strain, and in turn gastric upsets, headaches and apathy.

For over a century, the chief disagreement regarding Darwin's possible ailments has been between proponents of strictly physical and exclusively psychological origins. Among the former, the voyage of the *Beagle* still dominates research that must by its nature remain at some remove from medical evidence. In 1959, the parasitologist Saul Adler drew attention to a passage in Darwin's *Journal of Researches* in which he recalls having been bitten by 'the great black bug of the Pampas' during his time in Argentina in 1835. Adler concluded that he had contracted Chagas's disease, a disorder that could account for both his intestinal trouble and his later heart disease. In 1971, John H. Winslow published a small pamphlet entitled *Darwin's Victorian Malady: Evidence for its Medically Induced Origin*, in which he rejected all psychogenic theories and insisted that Darwin's symptoms were consistent with his having taken arsenic medicinally – though there is no clear evidence that he ever took it – for many years, leading to eczema, headaches, palpitations and gastric upsets. In both of these cases, countless arguments have been advanced for and against the causes in question, to no very conclusive end. Adherents of a psychological explanation, working from Darwin's own diaries, autobiographical texts and correspondence, as well as numerous memoirs written by friends, family and colleagues, have described him as neurotic, neurasthenic, obsessive, depressive and prey to unresolved antipathies towards his father and feelings of grief for his deceased mother. Despite all this conjecture, the true nature of Darwin's illness remains unknown. Its effects, however, and the curious treatments to which he submitted in the hope of curing it, may be more telling than its explanation.

*

In 1846, Dr James Manby Gully – born in Kingston, Jamaica, in 1808, and as of 1842 proprietor of a Hydropathic Establishment at the spa town of Malvern in Worcestershire – published a book entitled *The Water-Cure in Chronic Disease*. The volume has been described by one Darwin scholar as 'lucidly written and widely read'; the latter is believable, but even by the obfuscating standards of popular quackery then and now, the book is an indigestible bolus of common sense and wild speculation, expressed in turgid, often agrammatical prose. It is also fascinating as a guide to the practicalities, and the metaphorical possibilities, of chronic ill-health in the middle of the nineteenth century. *The Water-Cure in Chronic Disease* is not only a defence of (and advertisement for) the use of hydrotherapy in treating intransigent illness, it is also a picture of a certain popular medical imaginary: a map of what it was possible to believe at the time about body and mind.

The discovery of the water cure of which Gully was a prominent popularizer in Britain is attributed to one Vincent Priessnitz, a Silesian peasant born in the hamlet of Graefenberg in 1799. At around eight years of age, on the family farm, he came across a young roe that had been shot in the leg. Over several days the animal, he said, immersed its wounded limb in a local spring, and its condition improved with each 'treatment'. At eighteen, by which time he had become an unofficial medical authority for his neighbours, Priessnitz was badly injured in a cart accident and informed by a surgeon that he would never work again. He treated his broken ribs with a cold compress, recovered fully and began to proselytize on behalf of cold water and a sponge as all the *materia medica* required for the treatment of fractures, bruises and external injuries. By the 1840s, Priessnitz was attending to hundreds of patients himself, and the celebrity of his methods – which demanded exercise, modest diet and abstention from alcohol, as well as bathing in, and drinking, copious amounts of cold water – had spread to Britain, where Gully was among the first to establish a business around the new treatment.

Central to Gully's apologia for his profession is the notion of a natural sympathy between one organ and another. According to this doctrine, a popular one in Western medicine since the seventeenth century, the brain, for example, may be adversely affected by physical events elsewhere. The mental disorders that exercise Gully most are nervousness, hysteria and hypochondria. What Gully called 'the capricious storms of hysterical passion' were stirred, as medical convention had traditionally had it since the Greeks, by disorders of the uterus. In a sense, female hysteria provides Gully, as often with writers on hypochondria, with a model for ailments that afflict mostly men. The stomach is in this metaphorical sense the male womb: the organ to which the onset of countless physical symptoms may be ascribed, and the cause of many emotional disturbances. Irritation of the stomach, argues Gully, leads to stimulation of the blood vessels of the brain, resulting in a feeling of fullness in the head, impatience and irritability of temper, 'apoplectic congestion', 'paralytic congestion', hypochondriasis and, in the worst cases, insanity or 'drivelling imbecility'. Pains in the shoulders or the head; chronic irritation of the liver; tic douloureux of the face, arms, fingers or thighs; asthma or consumption; tetter, scurf, acne, psoriasis and dandruff; tenderness and swelling of the feet; the exquisite pain of gout: all of these and many more may be blamed on the sympathetic effect of the ailing stomach upon the body and mind of the patient. At the furthest extreme of his acute new sensitivity, he may feel so tender and transparent that he can actually feel 'a cloud passing athwart the sky'; he may report changes in the wind during the night, or predict snowfalls ten or twelve hours before any other sign appears – uncanny powers that ought to remind us of Roderick Usher's bizarre susceptibility to the atmosphere that surrounds his house. All such symptoms, scolds Gully, can be traced back to the stomach: 'You establish chronic irritation at the centre, and thereby keep it up at the periphery. The rule is invariable.'

By way of illustrating the extremes to which the hypochondriacal patient may be brought, Gully cites the case of a man, aged forty-seven, who had sought his help in January 1843. After twenty years as a commercial traveller – his job had required eccentric hours of eating and sleeping – this man had developed a morbidly great appetite. The result, writes Gully, was 'nervous dyspepsia': 'the fiend of hypochondria had fairly entered him, and began to feed on his body, for he grew emaciated as well as miserable. At length a celebrated surgeon of London recommended him to come to me and try the water cure; and, with much quaking, he came.' On his arrival at Malvern, the hapless patient complained of 'obstinate bowels'; his tongue was swollen, split and foul; his breath foetid; his skin colourless and dead to the eye. He had grown pecu-liarly sensitive to the smallest alteration of temperature; creeping, crawling and cold trickling sensations disturbed him constantly. His willpower was badly affected: he found it almost impossible to get out of bed. Once risen, he regularly quailed before the momentous decision about which chair he ought to sit in. On presenting himself to Gully he wept like a child, deplored the slow and certain death that he knew was coming, and rejected all assurances that at the Hydropathic Establishment his symptoms could be alleviated and, if he followed the regime prescribed by Gully to the letter, his illness actually vanquished.

It is clear from Gully's description of his patient's symptoms and fears that the latter were not simply, as far as the hydrotherapist was concerned, emotional responses to the former; they were the result, rather, of a physiological action of one organ upon the other. The stomach and the brain together constituted a kind of feedback loop by which gastric symptoms affected the brain and nervous feelings were transmitted to the viscera, where they manifested as renewed or redoubled discomfort. Darwin was by no means the sole Victorian dyspeptic of note whose suffering may be compared to that of Gully's commercial traveller. Thomas Huxley, for exam-ple, blamed his illness on his having (so he thought) been poisoned at the age of thirteen or fourteen while assisting at a post-mortem examination. A 'strange state of apathy' had come over him. From that time, he later wrote in rather purple terms, 'my constant friend, hypochondriacal dyspepsia, commenced his half-century of co-tenancy of my fleshly tabernacle'. Like Darwin, Huxley sought to obviate its effects with a strict daily routine, convinced as he was of an intimate connection between intellectual work and gastric upset. 'I have not now', he wrote from one of the health resorts to which he fled, 'nervous energy enough for stomach and brain both, and if I work the latter, not even the fresh breezes of this place will keep the former in order.'

Gully numbered among his patients Alfred, Lord Tennyson; Henry Hallam (about whose brother, Arthur, Tennyson had written *In Memoriam*); Charles Dickens; Wilkie Collins; and Thomas and Jane Carlyle. ('Here we are,' wrote Carlyle to Emerson in the summer of 1851, 'assiduously walking on the sunny mountains, drinking of the clear wells, not to speak of wet wrappages, solitary sad *steepages* and other singular procedures.') George Eliot, too, was among those who frequented the Hydropathic Establishment – her diverse symptoms, all quite congruent with a diagnosis of dyspepsia and resulting hypochondriasis, included violent headaches; indigestion; vomiting; frequent colds; influenza; palpitations; weakness and fatigue; red and streaming eyes; swimming head; sleeplessness; aching limbs, face and back; acute laryngitis; and depression or melancholia. The continuum from disorders of the stomach, through sympathetic ailments elsewhere in the body, to hypochondriacal terrors regarding chronic debilitation and death: all of this made up a frequently observed constellation of complaints, for which Gully's vaunted water cure claimed to offer a single treatment.

*

In the 1840s, Darwin reached many of the scientific conclusions for which he would later become famous. During the winter of 1843–4, around the time that the second volume of his account of the journey of the *Beagle* was published, he wrote up an initial draft of his theory of species, but held off publication, declaring himself, in a letter to Hooker, 'almost convinced (quite contrary to the opinion I started with) that species are not (it is like confessing a murder) immutable'. It was a period of intense anxiety; his growing celebrity in the scientific community was such that in 1844 an anonymously published defence of the theory of evolution, *Vestiges of the Natural History of Creation*, was widely attributed to him, and the argument of the book roundly condemned by religious and scientific authorities. 'I ought to be much flattered and unflattered,' he wrote; it was not the moment to risk publication. In the years that followed, Darwin immersed himself in family life and the administration of the local parish. In 1848, his father died, and his health, which had continued to be perilous – illness had even prevented him from getting to his father's funeral on time – now rapidly declined. He was tortured by anxiety, and suffered vomiting, flatulence, fainting sensations and black spots before his eyes.

On the 10th of March 1849, having read *The Water-Cure in Chronic Disease* with mounting interest and apprised himself of the fees charged at Malvern, Darwin took Emma and their six children, as well as a governess and servants, to the spa town. Installed in a rented house – his outpatient status was unusual: most of Gully's charges stayed at the Hydropathic Establishment itself – he gave himself up daily to the aquatic ministrations of Gully's staff. The precise regime that Darwin followed is described in detail in a letter he wrote on the 19th of March to his sister Susan. He rose, he said, at a quarter to seven, and was immediately scrubbed for two or three minutes with a rough towel that had been drenched in cold water; his personal 'washerman' scrubbed from behind, Darwin himself in front. (After a few days of this treatment, he confided, he began to look and feel like a lobster.) He then drank a tumbler of water, dressed himself and walked for twenty minutes: 'I like all this very much.' He alludes to a wet compress worn throughout the day – it was refreshed by dipping in cold water every two hours – but does not say where exactly about his person it was placed. Breakfast followed his walk: it 'was to have been exclusively toast with meat or egg, but he [Gully] has allowed me a little milk to sop the *stale* toast in. At no time must I take any sugar, butter, spices, tea, bacon, or anything good.' At midday, his feet were immersed in cold water and mustard, then violently rubbed by his attendant; though his feet ached at first, he found in time that they were less cold than before this course of treatment began. Another walk of twenty minutes preceded dinner at one: 'He has relaxed a little about my dinner and says I may try plain pudding, if I am sure it lessens sickness.' After dinner he lay down for an hour and tried to sleep. At five, his feet were immersed again in cold water, and he set out for another twenty-minute walk. Supper followed at six o'clock. 'I have had much sickness this week,' he complained to Susan, 'but certainly have felt much stronger and the sickness has depressed me much less. – Tomorrow I am to be packed at 6 o'clock for 1 & ½ hrs. in Blanket, with hot bottle to my feet and then rubbed with cold dripping sheet; but I do not know anything about this.'

Darwin felt the beneficial effect of Gully's personality before that of his treatment: 'I like Dr. Gully much – he is certainly an able man: I have been struck with how many remarks he has made similar to those of my father. He is very kind and attentive.' Before long he also reported himself feeling stronger, and his stomach somewhat improved: 'I expect fully that the system will greatly benefit me, and certainly the regular Doctors could do nothing . . . Physiologically it is most curious how the violent excitement of the skin produced by simple water, has acted on all my internal organs.' Late in April, he noted that he had begun to gain weight – 'I am turned into a mere walking and eating machine' – and after four months declared: 'The Water Cure is assuredly a grand discovery.' He was so recovered as to have recently passed a whole twelve hours without any flatulence at all.

Darwin's faith in Gully wavered, however, over the years. He was unimpressed, for example, by the hydrotherapist's eager recourse to other popular remedies for physical and spiritual ills: homeopathy, mesmerism and clairvoyance failed to convince him. (Coaxed by Gully into visiting a clairvoyant, he was alarmed, as his son George later wrote, to hear her paint 'a most appalling picture of the horrors which she saw in his inside'.) 'It is a sad flaw,' he wrote; 'I cannot but think in my beloved Dr. Gully that he believes in everything.' His attitude to the establishment was altered too when in March 1851 he brought his ailing daughter Annie, aged ten, to Malvern: she died the following month and was buried at Malvern Abbey.

In the decades that followed, Darwin visited two other hydro-therapy establishments. In 1857, plagued again by anxiety and illness while he was preparing *On the Origin of Species* for publication, he repaired to Moor Park, under the supervision of Dr Edward Wickstead Lane. Darwin found it '*much* better as a place than Malvern', and its physician 'a gentleman & very well read man' who neither pretended to understand the precise nature and origin of his patient's ill health, nor tried to convince him of the efficacy of therapies that Darwin found far-fetched in comparison with the water cure. In an account he wrote later of Darwin's time under his care, Lane ventured that he was:

. . . a great sufferer of dyspepsia . . . In the course of a long professional experience I have seen many cases of violent indigestion, in its many forms, and with the multiform tortures it entails, but I cannot recall any where the pain was so truly poignant as in his. When the worst attacks were on him he seemed almost crushed with agony, the nervous system being severely shaken, and the temporary depression resulting distressingly great. I mention this circumstance because it was then that I first perceived the wonderful sweetness and gentleness of his nature, his patience, and the gratitude with which he received the most ordinary services and tokens of sympathy . . . Of course such attacks as I have spoken of were only occasional – for no constitution could have borne up long under them in their acute phase – but he was never to the last wholly well.

In 1859 – the *Origin* was complete but not yet gone to press, and its author left feeling 'as weak as a child' – Darwin travelled to the grand establishment, built in the Scottish baronial style, which had been founded in 1843 by Hamer Stansfield, former Lord Mayor of Leeds, at Ilkley, Yorkshire. He submitted himself again to the rigours of the affusion (sitting in an empty bath, the patient was doused about the neck and shoulders), the dripping sheet, the shallow bath, the douche, the sitz bath and the wet sheet envelope. At Ilkley, the innovation of a compressed-air bath had been introduced. ('Of air, it may be said', wrote Gully, 'that an invalid cannot have too much, provided it be of the right temperature and hygrometric quality.') The apparatus was constructed of iron plates, and fitted with a door and several small windows; the interior was lined with wood and furnished with seats and a couch for the weaker patients. A sign warned: 'Parties not to laugh or discuss in the Air-bath!' As the pressure rose to about seven and a half pounds above the ordinary pressure of the air, Darwin would have found himself totally sealed off from the outside world, atmospherically autonomous for once, untroubled by the demands of family or colleagues (though the design of the air bath included a contrivance for passing letters back and forth without disturbing the seal). He wrote from Ilkley in 1859: 'I like the place very much, and the children have enjoyed it very much, and it has done my wife good. It did H[enrietta] good at first, but she has gone back again. I have had a series of calamities; first a sprained ankle, then a badly swollen whole leg and face, much rash, and a frightful succession of boils – four or five at once. I have felt quite ill, and have little faith in this "unique crisis" as the doctor calls it doing me much good.' As he awaited responses to the first complimentary copies of *On the Origin of Species* that his publisher John Murray had sent out, he professed himself to be 'living in Hell', covered in rashes and 'fiery Boils'.

At the centre of the hydropathic archipelago – with its violent douches and cold baths, its attendants advancing with sopping sheet in hand, its dietetic rigours and open-air excursions – sits the sodden, apprehensive figure of the hypochondriac. At mid-century, he was essentially indistinguishable from the grumbling, gassy dyspeptic: both were victims of a malign relay between stomach and brain, both prey to countless varied and maddening symptoms elsewhere in the body, both subject to sickening fears respecting their future ill health or coming demise. No doubt many of the gastric symptoms described by Gully's more celebrated inmates may be attributed to the rich diets of the Victorian middle and upper classes, but it seems clear too that a diagnosis of dyspepsia was sufficiently capacious as to also map many outlying ailments. The dyspeptic may be seen as a species of the hypochondriacal genus: his symptoms, traced back to an initial disorder of the stomach, radiating from this sole cause to countless irritating effects, are in a sense more specific than those of the nervous patient of the eighteenth century. On the other hand, they seem to proliferate, to ramify to such a degree that dyspepsia, whatever its physical starting point, begins to look like a catch-all diagnosis or the description of a character type rather than a set of discrete symptoms. Darwin's self-identification as a dyspeptic was thus an utterly conventional one for the time: the illness is as thoroughly cultural as the related afflictions of melancholia, hysteria, nervousness and hypochondriasis itself.

*

In a letter to the pioneer eugenicist and physiological taxonomist Francis Galton in 1879, Darwin admitted: 'I have never tried looking into my own mind.' He seems to have been mostly oblivious to the possibility of his illnesses having emotional origins. An incapacity for introspection, one might plausibly say in the light of the psychological theories of the last hundred years, seems guaranteed to end in somatic manifestations of some sort: the body feeling what the conscious mind cannot, or will not. It is not only because Darwin would not have countenanced this way of thinking that we ought to be wary of it. It is possible that the real meaning of his hypochondria – the combination of actual illness, perceived illness and the uses to which he put the two – lies not in its origin but in the temporal texture of his working life, in the retreat from extraneous duty that ill health allowed him, in the select society of the drenched and shivering that Gully's hydrotherapy led him to join, in the quintessentially Victorian cultural type – the chronic invalid – that he became in the course of his career.

There is but one reference to hypochondria in the sole book that Darwin devoted to the emotions. In truth, *The Expression of the Emotions in Man and Animals* is not really about emotion so much as its visible evidence. In numerous photographs and engravings (themselves taken from photographs by the French neurologist Guillaume-Benjamin Duchenne de Boulogne) the book, published in 1872, attempts to anatomize and typify the gestures common to humans and sometimes shared by animals: joy, love, devotion, hatred, anger, contempt, disgust, surprise, horror and shame. (The reputation of Darwin's study of the emotions has declined in comparison with his works on evolution, largely because he was committed to a view of human gestures as universal and timeless – a view that was much disparaged in the course of the next century.) In a chapter devoted to 'Low Spirits, Anxiety, Grief, Dejection, Despair', Darwin outlines the furrowing of the brow, the down-turning of the mouth, and the arching of the eyebrows that attend feelings of grief, by which term he meant all feelings of emotional pain or distress. To aid in his research into this expression, he suborned Dr James Crichton Browne, director of the West Riding Asylum at Wakefield, to attend closely the faces of his insane patients. In cases of melancholia, wrote Browne, and especially of hypochondria, the grief muscles are much exercised and the face persistently lined or furrowed. Browne carefully observed three cases of hypochondria. One of the three, a widow aged fifty-one, fancied that she had lost all her viscera, and that her whole body was empty. 'She wore an expression of great distress, and beat her semi-closed hands rhythmically together for hours. The grief-muscles were permanently contracted, and the upper eyelids arched. This condition lasted for months; she then recovered, and her countenance resumed its natural expression. A second case presented nearly the same peculiarities, with the addition that the corners of the mouth were depressed.'

There are no photographs of those wracked and, one assumes, unforgettable faces: faces that, if subjected to the photographic technique developed by Darwin's friend Galton, whereby several portraits of criminals were superimposed and averaged out to produce a single criminal type or composite physiognomy, would allow us to look into the eyes of that historically and medically obscure character: the Victorian hypochondriac. Darwin was himself photographed many times: pictured in a daguerreotype of 1842 with his eldest child, William, sitting on his knee; photographed looming, almost phantom-like, from the darkness by William himself in 1863; framed, in what is thought to be the final photograph of him, by Herbert Rose Barraud in 1881, a year before he died. In this last image, he is the familiar Darwin of icon and caricature: full white beard, beetling brows, deep-set eyes and bald head. Here, of course, at the age of seventy-two, Darwin's forehead is furrowed, his mouth turned down. It is impossible – and looking back through earlier photographs of him, reversing the flow of time that his concern for his health did so much to control, it is still impossible – to say whether his is the face of a hypochondriac in the sense that he, Crichton Browne or Dr Gully understood the term. There is a look about the eyes, in photographs from any period of his adult life, that might be resignation, grief, physical suffering or even fear. But it might as easily be a kind of relief: at his not having to submit himself to this protracted sitting for much longer, at having to hand a ready explanation for his retreat to study or bedroom, at the continued uses of invalidism and hypochondria.

4. Florence Nightingale and the Privilege of Discontent

'She found the machinery of illness scarcely less effective as a barrier against the eyes of men than the ceremonial of a great palace.'

Lytton Strachey, *Eminent Victorians*

In June 1858, Londoners long inured to the filth and stench of the city found their senses assaulted to a degree that even they felt intolerable. For many years, the sewers of London had discharged directly into the Thames – a state of affairs that was certainly an improvement on the accumulation of human ordure in domestic cellars (as had been the practice only decades earlier) or the piling up of turds in the street to the height, as one visitor to Spitalfields had noted in the 1840s, 'of a tolerably large house'. But the river's transformation into a de facto open-air sewer had singularly disgusting consequences. In the midst now of an early summer heatwave, it had begun to smell like nothing on earth. A hundred yards from its south bank, railway travellers leaving London Bridge station were seized by attacks of vomiting. By the middle of the month, the Great Stink, as the press had begun to call it, became so powerful that Parliament was forced to close. On the 18th, *The Times* reported that a few brave MPs had recently ventured into the library at Westminster, directly overlooking the foetid river, with a view to studying the pollution for themselves. They had been forced back at once, handkerchiefs clasped to their faces, by the astonishing reek, which seemed almost to have solidified around them.

For the Londoners of the 1850s the smell that rose from the

river was a malign entity in itself: the miasmic bearer of many diseases, cholera the most feared among them. (It was in fact the failure of the fetor of 1858 to start an outbreak of cholera that forced adherents of the miasma theory to consider the possibility that the disease was spread in drinking water.) We may imagine the terror that gripped the city as the Great Stink escaped the districts immediately fronting the river and oozed through adjacent streets and outlying squares. It would soon have troubled strollers in St James's Park, to the north, and appalled the tenants of Buckingham Palace, before insinuating itself into the respectable enclave of Mayfair. Even if the stench, in the weeks to come, did not reach the nearby Burlington Hotel, we may assume that one of its long-term residents was especially troubled by the approaching miasma. She might have added it to the catalogue of public health and hygiene problems that she had resolved to overcome, but also to the growing list of private reasons for her absenting herself from London as soon as possible.

Florence Nightingale left London with her aunt Mai, who was by now her constant friend and helper, and her aunt's son-in-law, the poet Arthur Hugh Clough. Leaving the city, she was recognized at the station, and a crowd encircled her small party before they could board their train. Railway staff held back the craning onlookers, many of whom were probably surprised to see the reclusive Miss Nightingale alive, if not exactly well. (She had come home after hostilities ceased in the Crimea in 1856, but she had since avoided public appearances.) The lean, soberly dressed woman of thirty-eight who appeared on the platform was apparently unable to walk unaided; a group of soldiers, representative of the thousands she had personally nursed and the many thousands more who had been under her administrative care, bore her towards the train on a chair, rather as if she were a plaster Madonna and the mid-morning crowd, transfixed by her fame and the maddening heat, a fervid congregation. We may guess that, once entrained, she sank with relief into her carriage, thinking this reminder of her reputation unseemly and irritating. It came at the end of a summer during which the city, the weather, her friends, her family and the very air itself seemed to be against her, conspiring to drain what little energy she had and deflect her from the tasks that she longed to complete. Perhaps she tried to use the hours between London and Malvern, secluded in the stifling carriage with two of her most trusted assistants, to plan the next phase of her campaign to improve the lot of the injured or sick British soldier. Perhaps, for the first time in months, she felt safe from importuning relatives, foreign and domestic dignitaries seeking moral grace by mere association, and the countless small physical inconveniences that together made her daily life in London such an ordeal. Perhaps, at last, she rested.

This was not Florence Nightingale's first visit to Malvern, nor the first time, since her return to England, that she had been incapacitated by illness. In the summer of 1857, scarcely able to rise from her sofa during the day, and unable to sleep for more than two hours at night, she left London for Malvern, accompanied only by a footman. Installed at the resort, she was treated with two cold-water packs a day to slow her racing pulse. She tried to carry on working, writing letters and reading official reports; after half an hour of activity, however, she would fall back exhausted, and sometimes even faint. In London, the journalist Harriet Martineau, on hearing of her friend's state of prostration, hastily wrote her obituary – the text was set, in readiness, by the *Daily News*. (Martineau was herself a prominent invalid of the period; she would write to Nightingale the following year: 'Every stroke of work is more likely than not to be the last. Yet I may go on, as I *have* gone on, – much longer than could be expected.') Nightingale's father visited her; he stayed only for a few minutes, and wrote, horrified, to his wife, Fanny, saying he was sure that their daughter's days were numbered. Dr John Sutherland, a long-standing ally in the struggle to improve the sanitary conditions in which British soldiers lived and died, implored her to abide by the regime at Malvern – 'do not gull Dr. Gully' – and especially to eat, which she had scarcely done in the month preceding her crisis. 'The day you left town,' he wrote, 'it appeared as if all your blood wanted renewing and that cannot be done in a week. You must have new blood or you can't work and new blood can't be made out of tea at least as far as I know . . .'

We might expect her reply to this solicitous letter to sound brave, resigned, hopeful or simply exhausted. Instead, Nightingale wrote back in fury, accusing Dr Sutherland, her family, her friends and her colleagues of having harassed her to distraction about her health, precisely at the moment when she had more pressing problems (matters, after all, of life and death) to attend to:

Let me tell you Doctor, that after any walk or drive I sat up all night with palpitation. And the sight of animal food increased the sickness . . . Now I have written myself into a palpitation . . . I have been greatly harassed by seeing my poor owl lately without her head, without her life, without her talons, lying in the cage of your canary . . . and the little villain pecking at her. Now, that's me. I am lying without my head, without my claws and you all peck at me.

Though written in anger and ill health, this letter is an impressive instance of Florence Nightingale's ability, at the moment of her greatest influence on those around her, to make herself appear weak and put-upon, subject to the spites and whims of her family, her allies and her professional foes alike. Today, we might dismiss such behaviour as 'passive-aggressive'; but that term does nothing to discern the motives behind such studied enfeeblement, nor to understand its supreme usefulness in the face of constraining circumstance. That Nightingale saw others' concern for her health as a maddening imposition is but the first of many ironies at the heart of her hypochondriacal character. She was, in her insistently valetudinarian attitude and in the scope of practical accomplishments she managed in spite of her ill health, the most ambitious of the high Victorian hypochondriacs. It has been suggested by Lytton Strachey and by several of her other biographers that she succeeded precisely because she was unwell. Where Darwin parlayed his illness into an essential solitude and freedom from public responsibility, Florence Nightingale, according to this argument, retreated from the world the better to engage and control it. If nothing else, we may be sure, her illness gave an urgency to her work that she never ceased to convey to others. Apparently lingering at the point of death for decades, she quickened the hands and minds of her helpers with the thought that each campaign was her last, then survived to lead the next charge. She liked to compare herself to an owl, but spent half her life perfecting her phoenix act.

*

Nightingale's escape from the scenes of human devastation that she had attended during the Crimean War must have seemed itself a sort of resurrection. The precise nature of the horrors that she witnessed, and the prodigious labour she undertook in Constantinople, have remained, even after a century and a half of scholarship, somewhat occluded by the bright myth of the Lady with the Lamp. Her earliest biographers scanted the details of what she discovered at the Barrack Hospital in the suburb of Scutari, on the eastern shore of the Bosphorus, in November 1854. To be precise, they hid the extent to which the daily life of Miss Nightingale, her nurses, the hospital's surgeons and the soldiers in their care was dominated by the problem of human faeces. Her patients lay wrapped in great-coats that were stiff with dried blood; they drank water that, it was found on examining the source, flowed through the decaying carcass of a horse; they lost teeth, and even toes, to scurvy. When a clergyman bent over them to write down their dying words, his page was overrun with lice. The fortunate perished before submitting to the operations and amputations, carried out without anaesthetic or disinfectant, that would have killed them anyway. But the most overpowering impression with which a visitor came away was that the hospital was drowning in shit. The latrines were blocked; there were twenty chamber pots to a thousand men, and all of those men had diarrhoea. In the wards, the few windows were so small, and placed so low down, that even had they been opened (which they never were), the hot, foul air would still have hovered, unmoved, above their level. The filth and stench were so extreme that doctors, fearful of contagion, refused to enter these wards. Nightingale, however, insisted on nursing the men herself. It is perhaps not too fanciful to conclude that she returned from Scutari feeling, even after she had done all in her power to reverse these conditions, as though for two years she had been on the verge of asphyxiation.

On her return to England, she embarked on a campaign to improve the living conditions of British soldiers at home and abroad. She pushed for the establishment of, and then gave evidence before, a Royal Commission on the Health of the Army. She enlisted among her supporters Queen Victoria and Prince Albert, who invited her to Balmoral in September 1856. She prepared her *Notes on Matters Affecting the Health, Efficiency, and Hospital Administration of the British Army*, an 830-page report which she had printed and privately circulated in 1858, and in which she concludes of contemporary conditions that 'Our soldiers are enlisted to die in barracks.' She wrote countless letters to interested parties, and composed articles on the design of hospitals for the journal *The Builder*. The failings of the current sanitary regime were such, she wrote, that '1500 good soldiers are as certainly killed by these neglects yearly as if they were drawn up on Salisbury Plain and shot.' Her vision of hospital and barrack hygiene demanded extensive reform of the Army's attitude to architecture, diet and clothing. Most of all, Nightingale was exercised by the necessity for fresh air; 'all foul smell indicates disease,' she thought, and proper ventilation was the only counter to contagion. As her most recent biographer, Mark Bostridge, has put it, she was 'unconcerned with the finer points of medical theory', and roundly rejected the mounting evidence that many diseases were carried by germs rather than engendered by bad air. Scientifically wrong-headed though they may have been, in practice her methods most likely still led to improvements: they destroyed germs in the course of eliminating dirt and human waste.

In more than one sense, however, she failed to take her own advice regarding the effects of fresh air upon the body. That is to say, she secluded herself behind a real and metaphorical barrier, air-locked herself from the world outside, save for the ministrations of her immediate family and necessary visits from her campaigning colleagues. She refused all invitations, whether public or private, and wrote in August 1856: 'The publicity and talk there have been about this work have injured it more than anything else, and in no way, I am determined, will I contribute by making a show of myself.' Her family heard her pacing in her room at night, and she rarely emerged from it during the day, though 'the work' occupied her mind at all times. Her body, meanwhile, appeared equally to recoil from the world: she was overcome by nausea at the sight of food; she suffered from palpitations and had difficulty breathing, as though she were still in the sweltering wards at Scutari. News of her illness escaped the circle of her wealthy family, and her mother received an anonymous letter: 'I hardly know how to express myself about your daughter's delicate health. She has the sympathy of two continents (one might say of all humanity).'

The Nightingales were in the habit of setting themselves up at the Burlington during the late spring and early summer – for the duration, in other words, of the social 'season' then observed by the English upper classes. In the autumn of 1856, Fanny and her elder daughter Parthenope (known within the family as Parthe) had stayed in London well beyond the end of the season, and while their concern for Florence forbade them from leaving, this continued displacement of the Nightingale household was becoming tiresome.

The layout of their apartments at the Burlington allegorized certain long-standing tensions within the family. Florence retreated to her bedroom, or worked in a small private dining room, while Fanny and Parthe entertained friends in a larger drawing room. In November, while Florence was preparing for her first interview with the Secretary of State for War, Lord Panmure, Parthe fell ill with a severe cold; a fever followed, and she insisted on being nursed by her sister. As Parthe began to lose her voice, she made it clear that she blamed Florence for the illness: she had only remained in London past the end of the season out of duty and compassion. Now the two of them were trapped in the airless Burlington apartments, which the sun barely penetrated. In the summer, from the streets below, they had heard the sound of wheels moving slowly on cobblestones, as water carts advanced through Mayfair in an effort to quiet the dust that rose everywhere in clouds. The water used was polluted, and only added to the hot stench of the city, as though London were steaming under glass. As winter approached, Florence, Fanny and Parthe seemed to inhabit their own torrid microclimate, a hothouse filled with tender but toxic plants.

Florence Nightingale's working habits, in the summer of 1857 and beyond, can scarcely be credited, in light of her illness and the varied pressures upon her, not to mention the physical atmosphere in which she laboured. In May, her mother recorded that she had spent the morning in Belgrave Square with Sidney Herbert – another long-serving accomplice, who had been Secretary at War during the first year of the Crimean War; it was he who first invited Nightingale to take charge of the nurses at Scutari – and the afternoon with John Sutherland, before returning to her rooms at the Burlington to work late into the night. The following day she worked from nine in the morning till after dark. The day after that she was at Highgate from half past eight in the morning until half past seven in the evening, then back to the Burlington before visiting Herbert again till after eleven. Following each such bout of concentrated effort, she invariably collapsed, and had to be fed like a child by Fanny or Parthe – that is, when she could be persuaded to eat at all. The drama played out mostly among the three women, with a supporting cast of Florence's advisors and minions. Watching such ministrations from a distance, her father seems frequently to have been unable to bear the sight, and was constantly in the act of retreating from the scene, convinced that Florence was going to die and that Fanny and Parthe had had their health ruined.

So far as Florence was concerned, the latter could not have been further from the truth. She wrote: 'The whole occupation of Parthe and Mama was to lie on two sofas and tell one another not to get tired by putting flowers into water. It is a scene worthy of Molière, where two people in tolerable and even perfect health, lie on the sofa all day, doing absolutely nothing and persuade themselves and others that they are the victims of their self-devotion for another who is dying of overwork.' As Bostridge points out, this portrait of martyred lassitude is not exactly accurate: Fanny and Parthenope were in fact willing and proud to assist Florence in her campaign, though they fretted constantly about what the workload meant for her health. It was not so much the disparity between their leisure and her labour that tormented Florence; rather, it seems, the mere physical presence of her mother and sister was enough to drive her to distraction. Having spent two years in the midst of a throng of humanity that was simply unthinkable for most women of her class – thousands of men, and their nurses, thrust together without regard for the modesties of Victorian social and domestic life – she now felt poisoned by the physical and emotional proximity of Fanny and Parthe. It was this dramatic response to the intimacy of family life that first led her to flee to Malvern. On the 11th of August she suddenly exclaimed to Parthe: 'I must be alone, quite alone . . . I have not been alone for four years.' She could not live, she explained to her sister, without silence and solitude.

She was, one might say, running out of air. She could not breathe

– the atmosphere of London, and especially of the Burlington, stifled her. Worse, it reminded her of the sickening air at Scutari, and of the dead air that even now was threatening the lives of soldiers and civilians alike in hospitals across the land. But she was being suffocated too by more metaphorical forces: the weight of bureaucracy that stood in the way of the reforms she envisaged; and the equally massive and immovable heft of her very allies in that struggle, who seemed unable to think at a tenth of the speed that she did, never mind act with the alacrity which was her natural response to a crisis. She longed to escape, to breathe the fresh air of personal and professional freedom that her male colleagues inhaled without a second's thought.

*

What exactly was the matter with Florence Nightingale? Her symptoms, as we have seen, were sufficiently alarming to convince her, and many of those around her, that she was about to die, and severe enough too to debilitate her for many years. Her strength and mobility were often compromised, and after an especially enfeebling attack in 1861 she was left unable to walk. She suffered, we know, from insomnia, headaches, palpitations, breathing difficulties, back pain and a marked loss of appetite. Still, a precise diagnosis eludes us, as, it seems, it eluded her doctors. Like Darwin, she presents such an array of ailments, obscurely bound up with fear, resignation and a desire for control, that it is hard to say where her physical suffering ended and its psychological ramifications began. The most comprehensive of her early biographers, Sir Edward Cook, refers to her as a 'hopeless' and 'incurable' invalid, even as he describes her amazing energy and details her many achievements. The confusion among her physicians survives in Cook's account, which was written only three years after her death in 1910: Nightingale's malady is variously a matter of nervous disorder, serious heart disease, a generalized exhaustion of the vital organs and a vaguely defined psychological condition.

Cook eventually concludes that she suffered both 'dilatation of the heart and neurasthenia' – which combination could be treated only, according to the medical wisdom of the period, by total rest and immobility of mind as of body.

Nightingale had already, as Cook records, been close to death during the Crimean War. On the 2nd of May 1855, ten days short of her thirty-fifth birthday, she had left Scutari for Balaclava, where she was to inspect the military hospitals. She arrived on the 5th, and a week later was taken ill with fever and became delirious. 'She is suffering', wrote Dr Anderson, the chief medical officer at the General Hospital in Balaclava, 'from as bad an attack of fever as I have seen.' For two weeks her condition fluctuated with alarming rapidity – she was often critically ill in the morning, recovered by the afternoon and perilously unwell again by evening. By the 24th of May she was out of danger but still unable to feed herself or to speak above a whisper. By July she was well enough to return to Scutari, where her nurses found her pale, emaciated, very weak and looking much older than thirty-five. Early in October she travelled again to the Crimea to complete her inspection of the hospitals, but was soon admitted to a ward herself, suffering from agonizing sciatica. 'I have now had all that this climate can give,' she wrote: 'Crimean fever, Dysentery, Rheumatism.' She returned to Scutari at the end of November and saw out the year afflicted with earache, laryngitis and insomnia. Quite what she had meant by 'Crimean fever' is at first unclear, given that the British army recorded six distinct types of fever during that war, typhoid and typhus being the most lethal. It seems likely that she meant the third most feared type: remittent fever. Its symptoms included gastric upset, irritation and delirium. It was seldom fatal, but its course was protracted and at times dramatic, with, as in Nightingale's case, sudden remissions and relapses in the space of a single day.

Remittent fever was in time ascribed to a specific bacterium, isolated by David Bruce in 1887, and given a new name: brucello-

sis. Known also as Mediterranean, undulant or Malta fever, the illness was most prevalent in spring and appeared to be transmitted
through milk and other dairy products. It affected the spine, joints,
heart, liver, lungs, kidneys and nerves. Brucellosis, it is now recognized, takes two distinct forms: specific and non-specific. The first is
characterized by painful effects on the patient's nervous system,
including sciatica and cervical or intercostal neuralgia. The bones
and joints are also affected. In the non-specific form of the disease, the
patient might suffer from any combination of a frustratingly diverse set
of ailments: insomnia, anorexia, nausea at the sight of food, anaemia,
nervousness, depression, delusions, tachycardia, palpitations, syncope
or fainting, dyspnoea (shortness of breath), weakness, indigestion,
flushing, headache, nervous tremors, depression and frustration. The
longer the disease is active, the more deeply entrenched such symptoms become and the more difficult it is to tell the immediate effects
of brucellosis from the personality of the patient. Indeed, non-specific
brucellosis may be indistinguishable from neurosis, or from hypochondria itself.

A quick tally of Florence Nightingale's symptoms seems to
accord with this description of chronic non-specific brucellosis. On
her return to England in 1856 she was depressed, anaemic and nervous; she had lost weight and was sickened by the sight of food. In
August 1857, as we have seen, she suffered a renewed attack,
accompanied by palpitations and perhaps a degree of paranoia or
delusion regarding the actions and attitudes of those around her. In
August 1859 she suffered a similarly distressing episode: the same
symptoms were now accompanied by weakness, indigestion and
flushing of the face and hands. In 1861 she was prey to three further
attacks; during the last, she developed nervous tremors. By the end
of the year she was quite unable to walk, and she remained mostly
bedridden for the next six years, excruciated by pains in her back,
chest and right elbow. After 1870, most of her symptoms abated or
vanished completely, though insomnia and appalling headaches

remained. Her depression, and the feelings of failure and worth-lessness that had plagued her since her return to England, continued until around 1880, when at last she entered on a relatively cheerful old age.

A diagnosis of brucellosis sounds compelling – it was first proposed in 1995 by David Young, a former principal scientist at the Wellcome Institute in London, and is more or less accepted in Bostridge's biography – but there exists, of course, no proof. Nightingale herself seems to have believed that her chief complaint was of the heart, and to have acted in accordance with the common recommendation of the day in such cases. That is to say, she took to her bed. If indeed she had a heart condition, as Sir Edward Cook and others later believed, she may well have made matters worse by following this regime of rest. If her illness, on the other hand, was imaginary, she may have cosseted a healthy body and mind into morbidity. Such was the case among the many sufferers, in this period, from 'Da Costa's syndrome', a malignity of the imagination first identified by Dr J. M. Da Costa during the American Civil War (during which conflict it was also known as 'soldier's heart', 'irritable heart' and 'nervous heart') and later elaborated upon by physicians in the First World War. The diagnosis was not restricted to the military, but the army seems in both cases to have provided a set of subjects whose behaviour and possible motives could be more easily studied. The young soldier typically presented to the doctor complaining of pain in the area of the heart, breathlessness, palpitations, giddiness, sweating and other less common or less well-defined symptoms. His heart rate was in fact usually found to be raised, his face flushed and his breathing laboured. The symptoms, so the patient said, worsened with exercise and so, as was the wisdom of the day, he was ordered to rest. But it was soon discovered that those soldiers who disregarded the order recovered quickly, while those who accepted the diagnosis and its consequences seemed to decline further, although no organic cause could be found. The disease seemed to be a psychosomatic response to trauma; what these soldiers had in common with Florence Nightingale was an intimacy with the physical facts that we routinely designate by such tired phrases as 'the horrors of war'.

One short and persuasive answer to the mystery of her illness is that she was suffering from what today we might call post-traumatic stress disorder, that her symptoms were the somatic expression of what she had seen at Scutari, or (perhaps even more distressing in the long run) of what she had been unable to achieve there. At the same time, so generalized are the symptoms of brucellosis that it is perfectly possible that Nightingale suffered both from an organic disease with an infectious origin and from an array of psychologically determined ailments. As we shall see, she was herself well aware of the ways in which mental distress could translate itself into apparent physical illness, and conscious too that women, especially, were in her time often forced to plead physical incapacity or ill health in order to escape the pressures placed upon them.

*

Commenting on Nightingale's illness, and the standard treatment of the day, Sidney Herbert questioned the wisdom of a rest cure: 'I should doubt, with a mind constituted as hers is, whether entire rest, with a total cessation of all active business, would not be a greater trial . . . than a life of some, though very limited and moderate, occupation.' In 1859, Nightingale completed, and had privately printed, an essay that demonstrates how little even her ally Herbert had understood her terror of idleness.

She had begun writing *Cassandra* in 1852, calling it her 'family manuscript'. In its first draft, it took the form of a dialogue between two daughters and their parents; in the second, it had expanded to become an autobiographical fiction. She subsequently revised the text until it was an ostensibly impersonal polemic of considerable force and skill, rendered in her customarily heated prose. Its subject was the absence, for women of her class in England, of anything

to do. It was not that their lives were empty, but that they were
filled with activities of such mundanity or frivolity that they were
apt to drive women mad. 'Is man's time more valuable than
woman's,' asks Nightingale, 'or is the difference between man and
woman this, that woman has confessedly nothing to do?'

It is not only a matter, she argues, of women being expressly
disallowed an intellectual or creative life; rather, the conditions of
their daily lives are such that no ban of that sort is required. She asks
the reader to imagine a certain 'Mrs. A.', possessed of all the imagination and skill, for example, of the seventeenth-century Spanish
painter Bartolomé Murillo:

Why is she not a Murillo? From a material difficulty, not a mental one.
If she has a knife and fork in her hands for three hours of the day, she
cannot have a pencil or brush. Dinner is the great sacred ceremony of
this day, the great sacrament. To be absent from dinner is the equivalent
of being ill. Nothing else will excuse us from it. Bodily incapacity is the
only apology valid.

A woman's life, she says, is thus reduced to the contemplation of
trifling details: the desirability, for instance, of her daughter's
attending such-and-such a party, and sitting beside such-and-such a
person. A woman spends her days sitting in drawing rooms, desultorily gazing at prints, doing worsted work to make the time pass,
or reading insubstantial books. When she escapes the domestic
sphere for a few hours, it is only to ride in a carriage with her
mother, or to fetch up at another, almost identical, drawing room,
there to repeat once more the endless, deadening round of dining
and diversion. There is no time for either thought or action, still
less for solitude, 'and the difficulty is that, in our social life, we
must be always doubtful whether we ought not to be with somebody else or be doing something else'.

Early in life, Nightingale seems to have begun to develop ways of eluding the surveillant eye of Victorian sociability. She was given to fantastic daydreams, and twice, in 1837 and 1843, had heard, so she recalled, the voice of God summoning her to a higher task than her family and caste would tolerate. In *Cassandra*, she describes the Victorian woman's need for dreams, and the ways in which those dreams are dissolved in daily life:

Women dream till they have no longer the strength to dream; those dreams against which they so struggle, so honestly, vigorously, and conscientiously, and so in vain, yet which are their life, without which they could not have lived; those dreams go at last. All their plans and visions seem vanished, and they know not where; gone, and they cannot recall them. They do not even remember them. And they are left without the food of reality or of hope. Later in life, they neither desire nor dream, neither of activity, nor of love, nor of intellect. The last often survives the longest. They wish, if their experiences would benefit anybody, to give them to someone. But they never find an hour free in which to collect their thoughts, and so discouragement becomes ever deeper and deeper, and they less and less capable of undertaking anything.

Such was the future that Florence must already, as a young woman, have felt lay in wait for her. This perhaps explains her tendency, in her mid twenties, to poor health, and the apparent connection between her periodic illnesses and the problem of her occupation, or lack of occupation. The first of these attacks came on at Christmas 1843, when Florence spent several weeks in bed. The following summer, apparently recovered, she was forbidden by her family to help nurse the local poor who were suffering from scarlet fever, and her own sickness promptly returned. On her recovery, Henry Nicholson, brother of Florence's close friend Marianne, asked her to marry him. She refused, and immediately became ill again. She was at the point, her parents feared, of a complete mental collapse, when her grandmother and her childhood nurse both fell ill. Florence was allowed to tend to both of them, and her own health soon improved. She had become convinced that her vocation lay in treating the sick, but it seems the whole family was by now well versed in the uses of ill health, for each time that Florence mentioned her desire to work in a hospital, both her mother and sister were likely to fall into a faint, and required to be brought round again with smelling salts. 'It was as if', Florence wrote later, 'I had wanted to be a kitchen maid.'

In the autumn of 1847, she became ill again, and was sent to Italy to convalesce. Two years later she received, and refused, her second marriage proposal, from Richard Monckton Milnes (later Lord Houghton). Her family was furious, and Florence once more became ill. She could not have brought herself, she wrote, to abandon her dreams:

I have an intellectual nature which requires satisfaction and that would find it in him. I have a passional nature which requires satisfaction and that would find it in him. I have a moral, an active, nature, which requires satisfaction and that would not find it in his life. Sometimes I think I will satisfy my passional nature at all events, because that will at least secure me from the evil of dreaming. But would it? I could be satisfied to spend a life with him in combining our different powers in some great object. I could not satisfy this nature by spending a life with him in making society and arranging domestic things.

Quite apart from the domestic duties that attended the unmarried as well as the married state, Florence revolted, in person and in print, against a more insidious style of familial coercion. It took the form of an oppressive concern – or at least the appearance of concern – for the health and happiness of the wayward young woman. Society triumphs over women, she wrote in *Cassandra*, by indirection, expressing its disapproval as if it were sympathy. "'I like riding about this beautiful place, why don't you? I like walking about the garden, why don't you?" is the common expostulation – as if we were children, whose spirits rise during a fortnight's holiday, who think that they will last forever – and look neither backwards nor forwards.' This was the atmosphere in which she later lived at the Burlington: a persistent chorus of invitations and admonitions from Fanny and Parthe sought to snare Florence in a kind of perpetual present. She must not exhaust herself, they chided. She must be ready to be interrupted at any moment. Her time was literally not her own.

*

Nightingale referred to her rooms at the Burlington as 'the little War Office', to her fellow reformers as a 'band of brothers', to their meals as 'our mess'. She conceived of herself both as commander of this body of (mostly) men and at the same time as a kind of mother to the soldiers on whose behalf they laboured:

No one can feel for the Army as I do. These people who talk to us have all fed their children on the fat of the land and dressed them in velvet and silk while we have been away. I have had to see my children dressed in a dirty blanket and an old pair of regimental trousers, and to see them fed on raw salt meat, and nine thousand of my children are lying, from causes which might have been prevented, in their forgotten graves.

But she was also, in a sense, a child. On her return from Malvern in 1857, she moved into an annexe of the Burlington, with a double sitting room on one floor and three bedrooms and another sitting room on the floor above. She sent for her aunt Mai, who promptly shut up her own house and sent her husband and her children to stay with Florence's family. Aunt Mai brought her son-in-law, Arthur Hugh Clough, who became Florence's messenger. As she was at this time convinced that she was about to die, he also arranged with her the details of her funeral and took dictation of several letters to be delivered after her death. Arthur and Aunt Mai became her new family, and the latter especially the subject of a peculiar veneration. Florence wrote:

Probably there is not a word of truth in the story of the Virgin Mary. But the deepest truth lies in the idea of the Virgin Mother. The real fathers and mothers of the human race are NOT the fathers and mothers according to the flesh. I don't know why it should be so. It 'did not ought to be so.' But it is. Perhaps it had better not be said at all. What is 'Motherhood in the Flesh'? A pretty girl meets a man and they are married. Is there any thought of the children? The children come without their consent even having been asked because it can't be helped.

Florence's army was also, it seems, a nurturing family to be distinguished clearly from her natural one.

At the same time, she was aware that her relationships with her immediate circle were apt to be distorted by her monomaniacal pursuit of her goals. She began to refer to herself as a 'vampyre', such was the toll taken on the health and happiness of her subordinates. This self-knowledge did not, it seems, stop her from habitually expressing her frustration at what she thought of as her lieutenants' malingering. John Sutherland, whose forgetfulness, untidiness and unpunctuality were tiresome enough, 'once more fancies himself laid up with bronchitis', she complained in February 1857. In the summer of that year, Sutherland tried to elude her constant demands upon his time by hiding behind letters from his wife. Summoned from Highgate to the Burlington, he had Mrs Sutherland write: 'The rain is so tremendous that he would be drenched in five minutes so he hopes the Commander-in-Chief will excuse him for this once.' She did not. On another occasion, having already displeased her earlier in the day by missing the deadline for an urgent report, he was ordered to Mayfair again later in the evening. He refused; Florence collapsed; Aunt Mai hurried to Highgate with the news that Florence would die if he did not return. Florence took to calling him 'my pet aversion'.

It was Sidney Herbert, however, of whom she expected most and tolerated least in terms of his own ill health. As she lay in bed, working continually, he complained of headaches, weakness and nausea: the first symptoms of the renal failure that would eventually kill him. His responsibilities as Secretary at War and an MP had by 1860 become unbearable, and his doctors, having informed him that he was in the advanced stages of kidney disease, advised him to reduce his workload. He decided to give up the House of Commons. Nightingale wrote, towards the end of the year:

I hope you will not judge too hardly of yourself from these doctors' opinion . . . it is not true that you cannot (sometimes) absolutely mend a damaged organ, almost always keeping it comfortably going for many years, by giving Nature fair play . . . But I hope you won't have any vain ideas that you can be spared out of the War Office. You said yourself that there was no one to take your place – and you must know that as well as everybody else . . . I don't believe there is anything in your constitution which makes it evident that disease is getting the upper hand. On the contrary.

A month later she declared that she saw 'death written in the man's face'; but when, the following summer, following a collapse, he resolved to quit the War Office, she was furious, and would not accept that his strength was gone. At first she refused to see him, then assented to a meeting at the Burlington, where she told him: 'No man in my day has thrown away so noble a game with all the winning cards in his hands.'

Sidney Herbert died on the 2nd of August 1861. Nightingale told her father: 'He takes my life with him. My work, the object of my life, the means to do it, all in one depart with him . . . Now not one man remains (that I can call a man) of all whom I began to work with five years ago. And I alone of all men "most dejected and wretched" survive them all. I am sure I meant to have died.' She shut herself in the familiar hotel for a fortnight and wrote an account of his work that she had privately published. She then left the Burlington for ever. By the end of the year, she was dangerously ill once more, and became totally bedridden for the next six years. She wrote to her mother early in 1862:

All the others have children or some high and inspiring interest to live for – while I have lost husband and children and all. And am left to the dreary hopeless struggle . . . It is this desperate guerrilla warfare ending in so little which makes me impatient of life. I, who could once do so much . . . I think what I have felt most during my last 3 months of extreme weakness is the not having one single person to give one inspiring word, or even one correct fact. I am glad to end a day which never can come back, gladder to end a night, gladder still to end a month.

Nightingale was then forty-two years old. She would recover only gradually, working all the while on the Royal Sanitary Commission on the Health of the Army in India. At the end of the decade she was mobile once again, but her spirits had not rallied. She could not move without help, and her condition was not improved by her having changed address five times in three years. In 1865, her father bought her a house at 35 South Street, where she spent the rest of her life. Her family were forbidden from visiting her, and close friends and associates were kept at bay. Still, she complained constantly that she was lonely. Her mood was for many years melancholic and self-accusing. As Cook puts it: 'Overstrain still continued, and though she was no longer, it seems, expected to die of her past exertions, she was still supposed to be a hopeless invalid. She had always resorted to self-examination and self-criticism, whenever her full life had given time for thought. The will was strong but the spirit very sensitive, and now self-reproach and the sense of failure in the height and purity of motive wore upon the overwrought nerves and tended to morbidity of mind, and sometimes to self-pity.'

*

Nightingale's plight, in the face of overwhelming social and familial pressure, seems of a piece with that of countless women of the period, for whom ill health afforded the only respite from domestic responsibility. If woman's realm, for the Victorian imagination, extended little further than hearth and home, the sickroom must have seemed to many, paradoxically, to contain a kind of freedom. The invalid fled into an interior world, a kind of secret garden from which she had so far been barred by convention. (Though she may, as the metaphor reminds us, have been free to explore such a kingdom in childhood.) There is no doubt that Nightingale craved such access to her own inner life, as her regular flight into daydream attests. In this, she resembled less a celebrated recluse such as Emily Dickinson – for Nightingale was also, in her tireless campaigning, constantly in touch with the outside world – than the nineteenth-century figure of the male hysteric or hypochondriac.

The masculine type of this period that most accurately incarnates the conflicting desires of the hypochondriac, and with which Nightingale shares some characteristics, is, perhaps surprisingly, the dandy. Dandyism is in one sense nothing more or less than an intense, even sickly, awareness of one's own corporeal being. The dandy is extremely sensitive to the sensations, attitudes and affects of his body, and tries to control such vagaries by reducing that body to the status of a corpse. The deathliness of the dandified body was one of its defining characteristics for Charles Baudelaire – writing in 1863, he said that dandyism imposed upon its adherents 'the terrible formula: *Perinde ac cadaver!*' This is what the dandy shares with the hypochondriac: he wants to become entirely insensate, to approach the condition of an object: a commodity or a work of art. Feeling, which Romantic artists and writers had cultivated to a morbid degree, has been replaced by a studied insouciance with regard to emotion and sensation alike.

To achieve such a state, however, it seems that the dandy must first have passed through a phase of excessive feeling, of a sentience that brings him to a mental, moral and physical crisis, from which surfeit of sensation he then retreats into a new sort of distanced proximity to the world. The motif of dandified retreat is the subject, for example, of Joris-Karl Huysmans's 1884 novel *À Rebours* (translated as *Against Nature* or *Against the Grain*). Its hero, Des Esseintes, is the scion of an ancient French family whose line has become degenerate: an excess of lymph in the blood, we are told, has made latter generations weak and febrile. At the outset of the novel, Des Esseintes has vitiated his sensibilities to the extent that he can no longer even bear the presence of another person: 'Depressed by hypochondria and weighed down by spleen, he had been reduced to such a state of nervous sensitivity that the sight of a disagreeable person or thing was deeply impressed upon his mind and it took several days even to begin removing the imprint, the human face as glimpsed in the street had been one of the keenest torments he had been forced to endure.' Des Esseintes's hypochondria consists precisely in a desperate desire to construct for himself a refuge of some sort, both physical and metaphysical, from the presence of humanity.

To this end, the enervated aristocrat buys a house outside Paris and constructs an artificial and hermetic world: his servants are banished to invisible corridors so that he does not have to see their faces. The details of his bizarre home are the contemporary stuff of decadent fantasy: a room that looks as though it were underwater; an 'organ' whose notes are perfumes which Des Esseintes combines to form chords and melodies; a collection of the most revolting plants he can procure (including a flower that has the texture and smell of rotting flesh); a gilded and jewel-encrusted tortoise that is meant to set off the yellow and plum threads of an Oriental carpet. Strangely, the motivation for all of this perverse luxury is a kind of austerity – Des Esseintes's aesthetic inventions express his renunciation of the world, not a desire to flaunt his wealth. The hypochondriac hero is in love with 'the idea of hiding away from human society'. But his desire is thwarted: he starts to suffer from a real sickness, or rather from that disorder that is intimately connected to Victorian hypochondria – he becomes a dyspeptic. Unable to bear the sight or smell of most foods, he is eventually prescribed by his physicians the most objectionable course of treatment: a return to real life, an engagement with society, a renunciation of his artificial self.

The dandy aspires to be a thing – he not only withdraws from the world, but shies away from expressions of his own human agency. Once wrapped in the comfort of reclusion, he literally wants for nothing. In this, a hypochondriac such as Des Esseintes resembles one of the most rigorously reclusive and self-abnegating characters in nineteenth-century literature. Herman Melville's *Bartleby the Scrivener* is not on the surface a tale about a dandy, but it is a story about the urge to do and feel nothing, a desire pursued with a purity that resembles the aesthetic vision of Baudelaire or Des Esseintes.

The narrator of the short story is a New York lawyer, a man who has lived 'with a profound conviction that the easiest way is the best'. In a nervous, energetic and turbulent profession, he has long been considered by his colleagues to be 'an eminently *safe* man', and has habitually carried out his business 'in the cool tranquillity of a snug retreat'. Into this serene landscape there intrudes one Bartleby, a copyist hired by the narrator, who at first seems supernaturally industrious and never to tire of replicating his employer's written words. Until, that is, he is asked to assist the lawyer in proofreading a short document, and replies in a mild, firm voice: 'I would prefer not to.' Thus begins Bartleby's strange withdrawal from the world: he retreats behind a screen in the corner of the office, continues his work but can on no account be summoned to perform ancillary duties, not even to put his finger on a bit of red tape that the lawyer is tying about some papers. But Bartleby is not merely laconic and immobile; there is something almost saintly about him, as though he has a secret, exalted mission that he will not divulge to his employer or his colleagues. His silence and apparent sloth seem full of meaning, as though doing nothing and going nowhere were morally or aesthetically superior to a life of industry and sociability. At the last, as Bartleby expires in the gaol to which he has been consigned as a vagrant after the lawyer, driven half-mad, has had to abandon his chambers, there is something Christlike about his turning from the world.

Florence Nightingale was in a sense the anti-Bartleby. Like the scrivener, she inhabited an inner room where all that mattered was the document at hand: in Bartleby's case, the legal papers that he continued to copy; in Nightingale's, the countless letters and reports to which she had to attend, and her own voluminous correspondence. Like him, she refused to eat, rebuffed all expressions of concern for her well-being and withdrew into a circumscribed and private space, appearing to have given up all social contact, preparing herself for death. Like Bartleby's, her stasis and apparent passivity occasioned a frenzy of activity in those around her: friends, colleagues and family, whose sympathy and frustration were often impossible to tell apart, whose attraction for the saintly but tyrannical patient caused them too to struggle with melancholic thoughts and hypochondriacal fears. And yet: Nightingale's 'I would prefer not to' was actually the prerequisite for her extreme industry.

*

In 1930, two years after the first publication proper of Florence Nightingale's *Cassandra*, Virginia Woolf wrote an essay entitled *On Being Ill* in which she imagined the experiences that only sickness makes possible:

'I am in bed with influenza' – but what does that convey of the great experience; how the world has changed its shape; the tools of business grown remote; the sounds of festival become romantic like a merry-go-round heard across far fields; and friends have changed, some putting on a strange beauty, others deformed to the squatness of toads, while the whole landscape of life lies remote and fair, like the shore seen from a ship far out at sea.

Such is the universality of illness, writes Woolf, so great is the spiritual alteration that it brings, so strange the territory that is illuminated by ill health, that one may wonder why the sickbed has not,
with love and war and jealousy, been among 'the prime themes of
literature'. A slight fever brings on strange visions: 'precipices and
lawns sprinkled with bright flowers'. A more serious illness forces
us to contemplate the possibility of our own annihilation. We are
suddenly subtracted from the ranks of the living and 'cease to be
soldiers in the army of the upright'. Such a strange disintegration of
ourselves, such a secession from the union of the well, has un-
expected benefits: 'We float with the sticks on the stream; helter-
skelter with the dead leaves on the lawn, irresponsible and
disinterested and able, perhaps for the first time for years, to look
round, to look up – to look, for example, at the sky.' Illness is an
opportunity not only to dream fantastic dreams, but to look anew
at the real world and to dream what it might become.

Is this what illness allowed Florence Nightingale? Did it give her,
to borrow the title of Woolf's more famous essay of 1929, a room
of her own? Sequestered at the Burlington, she was able to duck
beneath the waves of her turbulent family life even as she appeared
to place herself in their way and at their mercy. The violent attacks
and fainting fits that she suffered when faced with recalcitrant colleagues or stubborn relatives are in this sense no more edifying than
the amateur theatrics of her mother and sister. The three women
were playing out a drama of blame, envy and manipulation that
seems almost to define the restricted realm in which women of
their era and class could act: there was nothing to do but engage in
such pantomimes. But Nightingale's illnesses caused her real suffering; they expressed somatically the frustrations of her domestic
position as much as they did the trauma she suffered at Scutari. At
the same time, they forced her to diagnose, in *Cassandra*, her familial disorder. They may even be said, as she retreated to her bed, to
have allowed her to widen the horizons of her imagination and

influence beyond what her family or her colleagues and political adversaries thought possible. She was in many ways the saint that Victorian sentiment wanted her to be, and in other respects a monster of self-belief, self-delusion and expertly deployed enfeeblement. In the end, her hypochondriacal tendencies perhaps prove that reclusion is never merely a matter of escaping from the outside world; it is always also a message to that world and a way of insinuating one's influence far beyond the confines of a room of one's own.

Late in life, her health began to improve. After many years of seclusion and inactivity, she was able occasionally to risk a short walk or to be taken out for a drive in a carriage in fine weather. Her spirits lifted, and in 1895 she wrote: 'There is so much to live for. I have lost much in failures and disappointments, as well as in grief, but do you know, life is more precious to me now in my old age.' At the same time, wrote Lytton Strachey in 1918, 'there appeared a corresponding alteration in her physical mould. The thin, angular woman, with her haughty eye and her acrid mouth, had vanished; and in her place was the rounded, bulky form of a fat old lady, smiling all day long. Then something else became visible. The brain which had been steeled at Scutari was indeed, literally, growing soft. Senility – an even more and more amiable senility – descended. Towards the end, consciousness itself grew lost in a roseate haze, and melted into nothingness.' In 1896, she retreated once more to her bedroom, where she remained, the last survivor of her natural and spiritual families, until her death fourteen years later.

5. The Exaltation of Alice James

'Her disastrous, her tragic health was in a manner the only solution for her of the practical problem of life.'

Henry James, in a letter to William James, 1894

On the 27th of May 1891, Alice James, the youngest sibling of Henry and William James, was examined at her house in London by the renowned physician Sir Andrew Clark. It was not the first time that Clark had been called to the bedside of the unmarried American, who was then aged forty-two and long settled into a permanent invalidism which, though grown habitual, still sometimes erupted into crisis – Alice referred to these episodes as her 'going off' or 'going to pie'. Precisely what fresh torment had troubled her in the spring of 1891, when Sir Andrew first called at her previous lodging in the South Kensington Hotel, is unclear. Her stomach was often in turmoil, her nerves regularly 'shattered', her legs in recent years so weakened that the few excursions she risked into the streets and parks of London were undertaken in a bath chair, steered by her companion, Katharine Peabody Loring, or by the nurse (unnamed in Alice's diaries and letters) who attended her daily. Perhaps the occasion of her first consultation with Clark was a simple worsening of her usual symptoms. In the autumn of the previous year, Alice had complained in her journal of 'squalid indigestions', while Katharine recorded her disease as 'stomachic gout': a diagnosis as obscure as any she received during a quarter of a century of almost constant illness. Early in the new year, it seems that

Alice, who now spoke and wrote often of her impending demise, had begun to look more ominously frail than usual, prompting Katharine to write: 'I have never seen any one so thin as she was, so full of pain, and altogether wretched.' Alice could only concur that after decades of ill health, years of wavering between the chronic and the acute, she seemed to be fading fast. 'If the aim of life is the accretion of fat,' she wrote in her diary, 'the consumption of food unattended by digestive disorganization, and a succession of pleasurable sensations, there is no doubt that I am a failure.'

The house at 41 Argyll Road, Kensington, into which Alice, Katharine and their small staff had lately moved was modern and spacious, of mid-century Italianate design, giving onto a modest garden and close enough to Holland Park that Alice could hear the rooks from her sickbed. Because she left an imprecise account of the consultation with Sir Andrew, we have to imagine the early summer sun streaming into Alice's room, the slightly disapproving ministrations of the starched and pious nurse and the tireless Katharine in the background: angular, bespectacled, pen and paper still in hand after an hour spent taking Alice's dictation or editing and improving her journal entries of the last few weeks. We know that Alice, who was addicted to medical opinion and whose descriptions of her encounters with various doctors verge frequently on a palpable eroticism, thought the distinguished Sir Andrew (physician to Gladstone and Edward VII) a figure of some fun, on account of his habit of always making the same joke at his tardy arrival, announcing himself as 'the late Sir Andrew Clark!'. ('Imagine the martyrdom of a pun which has become an integral portion of one's organism,' she mocked in her diary.) We know too that part of her dreaded these meetings: not because she feared the diagnosis – as we shall see, Alice James was a curiously fearless kind of hypochondriac – but because she felt herself exposed, degraded and reduced by the medical gaze. Writing to her brother William in 1886, she had sketched for him the mental and emotional battle to which a consultation came down: 'I must confess my spirit quails before any more gladiatorial encounters. It requires the strength of a horse to survive the fatigue of waiting hour after hour for the great man and then the fierce struggle to recover one's self-respect . . .'

There is no diary entry for the 27th of May, perhaps because in the hours and days that followed she was engaged in that struggle. Only on the last day of the month did the patient refer to what had transpired between her and the physician, and even then the details of the examination form no part of her account. What exercises her first in the entry for that day is the feeling she has had for years beneath the eye and, one assumes, the touch of the medical profession, of being treated like an idiot. She recalls that only one doctor, John Cooper Torry of the Royal College of Physicians, had not seemed to assume that because she was the victim of so many pains she was also, of necessity, mentally enfeebled. It is a strange emotion to have focused on, this intellectual shame, given what she goes on to tell us of Sir Andrew's visit. She has, she says, 'been going downhill at a steady trot': Clark has confirmed a 'most distressing case of nervous hyperaesthesia', a 'rheumatic gout' in the stomach, the 'spinal neurosis' that has made it difficult or at times impossible to walk, and certain cardiac complications that account in part for her general decline. But this is all merely 'a delicate embroidery' to the central diagnostic motif. For three months, apparently without mentioning it to anyone, she has had a painful lump in one of her breasts, now identified by Clark as a tumour. Nothing can be done for Alice but to alleviate her pain; it is only, she notes in a phrase that might belong to the doctor's repertoire of euphemisms or might well be her own laconic shrug in the face of mortality, 'a question of time, etc.'

Alice James's response to that implacable et cetera is among the more impressive reactions to impending doom in the canon of valetudinarian bravery; it is comparable to David Hume's writing, with seeming calm, 'I now reckon upon a speedy dissolution', or to Ludwig Wittgenstein's logical reaction to his last birthday gift:

'There will be no more returns.' Alice seems to have greeted the news of her imminent death not only with equanimity but even, allowing for the ironic turn of her diaries and correspondence, with a kind of joy. Four days after Clark's 'uncompromising verdict', she dictated to Katharine:

To him who waits, all things come! My aspirations may have been eccentric, but I cannot complain now, that they have not been brilliantly fulfilled. Ever since I have been ill, I have longed and longed for some palpable disease, no matter how conventionally dreadful a label it might have, but I was always driven back to stagger alone under the monstrous mass of subjective sensations, which that sympathetic being 'the medical man' had no higher inspiration than to assure me I was personally responsible for, washing his hands of me with a graceful complacency under my very nose.

She is not only relieved at the prospect of a real disease putting an end to her sufferings, but triumphant at the notion that she might have been a terminal case all along. It is as if, only now that the end is in sight, she starts to live for the first time, begins to emerge from the 'formless vague' of her protracted suffering and her long seclusion at the edge of her own life, and asserts at the last, in dying, her true individuality.

In the wake of the diagnosis, Alice at first informed William James merely that she was suffering from heart disease – news that would not have surprised him, and that only added to the long list of her diffuse and still enigmatic complaints. But at the end of June she had Katharine write to inform him about the tumour, the significance of which, should the growth prove malignant, would have been beyond doubt. The exchange of letters that followed between the siblings is of a piece with her life to date and with the curious culture of illness and death, peculiar even for the time, that the James family had contrived between them. On the 6th of July, William wrote back from his summer home at Chocorua, New Hampshire:

So far from shocked I am, although made more compassionate, yet (strange to say) rather relieved than shaken by this more tangible and immediately menacing source of woe. Katharine describes you as being so too; and I don't wonder. Vague nervousness has a character of ill about it that is all its own, and in comparison with which any organic disease has a good side. Of course, if the tumour should turn out to be cancerous, that means, as all men know, a finite length of days; and then, good-bye to neurasthenia and neuralgia and headache, and weariness and palpitation and disgust all at one stroke – I should think you would be reconciled to the prospect with all its pluses and minuses!

Alice's reply of the 30th of July is similarly affectionate and unsentimental: she thanks her brother for his forthrightness and declares that she would have been 'very much wounded & *incomprise* had you walked round and not up to my demise'. But there is more in the letter than a shared facing down of the void, gleaned from William's medical realism when presented with a fact of nature and from Alice's relief at the prospect of an end to her suffering. It is rather as if life opens up before her for the first time, and she surveys the prospect with an astonishing eagerness and anticipation: 'It is the most supremely interesting moment in life, the only one when living seems life, and I count it as the greatest good fortune to have these few months so full of interest and instruction in the knowledge of my approaching death ... I have a delicious consciousness, ever present, of wide spaces close at hand ...'

*

How was it that Alice James, at the age of forty-two, had attained such a vantage, both physically perilous and emotionally assured, from which to view her own life and impending death? What complex of fancied and actual ailments, of imagination and experience, could have conspired to produce such a happy embrace of her end? What, in short, was the matter with Alice? In one sense, hers is merely a heightened example of the travails of many women of her class and education in the late nineteenth century, her career as an invalid simply one more instance of the effects of various sorts of repression: emotional, intellectual, sexual and (despite her privileged birth) economic. Dulled ambition and frustrated desire, so a certain received wisdom about the period has it, must inevitably have found some morbid expression, and the only theatre in which the private drama of the constrained female psyche could then be performed was the female body itself.

In the case of Alice James, there is more than a little truth in this theory; nor is it only a retrospective, post-Freudian reading of her story: the problem of nervous, hysterical, neurasthenic women exercised physicians and social commentators throughout the nineteenth century, and the sociological and sexual origins of such disorders were by no means hidden to the Victorians. What seems to separate Alice James from the ordinary neurosis of the well-off women of her time is first of all an extreme self-consciousness about what was happening to her, and secondly an especially keen sense that illness was truly a career, a kind of intellectual and artistic work that was comparable, in the domestic sphere, with the public labours of her brothers. The James siblings were raised in an idiosyncratic and peripatetic fashion. Alice was seven years old when they first left for Europe, Henry James Sr installing his family in London, Paris and Geneva before returning them to the USA and settling in Cambridge, Massachusetts, at the end of the American Civil War. A moral and theological thinker and writer with hampered ambitions of his own, Henry Sr made it clear to his offspring that conventional achievement was not sufficient: they ought not, he advised, to choose 'to be something', but rather to live an original life, a life dedicated to being peculiar (in the old sense of particular or individual), a life unconstrained by the ordinary paths of profession or career. It was better to be an interesting failure in the eyes of the world than a success by its hidebound standards. To demand that one's children be above all interesting suggests a degree of personal disappointment or inadequacy in a parent; beneath an unusually affectionate nature that is the object of nostalgia and regret in his children's writings, Henry James Sr wrestled with his own highly involved frustrations. Physically compromised by the loss of a leg following an accident when he was seventeen, he suffered mentally too in later life. In May 1844, Henry Sr, his wife and two young sons were living in a cottage in Windsor. Sitting alone after dinner one evening, he was seized by an attack of terror. 'Suddenly,' he later wrote, 'in a lightning-flash as it were – "fear came upon me, and trembling, which made all my bones to shake." To all appearance it was a perfectly insane and abject terror, without ostensible cause.' He seemed to feel 'some damnèd shape squatting invisible to me within the precincts of the room, and raying out from his foetid personality influences fatal to life. The thing had not lasted ten seconds before I felt myself a wreck; that is, reduced from a state of firm, vigorous, joyful manhood to one of almost helpless infancy.' Resisting an impulse to rush for his wife's aid, or even to run into the street for help, he somehow held still in his chair; the immediate crisis abated, but his distress did not, and he was prescribed rest, fresh air and water cures.

It was in the wake of this breakdown that Henry Sr dedicated himself to the search for a moral, true and free mode of life. His attitudes, schooled on the writings of the Swedish mystic Emanuel Swedenborg, may have been at odds with conventional religious beliefs regarding good and evil, and his philosophy of parenting unusually liberal, especially in the affection he bestowed on his children, but their effects on the five James siblings were nonetheless tyrannical. The two younger brothers, Garth Wilkinson ('Wilky') and Robertson ('Bob'), appear to have been crushed by the weight of expectation; both felt that they had missed out on the family genius, Bob once commenting that he must have been a foundling. Henry and William may have seemed to flourish in just the ways their father hoped for them, but their worldly success was constantly undercut by the suspicion that literature and science were still too conventional as fields in which to excel. And while Henry Sr delighted in his daughter's intellect and wit, she was emphatically excluded from the vision of moral and creative achievement that her father had conjured for his sons. In 1853, in *Putnam's Monthly*, he published an article entitled 'Woman and the "Woman's Movement"' that stated, in the face of increasing demands for women's education and suffrage in the US, the precise degree to which they were inferior to men: 'The very virtue of woman, her practical sense, which leaves her indifferent to past and future alike, and keeps her the busy blessing of the present hour, disqualifies her from all didactic dignity. Learning and wisdom do not become her. Even the ten commandments seem unamiable and superfluous on her lips, so much should her own pure pleasure form the best outward law for man.' Such views were of course entirely conventional, but they combined in the James household with a level of conversation and intellectual competition, of which Alice was privately very much a part, that must have made her lack of formal education, and the knowledge that she would never put her obvious intelligence to any creative or public use, all the more frustrating.

*

Alice was not alone in responding to this fervid family atmosphere by becoming ill: sickness was shared among the siblings, if not equally then at least generously, just as they shared a sense of humour that found its sharpest expression among the trio of Alice, Henry and William. Their letters to each other are filled with wittily described symptoms. Headaches, back pain and digestive problems troubled them all. William suffered from a weak spine and severe eye strain for which no cause could be discerned. Henry's correspondence details with obsessive care the variable but always trying state of his digestion, and he too was wracked with backache for much of his adult life. Wilky, who died of heart disease at thirty-eight, and Bob, who struggled on against alcoholism and anxiety until the age of sixty-five, felt temperamentally even less hale than their siblings. All five suffered to different degrees from nervous disorders, thus emulating their father. It was William's crisis that most resembled the unsettling episode that Henry Sr called his 'vastation'. In *The Varieties of Religious Experience*, published in 1902, he presents the case of a French patient 'in a bad nervous condition'. The subject is in fact a poorly disguised William James, who writes:

Whilst in [a] state of philosophic pessimism and general depression of spirits about my prospects, I went one evening into a dressing-room in the twilight to procure some article that was there; when suddenly there fell upon me without any warning, just as if it came out of the darkness, a horrible fear of my own existence. Simultaneously there arose in my mind the image of an epileptic patient whom I had seen in the asylum, a black-haired youth with greenish skin, entirely idiotic, who used to sit all day on one of the benches, or rather shelves against the wall, with his knees drawn up against his chin, and the coarse grey undershirt, which was his only garment, drawn over them enclosing his entire figure . . . *That shape am I*, I felt, potentially. Nothing that I possess can defend me against that fate, if the hour for it should strike for me as it struck for him.

What William seemed to fear most in this vision was the mental and physical withdrawal from the world, the idea that if he gave in to the forces that lay just below the surface of his character, he might easily succumb to the obscurity of unreason. The experience was, he wrote, a revelation; henceforth he awoke every morning with a sense of dread, and for months was unable to venture out alone after dark.

In a sense, what threatened to befall William suddenly was just what happened to his sister slowly, over years and decades: a gradual retreat into seclusion and immobility, her giving in to a kind of 'idiocy' – at least in the eyes of her doctors – and drawing the thin covering of her self-possession about her ever more pathetically as she grew older. Except that Alice was no green-skinned idiot, but a woman of exceptional wit and insight into her own predicament and the characters of those around her. Like William, however, she felt that if she let go, if she allowed her authentic self to show too clearly through the grey garment of her public persona, she would 'go to pie' completely, would descend into madness and disgrace. She felt this, we know, from an early age, and learned to mask her true nature. In London, in 1890, looking back on her early life, she was to write:

Owing to muscular circumstances my youth was not of the most ardent, but I had to peg away pretty hard between 12 and 24, 'killing myself', as some one calls it, – absorbing into the bone that the better part is to clothe oneself in neutral tints, walk by still waters, and possess one's soul in silence. How I recall the low grey Newport sky in that winter of 62–3 as I used to wander about over the cliffs, my young soul struggling out of its swaddling-clothes as the knowledge crystallized within me of what Life meant for me, one, simple, single and before which all mystery vanished. A spark then kindled which every experience great and small has fed into a steady flame which has illuminated my little journey and which, altho' it may have burned low as the waters rose, has never flickered out.

In middle age, she was resigned to the fact that hers was a 'little journey', grateful that she had maintained a solid self at all, however secret, and had not succumbed like 'those poor creatures who never find their bearings'.

In medical terms, it is not exactly clear just what she had survived: the family correspondence refers to her delicate or nervous nature, her valetudinarian tendencies, her desire, expressed in letters that have not survived, to die. Though her symptoms were scarcely mentioned, her 'refinement' had already set her apart from the other young women in her circle, who in their late teens and early twenties were starting to fall in love around her, and within a few years to marry and embark on a life that Alice knew was not to be hers. William, writing home from Brazil in 1865, asked if she continued to wish she was dead; Henry Sr, in a letter to his daughter's friend Annie Ashburner, conveyed Alice's regret at being too unwell to attend the Museum of Fine Arts in Boston. In the autumn of the following year, her mysterious condition had worsened and she was dispatched to New York, to the Orthopedic Dispensary of Charles Fayette Taylor, near the junction of Broadway and 35th Street. A specialist in the treatment of diseases of the spine and hip joint among the children of the poor, Taylor also welcomed into his home older private patients whom he submitted to his celebrated 'movement cure'. In the months that followed, Alice seemed to improve under his care: she wrote, noted William, 'delightful' letters from New York and was seen, reported a cousin to her mother Mary James, 'looking as fat as butter' after some weeks. The cure, however, took longer than expected: early in 1867, Alice was still in New York, and a note of concern that she might be settling into the life of an invalid began to trouble the family's letters. In January, Mary wrote to her daughter that she had received 'such fine accounts of your blooming appearance that I shall expect to hear from the Dr. that the good work of restoration is almost complete'. A month later, after her parents had visited her, William wrote that they had given 'a "graphic" account of you well fitted to tranquilize anxiety & annul pity but not to kindle enthusiasm or excite envy'.

The treatment that Alice most likely received at Taylor's establishment had its origins in the contemporary understanding of female neurasthenia – a disorder that, according to an account written by George Beard in 1868, resulted from the depletion of nervous energy and led to a potential array of over fifty symptoms, including fainting spells, muscle spasms, headaches, morbid fears, menstrual irregularity, neuralgia, dilation of the pupils, tooth decay, irascibility, paralysis, weariness, constipation, insomnia, dyspepsia, lack of appetite, vomiting, fits of laughing and crying, lapses in concentration, temporary blindness, convulsions and a generalized sense of hopelessness. (The James family correspondence gives us clues only to Alice's weight loss and depression.) For Beard, such symptoms were clearly caused by the frenzy and strain of modern life acting on the fragile female constitution; the excessive stimulation effected by such products of scientific progress as steam power and the telegraph, as well as increased mental activity among women, led inevitably to a morbid deficit in nervous energy. A common remedy for such a condition was the rest cure proposed by the famous neurologist Silas Weir Mitchell. The patient was confined to bed, massaged, read to, overfed and helped to sit up, bathe and urinate. But the cure, Mitchell admitted, had its own attendant dangers: the patient might develop a 'morbid delight' in inactivity and in the constant attention she received. It was this danger that Taylor's movement cure or 'motorpathic treatment' was designed to counter. Drawing on the discoveries of a Swedish physiologist, Peter Henrik Ling (who claimed to have cured a case of gout in his own elbow by constant manipulation of the joint), Taylor submitted his inmates to a course of physical exercise, devised, he explained in his *Theory and Practice of the Movement Cure* of 1864, to reverse what he called the 'exaltation' of the nervous system. 'By exaltation', Taylor wrote, 'is not meant actual strength, but a use and waste of power which otherwise might be converted into nervous strength or endurance' – as a result of which depletion the other functions, mental and physical, became chronically 'depressed'. The woman's nervous system, overstimulated by emotional and intellectual activity, was 'literally *starved*' of vital force; the cure consisted in a repletion of physical energy, the 'counter-irritation' of physical exercise thus effecting in response a restoration of psychic vitality.

What had brought Taylor's female patients to their sorry neurasthenic state? In the pages of *The Theory and Practice of the Movement Cure*, and in an article entitled 'Emotional Prodigality' that he published some years after treating Alice James, some confusion is evident: an ambiguity that is perhaps typical of a period that half understood the enervating effects of domestic confinement and grudgingly, with a species of warped sympathy, recognized the frustrations fostered by what sparse intellectual stimulation was available. On the one hand, says Taylor, women's lives are lived too often in a state of heightened emotion; relegated to the realm of the family, they absorb and become obsessed by the emotional intrigues of their immediate milieu. On the other, he notes with disapproval, they have in recent decades been overtaxed even by the modest education they have received. Woman, he avers, is 'characterized as a sex with less manifestation of independent thinking, whether from a feebler endowment of reasoning powers, or whether because the intellect is so habitually subordinated to simple feeling, it is not necessary to discuss . . . While education in men makes them self-controlling, steady, deliberate, calculating, thinking out every problem, the intellect being the preponderating force, the so-called "higher education" for women seems to produce the contrary effect on them . . . While men are calmed, women are excited by the education they receive.' Such women, Taylor concludes, are ill fitted to marriage or to the rearing of 'rightly organized' children.

Leaving aside his manifest prejudices, Taylor's account seems to describe, from a skewed perspective, the problem that Alice James faced in 1866. Her emotions cultivated in the affective hothouse of the James household, her keen intellect sharpened by the conversation of her brilliant brothers and almost brilliant father, her nature both cosseted and condemned by her somewhat distant mother, she surely exceeded most of Taylor's neurasthenic patients in the extremity of her circumstance, if not her symptoms. We have no record of the details of her treatment, but it seems probable that in the winter of 1866 and the spring of the following year Alice's body was exercised to the full extent of Taylor's curative vision, in a fruitless effort to harden the musculature of her troubled mind.

*

Alice emerged from the Orthopedic Dispensary in May of 1867, returned home to Cambridge with her aunt Kate and began to renew her modest social life, attending dinner parties and being introduced to the new friends her family had made in her absence. Her mother wrote optimistically to William: 'Alice seems very bright and is an immense joy to us. Her presence is a perfect sunbeam to Father.' As her biographer Jean Strouse reports, the health of her brothers had in the meantime declined: Wilky and Bob had purchased a plantation in Florida, but Wilky had returned home with a fever and Bob, having taken up a post as a railroad clerk in Wisconsin, was suffering, wrote Mary, from constant 'catarrhal trouble'. Henry was plagued as usual by back pain and constipation, had resorted to massage and ice therapy (which he soon abandoned as 'pernicious') to relieve his discomforts, and planned to visit Taylor himself to be fitted for a 'spinal assistant': a brace or corset designed to alleviate strain on the affected portion of the spine. He would later devise a humorous theory to account for his 'degenerescence': the family, he conjectured, maintained among them a delicate balance of health and disease, so that while Alice and Wilky got better, the remainder of the James allocation of ailments was visited upon him in his turn. In 1867, however, the regulating mechanism seemed to oscillate wildly; Alice's apparent improvement was short-lived, and in June, scarcely a month after leaving New York, while visiting her friend Fanny Morse in Brookline, she succumbed to another attack. Mary, summoned to her bedside, now foresaw, so soon after her daughter's apparent cure, the life that inevitably lay before her. 'Alice I am sorry to say, from a little overexertion, has had one of her old attacks; and a very bad one. She will have dear child to live with the extremest care.'

The tedious round of Alice's lifelong indisposition now began in earnest; she was never afterwards properly well. The following year she fell ill again, this time more spectacularly, with what she would call in her diary, twenty-two years later, 'violent turns of hysteria'. According to a letter of her mother's written at the time of her collapse, the diagnosis seems to have been generally accepted by the family; Alice's was, she wrote, 'a case of genuine hysteria for which no cause as yet can be discerned'. Oddly, Mary James claimed that her daughter's mind was not involved in the episode at all – prompting us to wonder what the unnamed symptoms actually were – and that she seemed otherwise perfectly happy once the initial violence of the attack had passed. Alice's diary entry of the 26th of October 1890, however, sketches in retrospect a more troubled scene, and is worth quoting at length:

As I lay prostrate after the storm with my mind luminous and active and susceptible of the clearest, strongest impressions, I saw so distinctly that it was a fight simply between my body and my will, a battle in which the former was to be triumphant to the end. Owing to some physical weakness, excess of nervous susceptibility, the moral power *pauses*, as it were for a moment, and refuses to maintain muscular sanity, worn out with the strain of its constabulary functions. As I used to sit immovable reading in the library with waves of violent inclination suddenly invading my muscles taking some one of their myriad forms such as throwing myself out of the window, or knocking off the head of the benignant pater as he sat with his silver locks, writing at his table, it used to seem to me that the only difference between me and the insane was that I had not only all the horrors and suffering of insanity but the duties of doctor, nurse, and straitjacket imposed upon me, too. Conceive of never being without the sense that if you let yourself go for a moment your mechanism will fall into pie and that at some given moment you must abandon it all, let the dykes break and the flood sweep in, acknowledging yourself abjectly impotent before the immutable laws. When all one's moral and natural stock in trade is a temperament forbidding the abandonment of an inch or the relaxation of a muscle, 'tis a never-ending fight.

The feat of self-control performed in the library seems to point today too readily to a resentment towards her father that Alice, even from the perspective of middle age, was unwilling or unable to examine more closely. It may also have been invisible to her parents and siblings, who acknowledged the severity of her symptoms but failed to appreciate the extremity of her torment or to gauge the interior pressure, the explosive emotional force, that she struggled to contain.

Henry James Sr's favoured solution to his recurring unease and uncertainty about his own course in life had been to travel abroad; in adulthood, his daughter would regret her unsettled childhood. Still, faced now with her own 'vastation', Alice sought relief from her symptoms at first in vacations close to home – in 1869 she was at Pomfret, Connecticut, according to her mother, 'busy trying to be idle' – and then further afield, and for longer stays, in Europe. In 1872 she accompanied her brother Henry and her aunt Kate to England. Although none of her letters survive from her six months abroad, we know that she was at first impressed and invigorated by the experience. Henry, writing from the Queen's Hotel, Chester, reported that Alice was 'ravished and transported by what she finds here', while according to Kate she had acquired a new calm and fortitude during visits to such historic towns as Warwick and Exeter, and the dignified resort of Royal Leamington Spa. Though London was 'not hygienic' and thus unconducive to Alice's well-being, Paris was certainly to her taste. She seemed, wrote Henry, 'like a new – like a rejuvenated creature, and displayed more gaiety, more elasticity, more genuine youthful animal spirits than I have ever seen in her'. At Thusis in Switzerland, however, she suffered some undefined 'episodes': the air, Henry reported, 'seemed over-exciting to Alice. It made her nervous – rather acutely so – for the 1st time since we have been abroad.' It was a case, he claimed, of 'climatic antipathy': 'Alice's own impulse and curiosity is almost altogether towards cities, monuments, and the *human picturesque*, of which she has seen, during her lifetime, so little; I think one month of mountains has been a little over-solemn sort of entertainment for her.' Overwhelmed by the grandeur of the landscape, Alice's spirit was perhaps 'exalted' in the sense of which Charles Fayette

Taylor had warned. On her return home, however, Mary James found her happier, stronger and (again this telling phrase) 'more elastic'. She began once more to expand her social and intellectual horizons, this time becoming involved in the Society to Encourage Studies at Home, an organization dedicated to alleviating exactly the boredom and constraint suffered by women like her.

As before, the improvement in her condition did not last. In 1878, a fresh crisis, apparently of the stomach, laid her low once more. It was during this breakdown that Alice and her father had a conversation concerning the morality of suicide. The family had long ago grown used to her expressing a desire to die, but she now put to Henry Sr a stark and seemingly pressing question: would it be wrong, she wanted to know, to put an end to her life? He later wrote to his son Bob:

I told her that I thought it was not a sin except where it was wanton, as when a person from a mere love of pleasurable excitement indulged in drink or opium to the utter degradation of her faculties, and often to the ruin of the human form in him; but that it was absurd to think it sinful when one was driven to it in order to escape bitter suffering, from spiritual influx, as in her case, or from some loathsome form of disease, as in others. I told her so far as I was concerned she had my full permission to end her life whenever she pleased; only I hoped that if ever she felt like doing that sort of justice to her circumstances, she would do it in a perfectly gentle way in order not to distress her friends.

Alice, he said, had thanked him and assured him that, now that she saw she had the right to dispose of her body in extremis, she could never do it – it had before been a matter of asserting her freedom in the face of imprisoning circumstance, but now, she said, her licence to kill herself was enough to liberate her from the need to kill herself.

She continued to speak of her death as a welcome relief from her pain, then later (after the ultimate diagnosis) to welcome it as a positive culmination of her life, and to admire those who managed to do away with themselves, but she never again seriously expressed a determination to emulate them. Rather, she dated the process of her dying from her facing up to the real possibility of suicide in 1878; to her diary, over a decade later, she would write: 'The fact is, I have been dead so long and it has been simply such a grim shoving of the hours behind me as I faced a ceaseless possible horror, since that hideous summer of '78 when I went down to the deep sea, its dark waters closed over me, and I knew neither hope nor peace; that now it's only the shriveling of an empty pea pod that has to be completed.' From the moment that Henry Sr gave her permission to end her life, Alice's was a kind of posthumous existence.

*

In January 1882, Mary James contracted bronchial asthma and died. Alice's brothers concurred that they had rarely, in recent years, seen their sister so well, nor so lively and hard-working, as in the days she spent nursing her dying mother and the weeks that followed, during which she became responsible for the care of her increasingly infirm father. In the spring, they moved to a smaller house at 131 Mount Vernon Street, Boston; meanwhile Alice, in a sudden flurry of enterprise and activity, arranged to have a second house built on land she had bought the previous year at Manchester-by-the-Sea. Her father, however, had no intention of living now that his wife had died, and seemed determined on a gentle sort of suicide. Henry Sr simply refused to eat, and although he consulted a homeopath who assured him that mental and physical rest would soon cure his malaise, he was heard to pronounce impatiently that 'it is weary work, this dying' and to express often his wish to leave 'this disgusting world'. On the 11th of December, Alice's aunt Katharine wrote: 'he is very happy and perfectly comfortable'; he refused to allow his sickroom to be darkened, and lay facing the window, waiting frankly for death. Among the last words he spoke, according to Katharine, were these: 'Oh, I have such good boys –

such good boys!' and 'There is my Mary!' He did not mention Alice, who was being nursed in another room. On the 18th, he died.

Alice was now essentially alone. Already in a state of collapse at the time of her father's death, she struggled on at Vernon Street in the company of her brother Henry until he left to visit friends in New York and Washington in the spring of 1883. Early in May, Alice made her way to the Boston suburb of Jamaica Plain and placed herself in a newly opened institution for the treatment of nervous diseases. The Adams Nervine Asylum stood among sixteen acres of lawn and wood-land, an eclectic agglomeration of wooden buildings in a variety of styles: Queen Anne Revival, Second Empire, Colonial. The effect of the numerous arches, cupolas and balconies today (for the asylum is still standing) is of a fantastical flowering of Victorian Gothic. In an article published in the *Boston Daily Globe* in 1887, Mary Norton Brad-ford described a 'cozy homelike interior that is most attractive': there were rugs, engravings and books in profusion, and most patients had an airy and well-lit room of their own. Female patients worn down by the climate or the 'mad pursuit of the "mighty dollar"', reduced to a state of 'nervous prostration', were here treated, Bradford wrote, according to the latest therapeutic methods. She sketches for her readers the battery room and its strange machinery: 'Here the bright brass discs of a big electric battery glisten under a great glass case and hanging from the walls of the room are all sorts of queer apparatus for driving the lazy blood into new life, and giving the flesh and that it implies a gentle fillip to remind it that it is forgetting its functions. This is where you get "points" and have your hair combed by electri-city till you present the appearance of a very fretful porcupine.' We can be reasonably confident that the Holtz Electrical Machine, acquired by the asylum in 1883, was among the treatments applied to Alice during the three months she spent there.

The Adams Nervine had been founded in 1877 at the bequest of a neurasthenic sugar baron, Seth Adams. Its thirty women patients were drawn, according to an 1883 report by the resident physician,

Frank Page, from all classes of society. Nervous trouble was not, Page asserted, confined to the upper and middle classes, as was commonly thought, but brought on too among the working classes by sheer drudgery and constant anxiety. Teachers, especially, seemed to succumb, due to the combination of hard work in the classroom and unstinting care of dependent or invalid relatives outside of it. The treatment of such cases was a matter of delicate balance between rest (the regime recommended by Mitchell) and the new theories and technologies of invigoration. As Page put it in his report:

The value of 'rest and seclusion' as remedial agents is an exceedingly interesting question, in view of the rather indiscriminate application which has been made of this treatment to all forms of nervous disturbance . . . In hysteria it assists by its discipline in regaining self-control, but *not* in melancholia, either of a mild or severe type. On the contrary, its use in cases of *depression* invariably aggravates rather than soothes or mitigates the symptoms, and I do not resort to it in the treatment of this class of patients. In nervous exhaustion, so-called, whether of cerebral, spinal, or mixed types, it is more certain of satisfactory results than any other plan yet tried. It retards waste, checks morbid activities, and prevents the drains and lesser strains so fruitful in perpetuating this condition.

As Jean Strouse points out in response to this passage, Alice had in fact been diagnosed in her time as both hysterical and neurasthenic; her treatment seems to have included rest, electricity, hot air, massage and vapour baths. Early in August, she left the asylum for Katharine Loring's house by the sea at Beverly; Henry James reported that she was much improved, 'but there has been no miraculous cure'.

A year later we find her once more in New York, at the office of a Russian nerve specialist, one William B. Neftel. According to Neftel, Mitchell was profoundly mistaken about the proper treatment for neurasthenia; exercise rather than rest was the key, and electricity the medium by which the exhausted female body could be restored to health, removing the 'effete substances' that depleted nervous energy, and restoring fresh blood and lymph to the muscles. At first, the cure seemed effective; Alice wrote to Fanny Morse of a 'wonderful change quite as if I had been transformed . . . The doctor is as kind and easy to get on with as he can be and the only thing I have to complain of is that "Rome was not built in a day".' Seventeen years after her stay at Charles Fayette Taylor's Orthopedic Dispensary, however, New York no longer agreed with her; nor, as the treatment progressed, did Neftel live up to her initial impression of him: 'I was charmed at first with the Slavic flavour of our intercourse but I soon found myself sighing for unadulterated Jackson. To associate with and to have to take seriously a creature with the moral substance of a monkey becomes degrading after awhile, no matter how one may have been seduced by his "shines" at the first going off.' Yet again, she was thrown back on her own modest resources, and retreated to Boston to try to make a home and a solitary but stable life for herself.

*

Alice was now in her early thirties, and what hopes her family may once have had of her marrying had long since vanished. Katharine Loring, who was by the mid 1880s more often than not at her side, has been variously described as Alice's lover and as a close friend in the particular, domesticated, sense that for the Victorians did not (publicly at any rate) suggest a sexual relationship. Clearly, for the James family, Katharine's presence was both welcome – she held out the only prospect of the invalid's living a comfortable life – and a source of some anxiety and suspicion. It seemed that Alice's health declined every time she was separated from Katharine – or more accurately, every time Katharine was forced to leave her side to nurse her own, frequently unwell, sister Louisa. In 1885 Alice joined the Loring sisters, who had travelled to England the previous year, at Bournemouth, where she was even more incapacitated than usual: she could not move her legs at all, and stayed in bed for months.

When Katharine and Louisa left for London, planning to travel in Europe, Alice's spine became so painful that she was completely immobilized, and Henry had to rush to her aid from London. The nurse he employed soon quit when she discovered her charge would not obey her orders; Katharine was summoned back to her bedside. The pattern of slight recovery in Katharine's presence, followed by rapid prostration as soon as she left again, was now becoming routine; it seemed that Katharine would have to become a permanent fixture of Alice's household if she was to survive.

Surveying the prospect of his sister's permanent invalidism, and her now almost total dependence on her companion, Henry James wrote resignedly to his aunt Katharine:

The plan is doubtless subject to variations of detail, from possible fluctuations in Louisa's health, but what it means is that, *virtually*, Katharine comes back to Alice for a permanency. Her being with her may be interrupted by absences, but evidently it is the beginning of a living-together, for the rest of such time as Alice's life may last. I think that a conviction on K's part at *bottom*, beneath her superficial optimism, that it *may* not last long, has something to do with the arrangement – for evidently it is a kind of definite understanding between them . . . We must accept it with gratitude. One may think that her being with A. is not in the long run the best thing for A., but the latter is *too ill* to make the long run the main thing to think about. There *may* be no long run at all.

The possibility of an early end to Alice's suffering seems to have been ever present from this moment on; it is not too cynical to read in her brother's guarded comments about Katharine a sense of relief that her having found somebody to love her and look after her would also mean that he would no longer be charged with the responsibility of her care.

In the autumn of 1885, Alice and Katharine moved to Mayfair, a few minutes' walk away from Henry's house at the end of Bolton

Street. In the summer of the following year they visited the health resort of Royal Leamington Spa, in Warwickshire; its mineral springs had been thought beneficial to the health since Elizabethan times, long pre-dating the hydropathic craze of the mid nineteenth century that had caught Charles Darwin and Florence Nightingale, among many others, in its watery wake. Nathaniel Hawthorne, John Ruskin, William Makepeace Thackeray and Charles Dickens were among the notable Victorians who took the waters at Leamington, but Alice was drawn back there indefinitely in 1887 as much by the prospect of a genteel solitude as by the therapeutic reputation of the town. In a boarding house at 11 Hamilton Terrace, she spent her mornings in bed, rose at half past noon and occasionally, if her health and the weather permitted, risked an excursion in her bath chair. In the afternoons she lay on the sofa in the drawing room, where she sometimes received visitors but more usually read or wrote. It was there, as the decade drew to a close, that she embarked, with Katharine as her amanuensis, on the work (of sorts) that would be her lasting legacy: a work that vies, in its confessional, ironic and often surprisingly antic way, with the psychological insights then being elaborated by William and Henry James.

Alice's diary begins on the 31st of May 1889: 'I think that if I get into the habit of writing a bit about what happens, or rather doesn't happen, I may lose a little of the sense of loneliness and desolation which abides with me . . . I shall at least have it all my own way and it may bring relief as an outlet to that geyser of emotions, sensations, speculations and reflections which ferments perpetually within my poor old carcass for its sins; so here goes, my first Journal!' What follows, over the course of almost three years, is the record of her further retreat from the world as her health weakens. The narrative of her decline is interspersed with precise and frequently merciless descriptions of her visitors, many of whom seem to have disappointed her by their paucity of wit. Sometimes, she simply feels abandoned: 'There are some half dozen people who have come to see me once and who have never come again, causing me to feel like a Barnum Monstrosity which had missed fire.' At others, she expresses the exasperation of one whose mind, despite her physical confinement, has not ceased to roam: 'Another of my inspired circle said, on her return from London, when I asked her what she had heard – "It was all on public affairs and I never remember anything in which I am not concerned myself." This one was not a scion of an effete race, but is by way of having *Mind*!' Alice reflected no less mordantly on the public affairs by which her anonymous friend was unmoved. An admirer of Charles Stewart Parnell, she followed his downfall with as much exasperation at the canting of the British political establishment as at the moral failings of the man himself. Of the British army's massacre by thirst of hundreds of dervishes at Wadi Halfa in Egypt in June 1889, she wrote on the 5th of the month: 'The troops of her *Christian* Majesty are now engaged in killing 3,000 Dervishes, by depriving them of water. When the desperate creatures make a rush to the river they are shot down! Tommy Atkins is in the "best of health and spirits" – how rank with *Humbug* is this Nation!' In the diary entry for the following day, she praised the recently deceased Father Damien, a Belgian missionary who had worked among lepers in Hawaii.

Alice, in other words, kept up a lively interest in the world outside her drawing room. As her health worsened, the tone of the diary remained alert and satirical about the social and political quirks of her adopted home, alternately heedless and despairing regarding her own condition. In many ways she was a remarkably uncomplaining patient, and considered herself the precise opposite of the sickly George Eliot, whose letters and diaries Alice read in the summer of 1889:

I'm glad I made myself do so for there is a faint spark of life and an occasional, remotely humorous touch in the last half. But what a monument of ponderous dreariness is the book! What a lifeless, diseased, self-conscious being she must have been! Not one burst of joy, not one ray of humour, not one living breath in one of her letters or journals, the commonplace and platitude of these last, giving her impressions of the Continent, pictures and people, is simply incredible! Whether it is that her dank, moaning features, haunt and pursue one thro' the book, or not, she makes upon me the impression, morally and physically, of mildew, or some morbid growth – a fungus of a pendulous shape, or as of something damp to the touch. I never had a stronger impression.

Alice, by contrast with this lugubrious and dropsical specimen, was a dry character; her wit is an impermeable defence against the sentimentality (and stupidity) of others and against the potential outpouring of her own emotions. She maintained to the end a droll and distanced attitude towards her own medical and emotional predicament.

*

Why then describe Alice James as a hypochondriac? Because her very self-possession seems a kind of pathology; it insulated her against the physically and emotionally unsettling expression of her real terror, and her real loneliness. Hers is a hypochondria – and the pattern of her collapses in Katharine's absence is perhaps enough to make that label stick – that consisted in allowing herself to be just ill enough not to have to face the creative and emotional void at the heart of her short life. Ensconced at Leamington, and latterly in Kensington, where she died, Alice managed her secret self so well that she never succumbed to its true afflictions, and never recovered from the effects of its having been stifled. It would be trite to conclude merely that her never having married nor had children constituted the core of her suffering, but the diary does reveal an obsession with the facts of sex and reproduction. She is constantly exercised by the propensity of the English working class to produce large families, no matter their economic privation. It is as if she feels swamped by the fecund masses of the poor – her sympathy for their poverty is genuine, but her constant references to their burgeoning number are shot through alike with envy and repulsion. (In fact, at times she seems surrounded, at all levels of society, by women intent on reproducing: she notes the tendency, less common at home, of well-off English widows to seek out a new husband with unseemly haste.) Disgust and jealousy mark too her frequent references to cases of suicide reported in the newspapers: she lights on them with an appalled admiration for those willing to admit that they no longer have the stomach for 'the game' of life.

In 1890, Alice discovered an especially apt vocabulary for the concealed version of herself that leaked out in the diaries in the form of a fascination for the births and deaths of others. Her brother William's essay 'The Hidden Self' had appeared in the March issue of *Scribner's Magazine*; on the 26th of October, Alice wrote:

William uses an excellent expression when he says . . . that the nervous victim 'abandons' certain portions of his consciousness. It may be the word commonly used by his kind. It is just the right one at any rate, altho' I have never been able to abandon my consciousness and get five minutes' rest. I have passed thro' an infinite succession of abandonments and in looking back now I see how it began in my childhood, altho' I wasn't conscious of the necessity until '67 or '68 when I broke down first, acutely, and had violent turns of hysteria.

She uses the word, which appears several times in the diary entries that follow, in an ambiguous fashion: it seems for her to describe both the deliberate suppressing of a part of herself and the letting go of conscious control of that inner self. She speaks of having to forge a temperament 'forbidding the abandonment of an inch or the relaxation of a muscle', then, on the 7th of November, of having to '"abandon" the rhetorical part of me . . . The seething part of me has also given out and had to be abandoned.' Either way the word is read, it is clear she feels a certain splitting of the self to be fundamental to her suffering.

William James intended the term in a more specific sense. 'The Hidden Self' describes a set of symptoms which he says are typical of the female hysteric, who abandons or suppresses a part of herself only to have it reappear as another, entirely discrete self or series of such selves. While the hypothesis might seem to denote both the unconscious as it was later described by Freud, and the more controversial notion of a division of the self into what were once called 'multiple personalities', it begins for James, unexpectedly, in the realm of the occult. There exists, he writes, an excess or remainder in the human psyche that has not yet been thoroughly studied; it has, in fact, so far only been described or expressed in mystical or Spiritualist terms, that is in a vocabulary from which the nascent science of psychiatry has sought to distance itself. Lately, however, science has seemed to suggest a certain truth behind the superstitious idea of possession and the disreputable theory of animal magnetism. Drawing on recent studies by Pierre Janet, James takes up the contention that the mind (and thus the experience and behaviour of the body) can split itself in two:

the original sin of the hysteric mind . . . is the *contractions of the field of consciousness*. The attention has not sufficient strength to take in the normal number of sensations or ideas at once . . . Our minds are all of them like vessels full of water, and taking in a new drop makes another drop fall out; only the hysterical mental vessel is preternaturally small. The unifying or synthesizing power which the Ego exerts over the manifold facts which are offered to it is insufficient to do its full amount of work, and an ingrained habit is formed of rejecting or overlooking certain determinate portions of the mass.

The result of this unbalancing of the mind, according to Janet, is that the patient effectively becomes more than one person; alternate selves may emerge under hypnosis, or, as in the examples of his patients, in hysterical reversion to another, entirely distinct and hitherto buried, personality.

The case of Janet's that strikes William James most forcefully is

that of Léonie, a 45-year-old woman who has had attacks of somnam-
bulism since the age of three. At sixteen, this peasant girl began to be
subjected to the curious gaze of the medical profession: she was hyp-
notized many times and, Janet notes, spent a good deal of her early
adulthood shuttling between a simple life in the countryside and the
alien, sophisticated world of the doctor's consulting room. In her
'normal state', Janet writes, Léonie is 'a serious and rather sad person, calm and slow, very mild with everyone'. Under hypnosis, however, she becomes immediately more animated: 'she is gay, noisy,
restless, sometimes insupportably so. She remains good-natured, but
has acquired a singular tendency to irony and sharp jesting. Nothing
is more curious than to hear her, after a sitting when she has received
a visit from strangers who wished to see her asleep. She gives a word-
portrait of them, apes their manners, pretends to know their little
ridiculous aspects and passions, and for each invents a romance.'
Under further hypnosis, she reveals a third self: 'Léonie 3' thinks the
first Léonie 'stupid' and the second 'crazy'. At times, two of the
three selves cohabit in the same body: one self talks volubly to visitors
while the other is engaged in automatic writing.

Whether or not William James had spotted in the story of Léonie
a counterpart to his sister's 'abandonment' of her inner self, the
parallels between the two women are today hard to resist. By the
time she read 'The Hidden Self', Alice had developed a conscious
counterpart to the hysterical patient's cordoning off of her social self
from the character who wrote, satirically, her impressions of her
visitors. More than this, she was keenly aware that a deeper level of
her character, the Alice James she had struggled to contain as a young
hysteric, was still there: weaker now, perhaps, but no less tormented, no less liable to 'go off', to 'go to pie' in the face of constraining circumstance and physical debility. But there was also a
third version of herself, a shade of Alice that had hung around in her
own mind and in those of her family for years, and who was about to
show herself confidently and for the last time. She had long spoken

of herself as a terminal case, and even confessed to her diary that she felt as though she were already dead, such was the state of inaction to which her many ailments had reduced her. Now, 'Alice 3' revealed herself – she was not Alice the hysteric, the melancholic or neurasthenic, nor Alice the intractable invalid and would-be suicide. She was the dying Alice, irrefutably diagnosed and fast declining.

*

According to Sir Andrew Clark, Alice had only weeks, perhaps months, to live. In July 1891, an American doctor, William Wilberforce Baldwin (a friend of Henry's, resident in Florence), passed through London, and was recommended, as Henry later put it, to make some suggestion 'of more than British ingenuity, as to the alleviation of pain'. Baldwin saw Alice four times, and diagnosed her tumour as malignant. He concluded from the pain in her right shoulder blade and her earthy complexion that the cancer had originated in her liver. (As Jean Strouse points out, it is more likely that it had metastasized from the breast to the liver.) Baldwin's diagnosis ruled out the possibility of a mastectomy – an operation perfected only two years earlier at Johns Hopkins University by Dr William Stewart Halsted – though it is unlikely that Alice would have submitted to surgery even if it had offered the chance of survival. She was intent on dying. The cancer had dispelled the fog of ambiguity in which she and Katharine had lived for so long; to her diary, she expressed relief at its 'setting us within the very heart of the sustaining concrete. One would naturally not choose such an ugly and gruesome method of progression down the dark Valley of the Shadow of Death, and of course many of the moral sinews will snap by the way, but we shall gird up our loins and the blessed peace of the end will have no shadow cast upon it. Having it to look forward to for a while seems to double the value of the event, for one becomes suddenly picturesque to oneself, and one's wavering little individuality stands out with a cameo effect.' Though her life might now appear worthless and unproductive, it seemed to her, paradoxically, that as she neared the end she took on 'a certain value as an indestructible quantity'.

Quite what Alice thought that solid core of self to consist of in the last months of her life is not clear. She seems to have cared little for her immortal soul, that 'poor, shabby, old thing'; she expressly forbade anybody to try to contact her through the fashionable efforts of a medium – 'oh, the curious spongy minds that sop it all up and lose all sense of taste and humour!' – and baulked at the thought of an Anglican priest officiating at her obsequies. Having been denied baptism by her parents, and marriage 'by obtuse and imperceptive man', she would rather, she joked, supervise her own funeral: 'it seems too bad not to assist myself at this first and last ceremony'. For a time, she maintained an intellectual interest in current affairs, the city in which she was dying, and the literary endeavours of her brothers. She recorded her horror of the cramped living conditions in even the best English houses, and bemoaned the fragility, compared to the solid wooden dwellings at home, of the buildings in London that she would never see again. She regretted missing out on Henry's future plays (not knowing that his failure as a playwright was to be one of the great disappointments in his career): 'within the last year he has published *The Tragic Muse*, brought out *The American*, and written a play, *Mrs. Vibert* (which Hare has accepted) and his admirable comedy; combined with William's *Psychology*, not a bad show for one family! Especially if I get myself dead, the hardest job of all.' She found herself about to ask Katharine practical questions, then realized that knowledge was no longer of any use to her: there were no more 'some days' when facts might come in useful or prove diverting. The subjects on which she might once have exercised her wit were now drifting out of reach.

On the 3rd of September, she wrote: 'Like a sheep to the shambles, I have been led by K. to the camera! Owing to some curious cerebral condition, Annie Richards [*née* Ashburner, Alice's friend] was heard to say, "Alice has fine features": K. seized the psychologic moment of titillated vanity and brought the one-eyed monster to bear upon me; such can be woman's inhumanity to woman.' The resulting portrait shows Alice apparently seated, or lying, on a sofa, a patterned velvet or silk cushion behind her head, the folds and large ribbons of her dress hiding her emaciated body. Her features do look notably finer than in previous photographs – a result, no doubt, of her having lost weight as the illness advanced, but seeming to suggest too a kind of peace or refinement. As was often the photographer's custom at the time, the image is a vague oval at the centre of the frame, its edges blurred in a technique known as vignetting. The effect is to make Alice look as if she is floating, surrounded by an encroaching grey mass which will soon obscure her altogether: 'one suddenly finds that the months have slipped away and the sofa will never more be laid upon, the morning paper read, or the loss of the new book regretted; one revolves with equal content within the narrowing circle until the vanishing point is reached, I suppose.' But it is also a photograph of a kind of persistence or obstinacy. It is Alice's assertion of her 'picturesque' self. The reference to Katharine's 'inhumanity' in making her pose for the picture is an ironic one, for this is exactly how Alice wished to be remembered: peaceably facing her own mortality, she looks like herself for the first time.

By the winter of 1891, Alice was in a considerable amount of physical pain. Both William and Henry had recommended morphine in large doses, but the 'ineffable blessing', as Henry called it, had begun to disrupt her sleep and cause 'hideous nervous distresses'. She turned now, again at Henry's suggestion, to hypnosis. In December she read an article on the subject by Dr Charles Lloyd Tuckey, and Katharine summoned him to Kensington. The method worked, and once Katharine had learned it too, Alice had a practical means of dissolution, a precursor to her last fading away, ready at hand. Dr Tuckey, however, made the mistake of assuring his patient that she had a good while still to live:

I was terribly shocked and when he saw the havoc that he wrought, he reassuringly said: 'but you'll be comfortable, too,' at which I exclaimed:

'Oh I don't care about that, but boo-hoo, it's so *inconvenient!*' and the poor man burst into a roar of laughter. I was glad afterwards that it happened, as I was taken quite by surprise, and was able to test the sincerity of my mortuary inclinations. I have always *thought* that I wanted to die, but I felt quite uncertain as to what my muscular demonstrations might be at the moment of transition, for I occasionally have a quiver as of an expected dentistical wrench when I fancy the actual moment. But my substance seemed equally outraged with my mind at Tuckey's dictum, so mayhap I shall be able to maintain a calm befitting so sublimated a spirit! – at any rate there is no humbuggy 'strength of mind' about it, 'tis simply physical debility, 'twould be such a bore to be perturbed.

As Alice lay close to death, early in March of the following year, Henry James was by her side, and wrote to William of the 'supreme deathlike emaciation' that had rapidly come over her. No longer able to speak out loud, she whispered a final message to be telegraphed to William in Cambridge: 'TENDEREST LOVE TO ALL FAREWELL AM GOING SOON ALICE'. On the 5th of the month, wrote Katharine later, Alice was still making emendations to the diary: 'one of the last things she said to me was to make a correction in the sentence of March 4th "moral discords and nervous horrors".' In the days after her death, William would write to his brother of their sister's 'little life, shrunken and rounded in retrospect'; the particular burden of that life, he ventured, had been the problem of how to maintain one's strength of character in the face of chronic and later mortal illness, and in that respect, her life had been well lived. But it is perhaps not unrealistic to conclude that for Alice the problem had been more precise. It had been rather the problem of how to sustain a voice, a personality or a self, and in that regard her illness had been as much her literary subject matter as mind and morals had been for her brothers. Alice James discovered in her own death a way to keep on dictating, up to the last: 'The difficulty about all this dying is that you can't tell a fellow anything about it, so where does the fun come in?'

6. The Delusions of Daniel Paul Schreber

'The wonderful Schreber . . . ought to have been made a
professor of psychiatry and director of a mental hospital.'

Sigmund Freud, in a letter to Carl Jung, 1910

During thirty-five years of almost unremitting mental illness, Daniel
Paul Schreber – the German jurist whose extravagant madness is
chiefly known today via Sigmund Freud's short study of him, published in 1911 – was subject to paranoia, hallucinations and a bizarre
array of bodily tics and tremors. In 1903, in his extraordinary book
Memoirs of My Nervous Illness, Schreber – who had only partly recovered, and refused to accept that he suffered from delusions –
described the cosmic scale on which his symptoms appeared. He had
been tormented, he wrote, at the hands of family, physicians and
nurses. But most dramatically, he had been chosen by God to give
birth to a new race of men; to this end, he was slowly being transformed into a woman. Almost all of Schreber's lurid thoughts relate
in some way to his own body; his was a 'hypochondria' – this was in
fact his first diagnosis – swollen or dilated until it compassed all of
space and time. It seemed to Schreber that each appalling event that
took place within his body had consequences at the furthest reaches
of the universe, and for many centuries to come. In his life, in his
Memoirs and in the vexed interpretations to which his case has since
been subject, we learn a startling lesson about just how far an individual may stray from a realistic conception of himself.

Daniel Paul Schreber was born in Leipzig in 1842, the third of five children. His early life was carefully, perhaps cruelly, regimented according to his father's many theories regarding health, fitness and morality. Moritz Schreber is now best remembered in Germany as the inspiration for the *Schrebergärten*, small garden plots or allotments that dot the suburbs of German cities. His interests, however, went much further than the simple prescription of community, manual labour and fresh vegetables to a nervous or anomic urban population. In his book *Medical Home Gymnastics*, published in 1855, he claims there is a moral duty to uphold one's health, and outlines the techniques that may be employed to ensure ethical as well as physical wholeness. This insistence on the intimacy of bodily and moral well-being was not especially quackish or eccentric: callisthenics and gymnastics were at this time almost as popular, and just as freighted with a sense of duty, as physical exercise (or at least gym membership) today. Moritz Schreber, however, seems to have used his family as experimental subjects and his home as a kind of laboratory in which to test his hypotheses about exercise and, especially, posture. Illustrations in his writings show the corrective machinery that was brought to bear upon the bodies of Daniel Paul Schreber and his siblings. While Freud merely adverts to the father's fame as an enthusiast of air and exercise, subsequent readers of the *Memoirs* have discerned the origins of some of Schreber's fantasies in a system of straps designed to keep the child supine in bed, in the adjustable metal frame that kept him sitting upright as he studied, and in the regular eye-washing procedures to which it seems he was subjected from infancy. Schreber's father was omnipresent and all-powerful; he was also, after a concussion caused when he fell from a ladder in 1851, prey to recurrent depressions around the time that his son entered adolescence and early adulthood. He died in 1861.

Schreber had embarked on a law degree the year before his father's death. Having passed the state bar exam, he served in the civil administration of Alsace-Lorraine during the Franco-Prussian War, and on a federal commission was given the task of drawing up a new Civil Code for the Reich. In 1878 he married Sabine Behr, and was soon appointed administrative director of the District Court at Chemnitz. Six years later he ran as a candidate of the National Liberal Party in the Reichstag elections; he lost to a Socialist, Bruno Geiser, and appears as a consequence to have suffered a nervous breakdown. He was admitted to the psychiatric hospital of Leipzig University and treated personally by its director, Professor Paul Emil Flechsig. The illness passed, he later wrote in the *Memoirs*, 'without any occurrences bordering on the supernatural' – that is to say, he did not suffer any hallucinations or paranoid fantasies. At the end of his six-month stay, Schreber was profoundly grateful to Flechsig: 'I gave this special expression', he writes, 'by a subsequent visit and in my opinion an adequate honorarium.' His wife was still more impressed by the physician who, she said, had given her back the husband she was sure she had lost; she kept a photograph of Flechsig on her desk for many years – even, we may surmise, long after she had lost all hope of having him returned a second time. In the aftermath of his first illness, Schreber recalls, he spent eight years with his wife, 'on the whole quite happy ones, rich also in outward honours and marred only from time to time by the repeated disappointment of our hope of being blessed with children'.

At the university hospital, Flechsig had first diagnosed the 42-year-old judge as suffering from severe hypochondria. It seems that both doctor and patient intended by the word something rather different from what might have been meant half a century before. The hypochondriac of the 1880s was not merely a nervous or melancholic type; nor were his symptoms said to radiate from a specific disorder of the stomach. Rather, hypochondria denoted, for Flechsig and Schreber alike, a generalized sense that something was awry with one's body, a vague unease that condensed at times to the fear of a specific disease, or the conviction that damage had already been done to a particular organ or member. The hypochondriac felt that his body had revolted, or that it was under attack from certain external organic processes.

Schreber's hypochondriac crisis was followed by a protracted convalescence. In the summer of 1893, by which time all signs of his first illness had long since vanished, he was nominated to the post of presiding judge of the third chamber of the Supreme Court of Appeals, in Dresden. He was not due to take up this new position until the autumn; in the meantime, he dreamed on several occasions that the illness had returned. On waking, he tells us, he felt an immense relief and assured himself that dreams were mere shadows cast by the mind, things of no substance in the real world. Some time later, however, the boundary between dream and reality began to seem worryingly porous, and he was subsequently unable to tell whether he had been asleep or awake when a strange notion entered his head one morning: 'it was the idea that it really must be rather pleasant to be a woman succumbing to intercourse.' The thought was so alien to his nature, he writes, that had he been fully awake he would have rejected it with indignation; he cannot now, however, discount the possibility that the idea was planted in his mind by external forces.

On the 1st of October, Schreber took up his new post in Dresden. Presiding over a panel of five judges, almost all of whom were older than he, the ambitious but nervous *Senatspräsident* started to overtax himself mentally. Anxious to convince his colleagues of his unquestionable efficiency, he began to lie awake at night, worrying. He and his wife had no friends in Dresden, and there were few social engagements to distract his mind from the cares attached to his position. Early in November, still unable to sleep despite the doses of sodium bromide that he had begun to take, Schreber lay listening to a recurrent crackling noise from the bedroom wall. Time and again, as he was on the point of succumbing to sleep, the noise started up, gnawing at his already frayed nerves. At the time, he writes, he assumed it was the sound of a mouse, although it was certainly odd that a mouse should have found its way to the first floor of such a solidly built house. Since that time, he notes in the fourth chapter of the *Memoirs*, he has heard similar noises – or 'interferences', as he has learned to call them – on innumerable occasions. At the time of writing, he says, they continue to plague him, even during the day. He has in the meantime realized that they are 'divine miracles', that the noise in his bedroom wall was the first sign of the prodigious torments to come: '*in other words that right from the beginning the more or less definite intention existed to prevent my sleep and later my recovery from the illness resulting from the insomnia for a purpose which cannot at this stage be further specified.*'

In the second week of November, Schreber's condition began to assume what he would later call a menacing character. He had taken a week's sick leave, intending to consult Flechsig, in whom he and his wife still maintained an immovable faith. They travelled from Dresden via Chemnitz and, because it was a Sunday and the professor was unavailable, stayed a night there with relatives. Schreber had by now begun to suffer palpitations: walking up even a moderate incline brought on an attack of anxiety. That night at Chemnitz, he was injected with morphine and chloral, but his nervousness, insomnia and increasing despair proved intractable and he spent a wretched night. In the morning he and his wife went by train and cab to Flechsig's office at the university hospital. A long interview followed, during which, the judge recalls, Flechsig spoke persuasively of the advances made in psychiatric medicine since the first illness, of newly discovered sleeping drugs and other treatments, and of his conviction that such cases could be comprehensively cured if the patient could be lulled to sleep for long enough. Schreber must repose, he counselled, from three o'clock that afternoon until the following day. The patient's wife and mother did their best to ensure that the order was carried out, but it was nine o'clock by the time Schreber had taken some exercise, eaten a meal and been dosed with a sleeping draught. It failed to take effect, and his anxiety increased until eventually he sprang from the bed intent on hanging himself with a sheet or towel. Sabine Schreber woke and stopped him, somehow seeing him through to the morning. Professor Flechsig was summoned, and it became clear that admission to the hospital was now inevitable. At the university, Schreber was bathed and put to bed, though he did not sleep and the illness, he would later write, progressed rapidly in the days to come. Removed from the care of his family, he passed his first days there occupied almost exclusively with thoughts of death.

*

Memoirs of My Nervous Illness, the substantial volume in which Schreber recounts these events, was published against the advice of his physicians. (Schreber found a publisher who specialized in spiritual and occult writings and was untroubled by the book's sexual and scatological preoccupations, not to mention its many other peculiarities.) The book, a classic in psychiatric literature thanks to the interpretation given it in Freud's 1911 essay 'Psychoanalytic Remarks on an Autobiographically Described Case of Paranoia (Dementia Paranoides)', might as easily be ranked in the canon of imaginative literature. The tale of a respectable jurist's abduction by malevolent supernatural forces, his subjection to extraordinary rituals and perverse sexual practices, his efforts to convince the authorities of his sanity, and his constant dialogues with the dead and even with God himself: all of this might place the *Memoirs* in a fictional lineage that would have to include *Gulliver's Travels*, *Frankenstein*, the most unnerving of Poe's short stories, the institutional horrors delineated by the Marquis de Sade and the amazing, blasphemous, hallucinatory precursor of Surrealism that is the Comte de Lautréamont's novel *Maldoror*. At the same time, Schreber reads like an early Modernist: he discovers correspondences across space and time that rival those of Marcel Proust, and he is a ventriloquist of competing voices quite as inventive as James Joyce. In his picturing the fate of a physically deformed individual beset by an immovable bureaucracy, he seems to conflate different narratives from Franz Kafka. And yet – and this is what makes the *Memoirs* such an unsettling and affecting read – all of Schreber's prodigious imaginings were, as he saw them, totally real. His book is a memoir of what never happened, a true story that is also a work of prodigal fancy.

The other writer whom he resembles is Sigmund Freud. Throughout his book, Schreber writes with the forensic logic and rhetorical assurance of his profession, but also from a fascination for the workings of the human mind that is perhaps learned from his physicians, and especially from the nerve specialist Flechsig. Like Freud describing the machinery of the unconscious, Schreber works to convince the reader of the existence of creative and destructive forces beyond (or rather beneath) our everyday experience. He posits an essential malignity behind apparently innocent actions; he conjectures that seemingly insignificant events from the past can haunt us at great historical or biographical distances; he intimates (and here he is closer to Jung than to Freud) that a kind of collective unconscious, made up of the souls of the dead, underlies the visible stratum of our daily lives.

The truth that Schreber has divined, he tells us at the outset, is of a strictly spiritual sort: '*I do not harbour any personal grievance against any person. My aim is solely to further knowledge of truth in a vital field, that of religion.*' In an open letter to Flechsig that prefaces the *Memoirs*, he regrets that his former doctor's name appears so often in the book – he has no doubt, he says, of the moral worth and integrity of the director of the Leipzig hospital. Flechsig himself is perhaps not to blame, he ventures, for the injuries he seems to have inflicted at a distance, by means of invisible rays, on the person of his patient. Part of the physician's nervous system may well have been removed from his body by supernatural means, and then have ascended to heaven where it acted, unknown to its original host, out of 'ruthless self-determination and lust for power'. This bizarre claim is the first clue to the substance and design of the delusional framework that Schreber is about to elaborate.

The human soul, he writes, is contained in the nerves of the body. The nerves are not merely conduits for sensations of pain, pleasure, hunger, voluptuousness, etc., but themselves harbour sense impressions, desires, memories and even the biological impetus for life itself: 'The male seed contains a paternal nerve and combines with a nerve taken from the mother's body to form a newly created entity.' The soul, with its thoughts and desires and recollections, can be reawakened by the passage of the nerves to a higher state after death. God himself is essentially made up of such nerves: 'They have in particular the faculty of transforming themselves into all things of the created world; in this capacity they are called rays; and herein lies the essence of divine creation.' Ordinarily, God can converse only with the dead: that is, with the souls or nerves of the departed. These he sifts, purifies and raises to a blessed or heavenly condition. Until they have been thus rarefied, these bundles of neural-cum-spiritual matter remain in a kind of cosmic and moral purgatory, during which time they are known as 'tested souls'. It seems, says Schreber, that a portion of Flechsig's nervous substance has become something akin to a tested soul. Endowed, as are all such corrupt entities, with human faults, it has begun to act on the body and soul of the unfortunate judge.

It is in this context that we must understand the catalogue of physical ailments, injuries and deformities that Schreber proceeds to detail. His body, he claims in the eleventh chapter of *Memoirs of My Nervous Illness*, has without cease been the object of divine 'miracles', an inventory of which could itself fill an entire volume. Hardly an organ or limb has gone unassailed, scarcely a muscle has not been yanked or wrenched by miraculous forces. At the time of writing, he assures the reader, the forces that attack him from hour to hour would scare any other person to death; but Schreber, by dint of long habituation to horror and pain, has learned to treat the most agonizing assaults as trivial. The detail and variety of these attacks are worth sampling direct from the pages of the *Memoirs*. Here is Schreber recounting merely the afflictions of his chest:

The miracles enacted against the organs of the thoracic and abdominal cavities were very multifarious. I know least about those concerning the *heart*; I only remember that I once had a different heart – still during my stay in the University Clinic of Leipzig. On the other hand my *lungs* were for a long time the object of violent and very threatening attacks. By nature my lungs and heart are very healthy; but my lungs were so affected by miracles that for a time I seriously believed I had to fear a fatal outcome in consequence of pulmonary phthisis. A 'lung worm' was frequently produced in me by miracles; I cannot say whether it was an animal-like or a soul-like creature; I can only say that its appearance was connected with a biting pain in the lungs similar to the pains I imagine occur in inflammation of the lungs. The lobes of my lungs were at times almost completely absorbed, I cannot say whether as the result of the activity of the lung worm alone or also because of miracles of a different kind. I had the definite feeling that my diaphragm was raised high in my chest to almost under my larynx and that there remained only a small remnant of my lung in between with which I could hardly breathe. There were days when during my walks in the garden I reconquered my lungs anew with every breath.

The rays that were directed against him, Schreber concludes of this last episode, cannot help but counter their own destructive force by providing the subject with just enough energy to carry on, 'because to create is their essence and nature'. Schreber, it seems, is half-sustained by the very forces that have been arrayed against him.

There now began, he writes, a series of extraordinary amputations, evacuations and disappearances from within the unguarded precincts of his body. Some of his ribs were temporarily smashed, then reconstituted at a later date. His stomach absconded, the naturally healthy organ replaced by an inferior 'Jew's stomach'. (The switch was effected, he claims, by a Viennese nerve specialist called Starkewicz, whose aim was to make all of Germany Slavic, then Jewish; Freud draws no attention to this passage.) Frequently, Schreber went without a stomach – he recalls informing an attendant that he could not dine because it had suddenly vanished. Sometimes, just before he sat down to eat, a stomach was 'so to speak produced *ad hoc* by miracles', only to be removed again during the meal. On such occasions, food and drink simply poured into his abdominal cavity and from there began to fill up his legs. Had the same befallen any other person, he tells us, such an interior calamity would have led to the formation of pus, and the patient would have died from the infection – but in Schreber's case the rays which ceaselessly bombarded his body seem to have soaked up all impure matter and preserved him from harm. So impressed has he been by this phenomenon that he is now, at the time of writing, quite sure that he is immune to all disease, and even to otherwise lethal poisons. His organs have been damaged or destroyed so many times, and so often restored, that he doubts his own mortality, at least as long as his converse with the rays should last.

Schreber now tirelessly lists the attacks upon his extremities and against his reason. Into the drama of his physical degradation is drafted a cast of 'little men' who attempt, he says, to pump out his spinal cord; a considerable quantity of it emerges from his mouth in the form of small clouds, especially when he is walking in the garden. 'One can imagine the apprehension with which such events filled me,' he writes: it seemed to him that his reason might float away on the air along with these vaporous portions of his spinal column. (There are more 'little men' later in the text: 240 Benedictine monks, he tells us in a passage of fervid anti-Catholicism, have taken up residence in his skull.) Worse, there were efforts afoot to extract the nerves from his head and to implant them in the brain of the patient in the next room. But Schreber's nerves proved stubborn, and after being pulled halfway from his head they invariably retracted. His skull, however, fell victim to what he calls 'flights of rays' – 'a phenomenon difficult to describe, the effect of which was that my skull was repeatedly sawn asunder in various directions'.

Perhaps even more disturbing for Schreber than all of these violent assaults upon, or insidious forays into, his body is the mutation that has been unfolding since his first institutionalization under the care of Professor Flechsig: Schreber is being turned into a woman. We have seen that he was disturbed, shortly before the onset of his second illness, by a dream in which he thought how pleasurable it must be for a woman to have sexual intercourse with a man. Now, says Schreber, he knows that this was no random fantasy, but a presentiment of the real transformation to come. A process of 'unmanning' has begun. Several times in bed he has felt that his genitals were being retracted into his body, or softened by the approach of impure rays, to the point of being almost completely dissolved. Hairs from his beard have been removed, one at a time. His stature has even begun to alter: the vertebrae and thigh bones have been shortened, and he has the impression that he has shrunk overall by between six and eight centimetres: 'that is to say approximately [to] the size of the female body'. He has started to grow breasts and his skin has become softer all over, more feminine and, he notes, more susceptible to voluptuous sensations. He is frequently to be discovered at this time – so his physicians' reports inform us – posing half dressed at a mirror in his room, admiring his new physique; he can stand thus transfixed for hours at a time.

At first, it seemed to Schreber that his becoming a woman was designed to put him at the mercy of Flechsig – he assumed he was to be abandoned to the sexual whims of the director. In time, a more elaborate plan has revealed itself. Schreber is in fact, he now believes, the sole survivor of a human race wiped out by terrible plagues: the people he seems to see around him are already dead, and merely linger in the form of 'tested souls' or impure spirits. If the human race is to be reborn, it will be through the body of Daniel Paul Schreber, who awaits his inevitable impregnation by God. Until then, he watches the swell of his chest and feels the slow ramification of 'nerves of voluptuousness' throughout his body. These nerves will exercise a considerable power of attraction over God, and it has fallen to Schreber to reconstitute the order of the world by giving in to the divine caresses he inspires: 'mere common sense therefore commands that as far as humanly possible I fill every pause in my thinking – in other words the periods of rest from intellectual activity – with the cultivation of voluptuousness.'

*

There is more, much more, in this vein in the pages of *Memoirs of My Nervous Illness* – Schreber's delusional cosmology is mapped in all its deep strangeness and its peculiar proximity to the real world. The book is testament as much to its author's real suffering – subject to the taxonomic gaze and inquisitorial touch of the new discipline of psychiatry – as to the prodigious unreality of the mental world he inhabited. The grisly splendour of his imagination is a reminder, too, of the long history of delusions regarding the body. Burton, as we have seen, alluded to the fantasies entertained by the sufferer from hypochondriacal melancholia. The theorists of the disorder in the eighteenth century were similarly keen to stress the fantastical nature of the hypochondriac's apprehension of his own body. One might say that hypochondria as we know it today – the 'health anxiety' that has once more become a recognized, if not respectable, diagnosis – is a species of delusion: the patient imagines something about his or her body which is simply untrue. But what sets these earlier hypochondriacs and melancholics apart is the way in which their imaginings go far beyond the restricted realm of disease itself, and begin to encompass all manner of bodily transformations, hideous processes of atrophy or decay, the sudden disappearance of whole organs or limbs, the hollowing out of the body until it is an empty shell that in its turn may be filled with new sorts of physical substance. It becomes an alien body: not merely a body besieged by illness but a body demolished and entirely rebuilt according to a new plan. With this transformation, as in the case of Schreber, the patient is afforded a new kind of knowledge – of his own substance and that of others – and a fearful new insight into the relationship between body and soul.

In the history of such eccentric torments, none is stranger or more instructive than the so-called 'glass delusion'. From the late Middle Ages onwards, this remarkably specific and consistent notion appears time and again in the literature on melancholia and hypochondria. The patient, as the reader will have surmised, fancies that he or she is made of glass, either in part or in whole. (In a series of related delusions, patients may imagine that they have lost limbs, that they have been turned into animals, that they are dead, that they do not exist or, as in the case of an unfortunate baker who was afraid to go near his oven, that they are made of butter.) This has predictable consequences: the 'glass man' fears for his physical safety, avoiding not only hard knocks but in some cases any touch at all from another person, as well as such delicate operations as sitting or lying down. The broad outlines of the delusion – imagining that one is made of a brittle substance – were not unknown to antiquity: classical accounts of earthenware men abound, but the spread of glass in the Early Modern period brought with it the possibility of thinking oneself made of less sturdy stuff. One of the earliest named cases is that of King Charles VI of France (r. 1 3 8 0– 99), who allegedly refused to allow members of his court to approach him, and took to wearing thickly reinforced clothes to protect himself. A later instance – anonymous but possibly concerning a French prince – was recorded around 1 6 1 4 by Alfonso Ponce de Santa Cruz, physician to Philip II of Spain: on the advice of his doctor, the man in question lay, lest he break, on a straw bed, and left it only when his mattress caught fire. In 1 6 0 7, in his play *Lingua*, Thomas Tomkis presented as an object of comedy the glass man Tactus, who sits upright in bed, hands clasped in fear and prayer, tormented by the fragility of his own being. 'I am an urinal,' he declares, 'I dare not stir for fear of cracking in the bottom.' In the same year, Thomas Walkington wrote of a 'ridiculous fool' from Venice who imagined that his shoulders and buttocks were brittle and vitreous; he lived in complete reclusion for fear of bumping his 'crackling hinderparts'.

Among the more sustained accounts of the glass delusion is 'The Glass Graduate', a story published by Cervantes in 1613 – between the publication dates of the two volumes of *Don Quixote*, itself a study of a notable fantasist. The poor hero of the tale, Thomas Rodaja, is taken up at the age of eleven by two gentlemen students who pay for him to study law and humanities at Salamanca. Before graduating, he travels first to Italy as a soldier, then to Flanders and at length back to Spain, where he completes his studies. He comes to the attention of 'a certain lively lady who was up to all the tricks': she falls in love with him and, rebuffed, tricks him into eating a quince laced with a love potion. Poisoned, he languishes in bed for six months, during which time, writes Cervantes, he becomes 'completely dried up' and is reduced to skin and bone. At last he recovers, but is now possessed by the strangest form of madness ever seen: 'The poor wretch imagined that he was all made of glass, and under this delusion, when someone came up to him, he would scream out in the most frightening manner, and using the most convincing arguments would beg them not to come near him, or they would break him; for really and truly he was not like other men, being made of glass from head to foot.' Thomas's eccentricities are soon public knowledge: he walks carefully along the middle of the street in a robe and no shoes, looking up constantly in case a roof tile should fall and shatter him instantly. In summer he sleeps in the countryside, in the open air, and in winter at an inn, buried up to his chin in straw. His friends try to disabuse him of his glassy conceit by embracing him, but to no avail: 'He told them to speak to him from a distance and ask him what they wanted, because being a man of glass and not of flesh, he would answer them all so much the more intelligently; for glass being a fine and delicate material, the mind could work through it more promptly and effectively than through an ordinary, solid, earthly body.'

This last is one of the most curious attributes of glass men in general: their vitreous estate brings with it a new insight, or apparent insight, into themselves and the world around them. Thomas Rodaja answers 'very astutely' any question put to him on the subject of law, morality, politics, poetry, book publishing and so forth. After two years of delusion and fame – during which time, Cervantes assures us, Thomas was otherwise 'one of the sanest men in the world' – he is cured by a Jeromite monk; as befits this oddly schematic fiction, Cervantes does not say how the cure is effected. Thomas Rodaja takes his place in a long line of seventeenth-century glass men blessed with a kind of second sight, and especially apt to see the human body as a disintegrated system. Another was the hero of Tomkis's *Lingua*: 'Opening my breast, my breast was like a window / Through which I plainly did perceive my heart: / In whose two concaves I discern'd my thoughts / Confusedly lodged in great multitudes.' A more abstract kind of interior vision – and a case, perhaps, of the glass delusion by proxy – was imagined by the Spanish Jesuit writer Baltasar Gracián in 1651, in his *Criticón*: 'One notable character is the Seer of Everything, who claims to penetrate men's hearts and brains as if they were made of glass. Such perspicuity has taught him that many living people lack a soul.' If Gracián's seer reminds us of Schreber, for whom humanity has passed away and been replaced by a host of drifting and impure souls, this is but one of the affinities between the mad judge and his hypochondriac predecessors – between his body and theirs. Like him, they set in motion a constellation of amputated or abstracted body parts, a star chart of whirling organs, strangely dispersed in space and time. The fleshly envelope of the body starts to resemble a museum vitrine, and the mind a curator of an eccentric collection, a cabinet of somatic curiosities.

*

Schreber was moved from Leipzig to the asylum at Sonnenstein on the 29th of June 1894. He appeared 'completely inaccessible', standing or lying immobile, staring straight ahead in fear. His hands shook, his face twitched and his whole body was rigid; questions put to him by his new physician were ignored, or elicited only the most halting, agonized replies. There could be no doubt, writes Guido Weber, the director of the asylum, that the new inmate 'was continually influenced by vivid and painful hallucinations, which he elaborated in a delusional manner'. He demanded solitude and peace, protested the presence of doctors and other patients, who obstructed, he said, the powers of God – as did the activity of eating. Schreber refused all nourishment, and was eventually force-fed. He rejected any distracting activity, such as reading – every word he read, he claimed, was being shouted out to the whole world. At the same time, notes the physician, 'he retained his stool apparently deliberately, as far as he possibly could; he was therefore even incontinent at times.' He was also often discovered in his room, poring over pictures of naked women, drawing pictures of them himself, and comparing his own body to theirs. In a further accommodation to the feminizing process, he shaved off his moustache. The continuing transformation, records Weber, had begun to occupy his mind to a greater extent than the other attacks on his body: the destruction of his stomach, intestines, bladder and lungs; the smashed ribs, torn gullet and swallowed larynx. He was convinced that his whole body, like that of the glass man, had been altered.

There had been, suggests Weber in his report of 1899, some marked improvements in his patient's condition in the five years since his arrival at Sonnenstein. In the autumn of his first year there, his stiff posture loosened and he was at last able to speak coherently, though in an abrupt and staccato fashion. Even as Schreber's delusions began to expand, his day-to-day engagement with the restricted world of the asylum grew more predictable and encouraging. He still refused to read, but could occasionally be induced to play a game of patience. It was as if the more elaborate his ideas concerning his body and the universe became, the calmer he seemed to those around him and the better able to adjust to the regime of the asylum. On the one hand, the hallucinations tortured him with increasing violence: he grimaced 'in an extraordinary way' or bellowed threats and imprecations at the sun. He became so noisy at night – shouting, laughing, repeating certain stock phrases to himself for hours on end – that in June 1896 it became necessary to segregate him from the other patients. On the other hand, notes Weber, 'he was in many respects more polite and accessible towards the doctors and other persons, even if they surprised him during such noisy scenes, even answered simple questions about his condition, etc., though in a somewhat reserved and patronizing manner, said nothing of his troubles and was able to control himself for a little while quite well; he also started to read, play chess and piano as he had done before.' In the spring of 1897 a further alteration was noted in the patient's behaviour: he began to write lively and for the most part coherent letters to his wife and relatives. He had been very frightened, he told them, and had not been able to get himself to engage in any regular activity when he first arrived at Sonnenstein – but lately he had begun to feel more like his former self, and was grateful for the stimulating conversation he found among the staff and patients.

Weber's subsequent report of November 1900 was appended by Schreber to the published version of his memoirs in 1903. The report refers us back to the opening paragraph of the *Memoirs*, in which the author declares that he has decided to apply for his release from the asylum in the near future 'in order to live once again among civilised people and at home with my wife'. By the time the book appeared, he had in fact been released. The book's various addenda make it clear that the judge's efforts to free himself were drawn out and intensely frustrating. In the third addendum, Schreber's own text 'concerning the exposition of the facts in the judgment against which I appeal', we see a legal mind of impressive clarity and eloquence at work. But it is tethered to an imagination that flies to extremes even as Schreber approaches, with consummate calm and tact, the point of persuading his physicians and legal guardians of his sanity. 'I do not deny', he writes in July 1901, 'that my nervous system has for a number of years been in a pathological condition. On the other hand, I deny absolutely that I am mentally ill or ever have been. My mind, that is to say the functioning of my intellectual powers, is as clear and healthy as any other person's; it has been unaltered since the beginning of my nervous illness – apart from some unimportant hypochondriacal ideas.'

This is one of the most amazing features of Schreber's illness, and of his book. The conviction that he is in fact completely sane is to be expected, but the insight into his own case (however played down by that painful phrase 'unimportant hypochondriacal ideas') is unexpectedly lucid. It hints at the extraordinary force of will by which he must at times have striven to contain himself. His body threatened to decay and disintegrate before his eyes, or to disassemble itself like a wax anatomical model. And yet, Schreber contrived almost literally to hold himself together. He was capable of such self-possession that Weber eventually invited him to dine with his family. Schreber evinced, notes the director, a keen interest in, and detailed knowledge of, such subjects as law, politics, literature and social life. His humour and tact ensured that Weber could trust him not to bore or offend the ladies present at table. Only certain aporias of concentration or memory betrayed him: he would sometimes bring up as if out of the blue a matter that had already been discussed, and sometimes grimaced or touched his face repeatedly as the 'miracles' began to distract him from the topic at hand. He was able to restrain himself from bellowing until he had left the table; on his way to his room on such occasions, says Weber, 'one can hear his inarticulate sounds.' These improvements did not, however, indicate to Weber that his charge was ready to return to the outside world in the care of his family, still less that he would be able to manage his own affairs. 'During excursions into the neighbourhood,' writes Weber, 'while joining in some festive occasion, during a visit to the theatre, the patient was able to restrain *loud* outbursts, but that at times he felt very embarrassed could be seen from his distorted face, his humming, clearing his throat, short bursts of laughter and from his whole bearing; indeed even during a visit to his wife in Dresden he could not entirely repress the noises at table, so that a sign had to be given to the servant-girl not to take any notice; and although the visit lasted only a few hours he was strikingly keen to return to the Asylum.'

*

Sigmund Freud wrote surprisingly little on the subject of hypochondria. It seems that hypochondriasis was an abiding problem for him, but one that he was for many years reluctant to pronounce upon with any certainty. (Indeed, one commentator has written of a form of 'approach-avoidance behaviour on Freud's part' when it came to hypochondria.) Some sense of his perplexity on the subject can be read in his letters to colleagues in the quarter century before he composed his 'Psychoanalytic Remarks' on the case of Schreber. He made tentative gestures towards a description: writing to Wilhelm Fleiss in November of 1887, Freud complained of 'the difficult task of differentiating between incipient organic and incipient neurasthenic affections . . . In neurasthenia a hypochondriacal element, an anxiety psychosis, is never absent, whether admitted or denied, and betrays itself by a profusion of new sensations, i.e., paresthesias.' He had already surmised that the disorder might have a sexual origin; here he is writing to Fleiss again, in January 1895: 'The hypochondriac will struggle for a long time before he has found the key to his feeling that he is seriously ill. He will not admit to himself that it arises from his sexual life; but it gives him the greatest satisfaction to believe that his sufferings are not endogenous . . . but exogenous. So he is being poisoned.' A specific process, he conjectures, seems to lead from narcissism to hypochondria – a hypothesis that Freud appears to recall in 1911 when he suggests with aphoristic assurance, to a meeting of the Vienna Psychoanalytic Society, that hypochondria is 'the state of being in love with one's own illness'.

Freud's explicit statements on the subject are as likely, however, to involve the founder of psychoanalysis throwing up his hands in exasperation. He wrote to Fleiss in 1894: 'It is painful for a medical man, who spends all the hours of the day struggling to gain an understanding of the neuroses, not to know whether he is himself suffering from a reasonable or a hypochondriacal depression.' To the Society, in 1909, he averred: 'The position of hypochondriasis is still suspended in darkness.' To the analyst Sándor Ferenczi, three years later, deploying the same metaphor: 'I have always felt the darkness in the question of hypochondria to be a great disgrace to our efforts but have come up with nothing but supposition.' He suspected, he wrote, that hypochondria was 'the third neurosis', alongside anxiety and neurasthenia, 'but nothing consistent has come out of this and I don't want to force anything that doesn't seem ready'. Where he had fashioned new clinical categories and psychic processes from the historical remnants of such notions as neurasthenia and hysteria (and would do the same with melancholia in an essay of 1917), hypochondria somehow remained enigmatic and obscure, an ancient malady that refused to give itself up to the light of analytic reason.

It was not until 1914 (three years after he published the essay on Schreber) that Freud finally began to resolve the question of hypochondria. In his essay 'On Narcissism: An Introduction', he posited the precise libidinal origin of his neurotic patients' fears or delusions regarding disease. Narcissism, he writes, denotes 'the attitude of a person who treats his own body in the way in which the body of the sexual object is ordinarily treated – who looks at it, strokes it, fondles it till he obtains complete satisfaction from these activities'. The narcissist, argues Freud, has reverted to an infantile stage that follows the auto-erotic but precedes the capability for 'object love': that is, the libidinal investment in a world outside of oneself. This childish 'primary narcissism' is perfectly normal. But in the case of the adult narcissist, thrust back on himself for reasons that have predictably to do with upbringing and subsequent sexual relations, self-love may be directed at a particular organ, member or portion of the body, and not at the ego as such. The result is hypochondria: a withdrawal from conventional objects of desire and a morbid focus on one's body. In extremis, realizing at bottom that he has turned from the world in this way, the narcissist-cum-hypochondriac can conjure florid delusions about the external world; they are, says Freud, his desperate (and counterproductive) attempt to regain some purchase on external reality.

It all sounds, even in this super-compressed précis, rather like the case of Daniel Paul Schreber. In fact, Freud's interpretation of the judge's text is a kind of proving ground for his as yet (in 1911) prototypical theories regarding narcissism. But before embarking on his exegesis of the *Memoirs*, Freud seems to falter before his own intuitions regarding Schreber's case, the problem of narcissism and (by extension) the subject of hypochondria. He worries about the 'increased level of ingenuity' required not merely to make sense of this self-involved text, but to penetrate to its core of psychoanalytic truth; reading the *Memoirs*, outlandish as they are in themselves, requires of the analyst an imaginative, creative and in the end perhaps literary leap of his own. It is only natural, he writes, that some of what is to come may seem devious, contrived, implausible, even obscene, 'that one analyst will err in his work on the side of caution, another on the side of audacity' – that is to say: *caveat lector*. It is as if, writing about Schreber, Freud feels especially keenly the scepticism of his potential readers, and wonders about the persuasiveness of his own theories.

It is perhaps for this reason – as well as an obvious empathy for his subject's plight – that he stays close in much of the essay to a strict summary of Schreber's own narrative. He retells the story of Schreber's first hypochondriacal episode, his recovery and subsequent relapse, his descent into delusions and hallucination, his complex theological schema, his bodily torments, his hostility towards Flechsig and his slow transformation into a woman. At last, Freud ventures what he calls 'attempts at interpretation'. There is, he says, a 'simple formula' in cases of persecution: 'The person to whom the delusion ascribes such great power and in whose hands all the threads of the conspiracy are brought together is, if given a specific identity, the same one as was of no less importance for the emotional life of the patient before the onset of the illness or an easily recognized surrogate.' This figure is Paul Flechsig: the 'certain person' whom Schreber initially imagines he is to serve sexually, the malign presence behind the rays that penetrate his body, the instigator of the 'soul murder' that threatens his existence, the only character in the *Memoirs* apart from God who in any way vies with Schreber for a position at the centre of the universe of delusion.

The upshot of Freud's analytic audacity is that Schreber is a narcissist and a hypochondriac because he does not want to admit that he is a homosexual. Narcissism, Freud writes, 'consists in the individual, caught up in his own desires, assembling his auto-erotically active sexual drives into a unity in order to gain an object of love and first taking himself, his own body, as that object, before moving on from this to the choice of another person'. He may baulk before the reality of his desire, but the fact is that Schreber is in love with Flechsig. The proximity of the dream in which his illness returned to his disturbingly cross-gendered early-morning reverie, for example, now becomes clear: 'a yearning to the effect: I wish to see Flechsig again'. It was the struggle against this erotic awakening that occasioned the second illness and the projection of actual delusions onto Schreber's already hypochondriacal background. Certain details of his story confirm the suspicion, as for instance when, still living at home, he was left alone while his wife went to stay with her father; Schreber writes that he 'experienced a quite unusual number of emissions (quite half a dozen) all in the single night'. For Freud, it is clear that the judge's homosexual desires were kept at bay only while his wife was present. (It is also obvious, says Freud, that Schreber's fantasized pregnancy is in part a compensation for his wife's repeated miscarriages, while the 'little men' that surround him are fantasized homunculi, standing in for both his own sperm and his lost children.) Schreber's hostility towards the asylum's director is a displacement of his desire for him, his transferral of his energies to contemplation of God a way of freeing himself from his love for Flechsig. God in turn is a figure for his dead father. And the delusions regarding his body, Schreber's cosmically realized hypochondria, the disintegration and decay of his organs – this is nothing more or less than the soul of Daniel Paul Schreber turning on its host in a sadomasochistic frenzy, punishing the body for its urges, shrinking before the horrors that the body inflicts on the imagination, and at the same time longing for a lost intimacy between spirit and flesh.

*

We need not accept the interpretation of Schreber's sexuality to see that Freud has described very precisely the mechanisms by which the judge's mind turned towards his inner organs and away from the world. But the hypothesis of the patient's love for his physician is just the sort of readerly response that the *Memoirs* demands: it is a book that, in its epic or mythic structure and content, invites us to read it as an allegory of some fundamental truth about the author or the society of which he is part. Perhaps even more ambitiously than Freud, Elias Canetti, in his book *Crowds and Power*, contends that the *Memoirs* are a glimpse, from the turn of the century, of the egomania, mass mobilizations and pure horror of the totalitarian regimes to come. In his struggles with Flechsig and God, in his contending with the lumpen masses of 'tested souls' and 'little men', in his paranoid delusions about Jews and Catholics, in his extension of his imagined dominion over vast tracts of time and space, Schreber speaks, says Canetti, of distant galaxies and stars 'as though they were bus-stops just round the corner'. In other words, he rehearses the resentment, fear and appalling ambition of Adolf Hitler. His body and his book incarnate forces in the German soul, and in the politics of modern Europe, that neither country nor continent can yet recognize in themselves. Paranoia, writes Canetti of Schreber's fancying himself at the centre of the universe, 'is an *illness of power* in the most literal sense of the words and exploration of this illness uncovers clues to the nature of power clearer and more complete than those which can be obtained in any other way. One should not allow oneself to be confused by the fact that in a case such as Schreber's the paranoiac never actually attained the monstrous position he hungered for. Others *have* attained it.'

The *Memoirs* do not discourage such readings. Something is lost, however, when we read Schreber for the richness of what he suggests rather than the wracked truth of what he experienced. Freud's essay may be the one text, apart from his introduction to narcissism, in which he treats of hypochondria at length; but it is also the place where, having told Schreber's tale, he retreats from the topic itself – that is, from the fate of a body subject to fearful maladies and imagined atrocities. Schreber's physicians, Flechsig and Weber, the men against whom he railed in the *Memoirs*, are in a way the more sympathetic witnesses to his decline, and Weber in particular the chronicler of the patient's last brief clutching at health and happiness.

In April 1902, Weber recommended that his patient be released from the asylum. The sphere of Schreber's delusional ideas, he writes, 'has gradually become more sharply demarcated from the rest of his ideas, and has for some time led a relatively separate existence. Experience so far shows that his judgment and treatment of a number of important life interests were not significantly influenced by these complexes of delusional ideas, but have been carried out faultlessly. Present conditions do not entitle one to expect any great change in the appellant's mental state, e.g., deterioration, in the foreseeable future. Apprehension for the future, therefore, need not weigh as heavily to-day as previously in judging the overall situation.' And so, on the 14th of July, the Royal Superior County Court in Dresden ruled that Schreber should be freed from his legal tutelage and returned to his family. He went at first to stay with his mother and one of his sisters, but soon moved into a new house in Dresden with Sabine. In 1906 the couple adopted a teenage daughter, Fridoline, who in later years recalled that Schreber had been 'more of a mother to me than my mother': they liked to take long walks together, after which the former judge, now in his mid sixties, would read, play the piano or challenge his adopted daughter to a game of chess. Relatives recalled that during this time he spoke little of his illness, but also that he was given occasionally to short fits of bellowing and that the voices in his head had by now become a constant, unintelligible background noise to his newly discovered normal life.

The interlude came to an end in November 1907, when Sabine Schreber was incapacitated by a stroke. Within weeks, her husband had been hospitalized once more – this time, at a state asylum in the village of Dösen, outside Leipzig. His symptoms included excessive laughter, screaming, depressive stupor, suicidal gestures, insomnia and delusions of his own decay: at the beginning of December, he was heard to mumble about 'rotting' and an 'odour of corpses'. He was convinced that his body had begun to putrefy but that his head was still alive. His hospital notes record that he 'speaks only very rarely with the doctor and then only that he is being tortured with the food that he cannot eat, etc. Continually under the tormenting influence of his hallucinations. Sleep at night mostly poor. Moans, stands in bed, stands rigidly in front of the window with eyes closed and an expression of listening on his face.' From time to time he was observed to scribble words or phrases on scraps of paper: 'miracles . . . tomb . . . not eat'. Before his release from Sonnenstein, Schreber had written of his hope that 'when my last hour strikes I will no longer find myself in an Asylum, but in orderly domestic life surrounded by my near relatives, as I may need more loving care than I could get in an Asylum.'

He was never to leave the establishment at Dösen. He died on Good Friday – the 14th of April – 1911. Sigmund Freud was even then, though quite unaware of his subject's plight and having shown no interest in contacting the author of the *Memoirs*, preparing the essay, to be published in the same year, that would keep Schreber's name alive in the annals of delusion.

7. Marcel Proust and Common Sense

'He died of ignorance of the world and because he did not know
how to change the conditions of his life which had begun to
crush him. He died because he did not know how to make
a fire or open a window.'

Jacques Rivière, 'Proust et l'esprit positif'

Céleste Albaret, aged twenty-two, had been in Marcel Proust's employment for several months when, in December 1913, she was first entrusted with the delicate task of taking him his second croissant. The quotidian regime at 102 Boulevard Haussmann was for the most part precise and invariable, and Proust's requirements on waking remained imprinted on the mind of the village girl from the Lozère, only lately married and arrived in Paris. Six decades later, in the pages of *Monsieur Proust* – a memoir of her time with him, based on a series of tape-recorded interviews – Céleste would describe the ritual that was enacted quietly, so as not to disturb the still slumbering Monsieur, each afternoon. Having sunk himself in his novel long into the night and then slept briefly, if at all, Proust finally surfaced, often somewhat enfeebled, around four o'clock. According to his exacting instructions, a small silver coffee pot was prepared, containing just enough coffee – brewed slowly, until it was very strong, in a double boiler – for two cups. (The coffee itself, and the filters, had to be bought always from the same shop on the Rue de Lévis, in the 17th arrondissement.) Sometimes, if he was especially tired or ill, he did not ring for his breakfast until six o'clock. On such occasions, the coffee had to be readied all over again, lest his sensitive palate revolt against the stale brew. Nicolas Cottin, Proust's valet, was charged with depositing the coffee and a single croissant at his bedside. A second croissant remained ready in the kitchen in case he should call for it later, but it quite often went uneaten. It was usually Cottin's wife, Céline, who delivered this second croissant. Towards the end of 1913, however, Céline was taken ill, and her husband arranged that Céleste, the young wife of Proust's driver, Odilon, should take on this secondary, occasional but essential, role in the daily ritual. He explained that a bell would ring twice in the kitchen in the event that Proust had decided to extend his breakfast. She must then hurry down the long passageway from the kitchen, across the hall, through the drawing room to the bedroom door, and go straight in without knocking or saying a word unless M. Proust spoke first.

Several days went by before the kitchen bell rang. Céleste waited, growing nervous as she imagined her employer, silent and invisible at the other end of the apartment. At length, the signal came; clutching the saucer, Céleste made her way towards the bedroom, opened the door without knocking and pushed aside, as Nicolas had also instructed her, the heavy curtain that hung immediately on the other side. As she describes it in the second chapter of her book, a chapter entitled 'A Cloud of Smoke', the scene that greeted Céleste seemed almost hallucinatory. Nicolas had warned her that Proust was in the habit of burning medicinal powders while still in bed: his chronic and worsening asthma affected him especially on waking. Céleste, however, was unprepared for the dense fog that filled the darkened room, the windows of which were closed and heavily curtained against the fading winter afternoon. A few patches of illumination insisted out of the darkness: a green-shaded bedside lamp diffused a weak glow; the dull gleam of a brass bedstead and a small portion of white sheet were encircled by this halo, while just beyond it, on a bedside table, a silver tray and coffee pot composed a rival cluster of light. The rest of the room was a dull haze: when she left, Céleste was unable to recall any of the brooding furniture, too large even for this spacious bedchamber, that would later become so familiar to her. It was as if the bed and its occupant were floating in space, quite as unattached to the rest of the room, or to the apartment around it, as they were to the street outside and the busy world beyond. Of Proust himself, Céleste saw almost nothing, but she felt the intensity of his gaze upon her. Shaking, she made her way towards the gleam of the silverware and put down her saucer, bowing towards the half-imagined face at the head of the bed. An arm was raised to thank her, but Proust said nothing. Céleste retreated behind the thick curtain and closed the door.

It was only after she had left that she was struck by the aspect of Proust's bedroom that remains best known, and is probably the most resonant symbol of his protracted retreat from society, his monkish reclusion in the service of his novel, and his sensitive, neurasthenic or hypochondriacal character. The walls and ceilings, Céleste realized, had been lined with cork. The room reminded her of a childhood trip to a new quarry where, more curious than the other schoolgirls, she had found her way alone into a narrow stone corridor and stood in the dim light, almost encased in honey-brown rock. Proust, it seemed to her, had buried himself in his room; beyond it, she says, the apartment was mostly disused and, so far as her employer was concerned, a hostile environment to be avoided as far as was practical. He worked, ate, socialized and sometimes slept in his bed. It was a place of solitude, but also the scene of certain well-rehearsed domestic dramas: a carefully lit stage set that cast the rest of the room, and with it the real world, into darkness. The bed was a well-provisioned craft in which he set sail on a darkened ocean – or, in Walter Benjamin's beautiful image, the summit of a scaffold on which Proust lay flat, holding his manuscript above him, his face pressed against the upper reaches of his imagination, like Michelangelo painting the ceiling of the Sistine Chapel.

Beneath him and around him were spread the elaborate paraphernalia of illness and writing. The immediate environs of Proust's bed housed a sort of life-support system designed as much to maintain his book as his body, and with practicality rather than aesthetics in mind. Visitors to the Boulevard Haussmann whose impressions survive seem for the most part to have disparaged the heavy, unattractive and (by the time Céleste arrived) somewhat shabby furniture that Proust had inherited from his parents' home. (Oscar Wilde, invited to dine *en famille* at Rue de Courcelles, but finding that he could not abide the stuffy atmosphere no matter how charming the aesthete son, is said to have surveyed the Prousts' drawing room and declared 'how ugly your house is' before leaving abruptly.) Marcel appeared almost indifferent to the matter of interior decor, at least when it came to his own home – his bedroom was a functional cell (however stuffed with things) and a mnemonic machine, not an expression of his visual sensibility.

Its layout was both pragmatic and oddly inconvenient. At the far end of the room from the bed, between the two windows, stood a large rosewood wardrobe; in front of it, jammed so close that the doors of the wardrobe could not be opened, his mother's grand piano dominated the room. To the left of the piano, as one faced the windows, a massive oak desk, at which Proust never actually worked, was piled high with books. On the right-hand wall, there were two sets of double doors; only those closest to the windows could be used, access to the other pair having been blocked by two revolving bookcases. A small Chinese cabinet also stood against this wall. Its drawers held money and bank papers, and on its top stood framed photographs of Marcel and his brother Robert as children. The room was otherwise bare of images. On the walls of his previous bedroom had hung at least four pictures – a watercolour of trees, a photograph of the cathedral at Amiens, a reproduction of the *Mona Lisa* and a photograph of Whistler's *Portrait of Thomas Carlyle* – but it seems that Proust had felt he must rid his visual field of all extraneous imagery. Finally, a rosewood chest stood against this wall, on the marble top of which sat thirty-two black faux-leather notebooks that contained the first draft of *À la recherche du temps perdu*; these were later burned by Céleste on Proust's instructions.

In the immediate vicinity of the bed, recalls Céleste in her memoir, a more modest array of items responded to Proust's daily and hourly needs:

Apart from an exquisite five-panelled Chinese screen behind the bed, everything was very plain. The bed was of brass, with bars, the metal tarnished from the fumes of the Legras powder. Then there were his three tables, arranged within arm's reach. One was of curved bamboo, with a lower shelf that held a pile of books, a pile of handkerchiefs, and the hot-water bottles. There was also an old rosewood bedside table with doors, which held his work things: manuscripts, notebooks, a schoolboy inkwell, penholder, a watch, a bedside lamp, and, later on, several pairs of spectacles. A third table, of walnut, was for his coffee tray, and for the lime and Evian water at night. And all of this was very simple, like a little island in that vast room and all that massive furniture.

Céleste's account contains some details – the Legras powder, the lime-flower tea made with Evian water – to which we shall have to return, but for now the initial sketch will suffice. Here is Proust, propped up on pillows, warmed by hot-water bottles, supplied with fresh handkerchiefs and his habitual writing materials: a picture of fragile seclusion.

The image of Proust as air-locked and unstinting recluse is of course, when viewed from any serious critical perspective on his writing, a reductive one – that is, if all it is meant to do is convince us of his personal peculiarity and aesthetic refinement, or rehearse again the cliché of the artist as sole, involuted source of his own creation. *À la recherche du temps perdu* is hardly a novel that can be exhausted by reference to its author's own life, no matter how much of it he may have put into the book, nor how much he gave up so as to be able to write it. And yet, Proust's illness, his retreat from the world, his obsessive organization of his domestic space so that it both protected him from the world and allowed him to affect it, and be affected by it, at a distance – all of this suggests that what we may with confidence call Proust's hypochondria was an essential aspect of his working life as well as a recurring subject of the novel itself. Among the many signposts of advancing historical and cultural time in *À la recherche du temps perdu* we can count Proust's references to the telephone, a device that for a time he used enthusiastically and then banished from his apartment when it promised to intrude too regularly on his privacy. We might say that Proust nonetheless lived the last years of his life telephonically, speaking at a distance. He was able, thanks to his illness and the sensitivity that it fostered in him, to withdraw from the world and persist in acting as if he were part of it. In 1913, as she went about Paris carrying out errands on behalf of her employer, Céleste recalled, she often felt that he was directing her actions from his plush cell above the Boulevard Haussmann, as though his sensitive brain had sent out nervous threads into the city, letting it know his desires, feeling along its streets and into its shops and apartments, picking up signals from the world he had left behind.

*

Along with his doctors, his family and friends, as also many subsequent biographers and critics, Proust persisted in believing that his asthma was psychosomatic or self-induced – a view that was encouraged by attitudes towards pulmonary and 'nervous' disorders in the last decades of the nineteenth and first years of the twentieth centuries. There is no doubt that he suffered physically, nor that his symptoms nursed in him a super-sensitivity towards the physical world and a heightened sensation of his fragility in relation to it: the asthmatic, trying to force air into his lungs, is painfully aware of processes in his body that ought to carry on without the intervention of will or the knowledge of the conscious mind. In a story written in 1893 and entitled 'L'Indifférent', Proust writes: 'A child who since birth has breathed without being careful about it is unaware how essential to his life is the air which swells his chest so gently that he does not even notice. Will he suffocate on a convulsion during a feverish attack? In the most desperate effort of his life, it is almost for survival that he is struggling, and for the vanished calm he will rediscover only with the air from which he did not know it to be inseparable.'

Proust more than once claimed a knowledge of his condition, and of the dire prognosis that awaited him, that he ascribed directly to the fact that his father was a physician: the son of a doctor, he said, becomes a doctor himself. Adrien Proust was a leading figure in the growing field of medical hygiene, expressing his ideas on the subject most clearly in his 1873 *Essay on international hygiene, and its application in the treatment of plague, yellow fever and Asian cholera.* Four years earlier, he had travelled to Russia, Turkey and Persia to study the spread of cholera into Western Europe, and become convinced of the need to institute a *cordon sanitaire* between Europe and Asia. He went on to write twenty books – all of them, notes his son's biographer, Jean-Yves Tadié, 'void of literary qualities' – on epidemiology, neurology and neurasthenia. In a speech delivered towards the end of his life, he defined his concept of hygiene, speaking of 'the dangers of dust, when it transmits the germs of contagious illness', and of the need for new homes 'flooded with light and air, which are the two most powerful tonics and antiseptics we know'. Much of Proust's suffering, we might conjecture, may have been caused by his contradicting the latter while trying to heed the former. His self-sequestration from the poisonous effects of various pollens and dusts removed him also from the benefits of light and air, while behind the shuttered casements and curtained doorways dust bred on every surface and lay in mounting drifts in the untouched corners of his apartment.

Proust's first attack of asthma occurred in 1881, probably in the spring, when he was not yet ten years old. After a long walk in the Bois de Boulogne, Marcel was struck, according to his brother Robert, 'by a frightening spasm of suffocation which, with my terrified father watching, almost proved to be fatal'. His breathlessness was so severe that Adrien Proust did not expect him to survive – he and his wife would later grow used to sitting all night by their son's bedside, unsure if he would live until morning. During one of the worst attacks of his childhood, Proust later recalled, the doctor who had been summoned propped his pillows up behind him with big medical dictionaries of his father's; during another, he sent for a colleague who administered a morphine injection. The severity of Proust's attacks was apparently compounded by his having fallen in the Champs-Élysées around the time of the onset of his asthma and broken his nose, permanently weakening it. In 1921, having suffered from hay fever at the start of thirty springs, he wrote that he had submitted to 110 nasal cauterizations to counteract the effects of pollen. Both illnesses, asthma and hay fever, were thought at the time to be aspects of the same disorder, and their physical symptoms to arise from an underlying psychological malaise.

As the illness began to alter the rhythms of his life – he was often absent from school in the spring term – the young Proust began to devise ways of dealing with his periodic debility and putting it to good use. In the words of his biographer Ronald Hayman, 'if there was a phobic edge to his anxieties and a voluntary element in his sufferings, it's hard to locate the hairline crack between the unavoidable and the theatrical.' Told time and again by his parents that he lacked willpower, he seems to have embraced weakness, as Hayman puts it, as the only strength he possessed. While suffering greatly in reality, he also exaggerated his symptoms, using them in particular as bargaining tools in his relationship with his mother.

As an adult, Proust consulted numerous authorities, both in print and in person, on the subject of his emotionally over-determined disease. In Dr Édouard Brissaud's *Traité de médecine*, he read that asthma was 'a neurosis characterized by attacks of spasmodic dyspnoea'. In the same physician's *L'Hygiène des asthmatiques* – Proust's father had written the book's preface in 1896 – he discovered that the disease 'seems to choose some victims to make them pay for the invulnerability of others. Then the neurosis ceases to be protective. It impairs the organism so deeply, redoubles its attacks so relentlessly, that even the most robust have to succumb; at the least, if they do not die, they are reduced to a kind of *physiological misery*.' A general debility thus 'establishes itself in them step by step, makes them thin, enfeebles them, takes away all moral support; they abandon themselves, stop eating, no longer sleep'. Dr Brissaud appears in *À la recherche du temps perdu* in the guise of the nerve specialist Dr du Boulbon. A friend of the writer Bergotte, du Boulbon comes highly recommended by the celebrated neurologist Jean-Martin Charcot when he is summoned to the bedside of the narrator's dying grandmother. He tries to convince her that her illness is merely the effect of suggestions made by other physicians; she must, he counsels, submit to being called a neurotic:

You belong to that splendid and pitiable family which is the salt of the earth. Everything we think of as great has come to us from neurotics. It is they and they alone who found religions and create great works of art. The world will never realise how much it owes to them, and what they have suffered in order to bestow their gifts on it. We enjoy fine music, beautiful pictures, a thousand exquisite things, but we do not know what they cost those who wrought them in insomnia, tears, spasmodic laughter, urticaria, asthma, epilepsy, a terror of death which is worse than any of these, and which you perhaps have experienced, Madame.

Dr du Boulbon, in other words, is, like Brissaud, a theorist of hypochondria. Proust had had an appointment with Brissaud – then editor of *La Revue neurologique*, his book on asthma had yet to appear – and reported to his friend Léon Daudet that the physician was warm-hearted, ironic and intelligent, as well as sentimental and romantic. Though Brissaud was generally of the opinion that the asthmatic was the best judge of how his condition might be improved, in the case of Proust he recommended mercury washes; Proust declined, as he did with many of the treatments that were offered him over the years. Diets were recommended, sanatoria put at his disposal, but Proust usually refused to go along with the suggested regime. Instead, he devised complex and at best ambiguously effective treatments of his own, based on his patchy medical knowledge, the whims that his wealth facilitated and the habits of mind and body into which he had in any case fallen.

*

Proust lived at a time when asthma and hay fever, the ailments that afflicted him most severely (and to which his later maladies may be ascribed as secondary or reactive consequences), were among the diseases commonly thought to express the struggle between mind and body, pathology and personality. They were, in other words, prominent among the disorders around which the diffuse diagnoses of hypochondria and neurasthenia were most likely to condense. Of the two diseases, asthma is the more ancient diagnosis. In Hippocratic and Galenic medicine, the term denoted a shortness of breath, or dyspnoea. The Roman philosopher Seneca refers to the characteristic panting or wheezing of the asthmatic as a sort of continued 'last gasp' and ascribes it, as with so many other diseases, to an imbalance of the humours. It was only with the knowledge gained from anatomy during the Renaissance that the lungs were posited as the seat of the disease. In the seventeenth century, the English physicians Thomas Willis (in *The Practice of Physick*, of 1684) and John Floyer (whose *Treatise of the Asthma* was published in 1698) claimed to have observed the symptoms of asthma in several members of the same family and posited such external causes as dust, feathers, tobacco smoke, certain foods and excessive exercise or emotion. By the late eighteenth and early nineteenth centuries, asthma had been definitively distinguished from a simple difficulty in breathing and properly isolated as a disorder of the lungs. The organic peculiarities of the disease were speculated upon by Charcot and Ernst von Leyden, who claimed to have found colourless crystals in the sputum of asthmatic patients, and by Heinrich Curschmann, who professed to have observed spiral forms under the microscope that were typical of asthma.

At the same time, asthma came to be regarded as a form of hereditary neurosis that was typical of the leisured, educated upper classes. (By contrast, in the eighteenth century it had been thought primarily an artisan's illness.) In common with hay fever and tuberculosis, treatment for asthma often took the form of removing the patient to a place of cleaner, healthier air: seaside resorts and mountain retreats attracted many hopeful asthmatics in the same period that they welcomed less optimistic consumptives. Among the local and systemic treatments canvassed, recalls Mark Jackson in his book *Allergy: The History of a Modern Malady*, the use of opium was common, though deprecated by at least one physician, Henry Hyde Salter, on account of its potential to 'excite involuntary muscular action, and induce a tendency to spasm'. Salter recommended instead a wide variety of depressive, stimulating or sedative remedies, among them tobacco, tartar-emetic, ipecacuanha, coffee, chloroform, strabonium or belladonna cigarettes, cannabis, ether and lobelia. Proust was to experiment with most of these, alongside the Legras powders that had threatened to choke Céleste Albaret on her first entering his room.

Hay fever too was considered a refined or even an aristocratic affliction. In 1887, in a lecture to the West London Medico-Chirurgical Society, Sir Andrew Clark – who would treat Alice James four years later – claimed that 'once hay-fever appears, it exhibits still further the closeness of its relationship to the nervous system by choosing the man before the woman, the educated

before the ignorant, the gentle before the rude, the courtier before
the clown . . . it prefers the temperate to the torrid zone, it seeks
the city before the country, and out of every climate which it visits
it chooses for its subjects the Anglo-Saxon, or at least English-
speaking, race.' An apparent epidemic of such susceptibility over-
took Britain and America towards the end of the century. One
physician, Morell Mackenzie, commented in 1884 that as the ailment was 'largely confined to persons of cultivation . . . our national
proclivity to hay fever may be taken as a proof of our superiority to
other races'.

Despite their notably Anglophiliac sympathies in terms of language and literature, none of Proust's family seems to have suggested that his hay fever was a result of adopting Anglo-Saxon
customs. But the combination of hay fever and asthma does appear
to have inspired in him and his parents a sense of his special sensitivity, and a submission to whim and routine that was in itself, as
numerous critics and biographers have concluded, a kind of pathology. At first, Proust's parents tried to toughen him up, to resist his
sickly demands for comfort and affection, of which, early in his
novel, the narrator's famous demand for a maternal kiss before he
goes to sleep is just one exemplary instance. Jeanne Proust found
that she could rarely refuse the requests of a son whose frailty made
him a kind of domestic sovereign, an enfeebled prince, the greater
part of whose domain was the bedroom, where he demanded to be
kissed, caressed, tucked in at night and supplied with countless
small treats and luxuries. As her son grew older and his homo-
sexuality became the central unspoken secret in the Proust household, his main imperious demand was for privacy: a solitude that
allowed him to turn illness and writing into the supreme concerns
of his daily routine. Jeanne Proust concerned herself constantly
with the physical requirements of the invalid genius who would
sometimes disappear for a whole night and return pleading to be
left alone with his manuscripts and his symptoms; thus did Proust

deflect most parental inquiries into his intimate life outside the apartment. Even in the weeks before her death in 1905, when her son was thirty-four, Mme Proust, according to the nurse who attended her, was still treating 'little Marcel' as though he were four years old. In adulthood, his sense of having to be protected from the world had given rise to habits and fears that were now ingrained and essential to his sense of self and to his writing.

*

What exactly was it that Proust was afraid of? At least on the surface and on a daily basis, it was the sights, sounds and smells of his immediate environment, including those of his apartment. Once again, Céleste Albaret is our best witness to the prophylactic measures her employer took at his home on the Boulevard Haussmann. Smells, she tells us, seemed to threaten his constitution – visitors were warned not to arrive at the apartment wearing perfume or bearing flowers, even those that did not seem to smell at all. On a few occasions, Céleste writes, he asked to be driven by her husband Odilon to Chevreuse Valley, to see the hawthorn and apple trees in blossom. During these excursions, Proust would remain in the car, admiring the trees from a safe distance, then ask Odilon to cut off a branch and bring it closer so that he could examine it through the window. On at least one occasion, the branch was placed in the boot of the car and brought home to be left on the landing of the service stairs, where Céleste was sent to look at it. When it seemed to Proust that she had not peered intently enough at the flowers to render him a thorough description and appreciation of their perfections, she was sent out a second time and told to look more closely.

All manner of scents assailed the invalid's keen sense of smell. Once, a pair of gloves, readied on a silver tray as Proust was preparing to go out in full evening dress, offended him by their faint smell of benzine – they had recently been cleaned – and they had to be replaced before he could leave the apartment. Céleste was barred from sweeping or mopping the floors while Proust was at home, and so took the opportunity of a rare outing such as this to apply her carpet sweeper. Polishing the parquet, however, was quite out of the question, such was the disagreement of the lingering smell with his fine nose and ailing lungs. So sensitive was Proust's nose that only the finest handkerchiefs were to be left folded on his bedside table; having wiped his nose – he never blew it, for fear of the violence this would do to its delicate membranes – he would let the handkerchief fall by the side of the bed and reach for another. On one fraught occasion, Céleste tells us, she had sent for a fresh supply from Bon Marché, but the cloth proved too coarse for Proust's nose. Unconvinced, Céleste washed and replaced the offending items three times before Proust, enraged, cut one up in front of her with his nail scissors and announced: 'Handkerchiefs are like shoes: none but the finest are pleasant until they've been broken in. From now on, let's be satisfied with the old ones.' He was similarly exacting in the matter of towels, of which twenty or twenty-five had to be laid out at any one time in the bathroom that adjoined his bedroom. When Céleste risked the opinion that a great deal of money was wasted on laundering these towels, each of which Proust cast aside after a single, gentle dab at his person, he replied: 'My dear Céleste, you don't realise that if I use a towel twice it gets too damp and chaps my skin.' In this sense, Proust was a cultural and temperamental descendant of the dandy Beau Brummel, whose prodigious washing (prodigious, that is, for the time, in that he did it every day), and consequently vast expenditure on towels, was almost as legendary as the rate at which he got through fresh cravats.

Sounds, too, tormented Proust. The Boulevard Haussmann was not only lined with chestnut trees that were heavy with pollen in the spring, but was a principal thoroughfare of the city, not far from both the vast department store Printemps and the bustle of Saint-Lazare train station. In January 1912, almost two years before Céleste arrived, the Seine had burst its banks, and Paris begun to flood; towards the end of the month, cement barriers were erected at the end of the boulevard in an effort to keep the water out. The flood started to subside on the 30th, but Proust's ordeal had only just begun – the cellars had to be pumped dry and disinfected, causing carbolic fumes to rise to his apartment, and precipitating a series of asthma attacks 'from which nothing gives me any relief'. Workmen then set about removing rotten parquet from the basement apartments and hammering new boards into place. Plumbers, meanwhile, were hard at work by six in the morning, noisily installing new drains. The sounds penetrated even his inner sanctum where, having suffered from diverse noises from the street two years earlier, he had had the walls lined with cork. On that occasion, Proust had almost immediately suffered a violent asthma attack, which he blamed on the cork itself: it seemed that the assault on his senses was constant and easily transferred from one sense to another.

When Céleste moved to the Boulevard Haussmann, Proust was still in the habit of holidaying at Cabourg, on the Normandy coast, just as he had done with his family as a child. Early in September 1914, despite the recent outbreak of war and the personal and administrative chaos into which it had plunged Parisians, he announced to Céleste that he felt lonely in the capital – most of his friends had already volunteered, and he had been rejected on the grounds of his health – and must escape to the coast. A large canvas and cardboard valise was prepared, containing Proust's manuscripts, on which he intended to work at Cabourg, and a huge wheeled trunk was packed with clothes: outer garments, underwear and the jumpers in which he habitually wrapped himself while sitting in bed. The trunk was also stuffed with blankets – the hotel, Proust told Céleste, closed in winter, 'and no matter how much they air them their blankets smell of mothballs'.

At the Grand Hotel, Proust was given his usual room – number 137 – and assured that during his stay nobody would be allowed to set foot on the terrace above his third-floor room. Céleste was installed in the room next door, partly so that he could summon her by simply knocking on the wall, and partly so that he would not have to put up with the unpredictable noises of neighbours unknown to him. At Cabourg, Céleste tells us, Proust was in fact less sensitive and less of a recluse than at home in Paris: the curtains were drawn back in the afternoon and 'he himself seemed to open up much more'. He took walks on the terrace, or sat there until Céleste happened to pass by, when he beckoned her to join him and began to reminisce about his childhood visits to Cabourg, and the later visits, when his father's advice regarding the beneficial effects on his asthma of a change of air had suited him well, for many of his friends had stayed in the region each summer. In 1914, however, as the autumn wore on, the hotel was requisitioned for use as a military hospital. As no casualties had yet arrived from the front, Proust was allowed to retain his room; but the hotel was becoming deserted as guests drifted away. French banks were also in turmoil, and Proust, having run out of money, decided to return to Paris. Céleste recalls:

> I shall never forget that awful journey home.
>
> We were on our way, everything was fine, when M. Proust suddenly had a terrible choking fit. We were near Mézidon, in Calvados, and between attacks he told me it was always there that he had an attack – always passing through Mézidon, and always on the way home from Cabourg. I remember quite clearly his telling me right in the middle of it all:
>
> 'It always comes on here. There must be something in the air that disagrees with me – perhaps because it's haymaking time. On the way to Cabourg, I know I'm nearly there when we pass through here, and it doesn't have time to affect me much. But coming back . . . the very thought of all the distance still to go . . .'

While Proust suffered, Céleste realized that she had left his medicines and fumigation powders in the valise with his papers; at the next station, she rushed along the platform to the back of the train and retrieved the drugs. She does not record, as she describes Proust lighting his Legras powders and inhaling the fumes, whether in extremis he had had to use matches, the fumes of which he could not abide, instead of a small piece of paper lit in turn from a candle.

'I don't remember', writes Céleste, 'how we finally got back to boulevard Haussmann. But there more trouble awaited us.' Every year, while he was away, Proust's apartment was thoroughly cleaned with huge vacuum cleaners – he could bear neither the noise of the machines nor the great quantity of hot, noxious air, not to mention disturbed dust, that the machines produced. Now he returned to find the vacuum cleaners still hard at work. 'They must go away, Céleste, they must go away. I must go to bed,' he cried, before retreating to his room with a candle, a box of Legras powders and his hot-water bottles. Céleste discovered him streaming with sweat, choking as he hunched over the smoking powder. Terrified, she retreated to the kitchen, convinced that she would not see him alive again. Eventually the attack subsided; during the evening, Proust sent for Céleste again, and acknowledged that she must have been frightened, having never before seen him in such physical distress. It was then, she recalled, that M. Proust deliberately became a recluse, and then that he told her he would devote himself henceforth entirely to his novel: 'My dear Céleste, there's something I must tell you. I've just been to Cabourg with you, but that's all over. I shan't ever go again, to Cabourg or anywhere else. The soldiers do their duty, and since I can't fight as they do, my duty is to write my book, do my work. I haven't the time for anything else.'

*

It is as much a cliché to say that the book in which Proust determined to immerse himself on returning from Cabourg in 1914 is a novel about sensation, as to claim that it is solely 'about' time, memory (chiefly of the involuntary sort), sex, habit or literature itself. But the senses are assuredly one structuring principle among others, and at times the book's explicit theme. Consider the passage in which the narrator is alone in a barrack room, waiting to see Saint-Loup, and listening to the sounds coming from the fireplace – sounds that, had he been listening from another room, he would have felt sure were those of a man blowing his nose and walking about. This confusion continues as his attention strays to Saint-Loup's watch on the table: the source of the ticking had seemed to shift around in the room before he spotted it, then to have remained fixed in space. There follows a long disquisition on the pleasing effects of muffled sound, followed by a reflection on the aesthetic effects of complete deafness. The deaf person, writes Proust, experiences the world as a kind of tableau or stage set: 'for this stone-deaf man, since the loss of a sense adds as much beauty to the world as its acquisition, it is with ecstasy that he walks now upon an earth become almost an Eden, in which sound has not yet been created.'

That one sense may be heightened in this way by the diminution of another is just one of the sensuous curiosities that proliferate in the novel. More common in *À la recherche du temps perdu* is the phenomenon of synaesthesia, the confusion of one sense with another, so that at various points in the book scents are said to have shades; proper names to possess colours, tastes and scents; and air itself to solidify around the narrator. This is not merely a metaphoric tic. Rather, it acknowledges the constant lapses and slippages that come with being a sensitive creature. Quite often in Proust, as indeed in the novel's famous opening pages, this reflection on the senses is expressed with respect to sleep. The passage in *Du côté de chez Swann* that relates the narrator's waking in the middle of the night, momentarily at a loss even as to his own identity, is usually taken to describe a certain phenomenon of consciousness. But Proust is quite explicit about the level of awareness involved: 'I had only, in its original simplicity, the feeling of existence as it may quiver in the depths of an animal.' Later in the book, he describes his waking self precisely in terms of sensation, not thought:

My consciousness, still muffled from sleep (like those organs by which, after a local anaesthetic, a cauterisation, not perceived at first, is felt only at the very end and then as a faint smarting), was touched only gently by the shrill points of the fifes which caressed it with a vague, cool, matutinal warbling; and after this fragile interruption in which the silence had turned to music it relapsed into my slumber before even the dragoons had finished passing, depriving me of the last blossoming sheafs of the surging bouquet of sound. And the zone of my consciousness which its springing stems had brushed was so narrow, so circumscribed with sleep that later on, when Saint-Loup asked me whether I had heard the band, I was not certain that the sound of its brasses had not been as imaginary as that which I heard during the day echoing, after the slightest noise, from the paved streets of the town.

Proust's sensitivity to those moments when our senses are muffled or intensified – and often for him the two go together – gives rise to some of the more striking descriptions in his novel. It is as if he is particularly attuned to what it means to be a sensing creature, as though he can sense the senses themselves. This is not as abstract or needlessly awkward a notion as it might at first appear; there is a long, now rather occluded, medical and philosophical tradition that refers to a kind of sixth sense or 'common sense' that governs the others or somehow subsumes their sensations into one overall feeling. Or perhaps, because the precise operation of the common sense is unclear in the Greek philosophers (including Aristotle) who first described it, it is a layer of more fundamental feeling that grounds the five senses. Whatever its relation to the other senses, the common sense is an abiding, if uncommon, theme in literature and philosophy. It is present, for example, in Michel de Montaigne's account (in his essay 'On Experience') of his falling from his horse and almost losing all sense of himself: at the moment he hits the ground his senses desert him, except for a fragile feeling of still being Michel de Montaigne, a sense that is not reducible to thought. In his book *The Inner Touch: Archaeology of a Sensation*, the contemporary scholar

Daniel Heller-Roazen contends that the common sense, inner touch or *coenaesthesis* lies barely hidden in philosophical concepts such as John Locke's 'uneasiness' and Gottfried Wilhelm Leibniz's 'unrest': they name 'the incessant and infinitely minute perceptions' by which a body feels itself to be alive but which cannot be attributed to the five senses alone.

By the nineteenth century, says Heller-Roazen, the common sense had become more explicitly a medical than a philosophical idea. The term denoted those objectless sensations such as fatigue, hunger, nausea, itching, shuddering, aching, muscular resistance, desire and pleasure: all that could not be subsumed under one or another of the more familiar faculties. Under the rubric of *coenaesthopathy*, various disorders of the common sense were delineated: patients were observed to feel too little or too much the fact of their own feeling nature. In 1882, in the eleventh volume of the *Archives de neurologie*, Jules Cotard – a protégé of Charcot's and fellow student of Adrien Proust who lent his name to the character of Dr Cottard in Proust's novel – published an account of what he called a 'negation delirium', subsequently known as Cotard's syndrome. In several respects a precursor to Freud's study of Daniel Paul Schreber, Cotard's essay describes patients who claim to feel nothing because their bodies have been partly or wholly destroyed. Cotard quotes from his notes, taken at a psychiatric institution at Vanves:

Madame E., fifty-four years of age, married, mother, is put in the Vanves medical centre June 15, 1863, after having made various suicide attempts. Madame E. is in a state of anxious agitation . . . She imagines that she has a shrunken throat and a displaced heart. In paroxysms of agitation, she cries out and complains aloud, always repeating the same sentences. All her organs have been displaced; she cannot do anything about it . . .

Monsieur A., forty-eight years of age, put in the Vanves health centre in March, 1879, following a suicide attempt, is in a state of intense anxious agitation . . . His brain has turned soft; his head is like a hollow nutshell. He has no penis; he has no testicles; he no longer has anything at all.

Monsieur C., forty-five years of age, of a sturdy constitution, married, father . . . Sometime near March, 1880, he began to express negative and completely absurd ideas . . . Brought to Vanves in April, 1880 . . . Monsieur C. insists that he is not married, that he does not have children, that he has neither a father nor a mother, that he has no name . . . Monsieur C. resists all care taken as to his body; he refuses to don clothing because his whole body is nothing other than a large nut. He refuses to eat, for he has no mouth; he refuses to walk, for he has no legs.

Such cases are extreme, and easily remind us of the sufferings of the unfortunate Schreber. Nonetheless, the hypochondriac, according to Cotard, was not always to be considered insane – the sensations he reported were not simply imaginary. They were characterized, Cotard wrote shortly before his death in 1888, 'by an exaggerated psychological response. Not only visceral pains are amplified but also normal sensations cause anxiety . . . It is less a veritable hyperaesthesia than a dysthaesia, i.e., a hyperaesthesia linked to a blunting of sensation.' Cotard's syndrome typically involves a deficit of feeling, but this is just one sort of catastrophe of the common sense, which may as easily become excessively heightened as diminished. Hyposensitivity and hypersensitivity belong together on the same hypochondriacal continuum. Similarly, for Richard von Krafft-Ebing, in 1893, the hypochondriac was no mere fantasist, however outlandish his convictions regarding his body, but suffered from a disorder of the general feeling or common sense: 'hypochondria may be called a neurosis of the general feeling, with effects on the psychological sphere . . . The state of consciousness of the patient may extend from ideas of severe diseases to the most absurd interpretations of sensations that are actually experienced.' Or again, Baron E. von Feuchtersleben, in his *Principles of Medical Psychology* in

1847: 'hypochondriasis is in its essence nothing but a coenaesthesis abnormally heightened in all directions'. The hypochondriac, in short, feels normal sensations more keenly than others. He is not deluded but instead pathologically attuned to the smallest changes in his own body. He knows himself only too well.

*

We might call Proust, then, a kind of *coenaesthopath*. He regularly heard, through meetings with his father's colleagues, about discoveries and controversies in contemporary neurology, and the forensic interest his novel shows in the nature of sensations, especially at those moments when they are confused, intensified or attenuated, suggests that he was acquainted with the concept of the common sense. His own hypochondria was manifestly not of a delusional sort: Proust did not imagine that he had illnesses that did not exist, nor greatly fear the onset of such ailments, and a stoic resignation seems to have accompanied even his most distressing symptoms and his most painfully refined susceptibilities. The miracle is not that Proust kept going despite his disease – that he staved off asthma, bronchitis and pneumonia long enough to put an end to his novel, if not finish it to his satisfaction – but that he kept going despite his disastrous attitude to his disease: despite his self-neglect and unregulated self-medication, his inadequate and capricious diet, his immobility and insomnia, his immuring himself in a dusty and (towards the end of his life) unheated room.

Proust began to die, writes Céleste Albaret, at the moment he left the apartment on the Boulevard Haussmann:

The tragedy, for that's what it was, was aggravated emotionally by the circumstances in which it took place. M. Proust's aunt sold the building without letting him know, so that at the end of December 1918 he found himself faced with a *fait accompli*. The Varin-Barnier Bank had bought all the lower part of the house and intended to open a branch on the courtyard. The work began at the beginning of 1919, and M. Proust, who had

been desperately hoping to be able to stay on in spite of everything, realized there would be no more peace and quiet and that his life, like the
house he was so attached to, would be completely changed.

In June, Proust moved his small household to an apartment owned
by the celebrated actress Réjane. Most of the furniture at the Boulevard Haussmann was auctioned off, and such landmarks in Proust's
bedroom as the grand piano and the enormous wardrobe put into
storage. At his temporary home in the Rue Laurent-Pichat, the thin
walls failed to protect him from the sound of the outside world; he
lived, he said, 'in a house where you hear every word the neighbours say, where you know each time a window is opened, where
I have not slept for twenty days'. His temperature soared to a hundred and four degrees, and the emanations of the nearby Bois de
Boulogne worsened his asthma daily. The summer passed in a wel-
ter of noise and bad air, made comically bearable only by the fact
that one of his noisiest neighbours was another famous actor, Le
Bargy, who could be observed on the other side of the courtyard,
arguing with his wife and sometimes howling loudly. At the beginning of October, Proust finally moved again to an apartment on the
fourth floor in the Rue Hamelin.

There he set about replicating as far as possible the domestic
arrangements at his previous home. The Chinese screen behind his
head; the three electrical switches that were attached to a bell, his
green-shaded bedside lamp and a small kettle for his lime-flower
tea (he had a habit of letting this kettle boil dry); the bedside tables
containing his pens and paper and the Legras powders; the constant
supply of sweaters that he draped on his shoulders and then allowed
to slide down behind him until they formed, said Céleste, a sort of
throne; the heavy overcoat that hung on the tarnished bedstead and
which he wore as a dressing gown when he had strength to get out
of bed; his books ranged along the mantelpiece: all of this meant to
re-establish, unchanged, the requisite physical conditions for the

completion of his book, which was now all that mattered to him. As Céleste puts it, 'the magic circle was re-created . . . and the machinery of his habits resumed.' The new bedroom, however, was even less conducive to his maintaining his present state of health, let alone to any possible recovery. As before, he would not countenance the use of the central heating. When Céleste tried to light a fire in the tiny fireplace, the smoke billowed back into the room, and Proust began to choke. 'The smoke makes me ill, Céleste,' he said. 'I can taste it in my mouth and chest. I can't breathe. We will have to give it up.' He carried on writing, Céleste recalls, in the freezing cold, uncomplaining and swathed in sweaters.

By this stage Proust ate very little. Even while still at the Boulevard Haussmann, he had seemed to Céleste to be 'living on the shadows of foods he'd known and loved in the past'. Before the war, he had dined at the Ritz, or sometimes sent out to Larue's, on the corner of Rue Royale and Place de la Madeleine, or to the Louis XVI, a restaurant on the boulevard itself, for 'good plain' food. Occasionally, though he could not abide the smell of cooking in the apartment – his servants' food too had to come in from outside – he would ask Nicolas to cook him a sole. But after the war, his only meal of the day was the meagre breakfast: coffee and a croissant, sometimes a second. Even this, says Céleste, eventually dwindled: he failed to finish even one croissant, and in the end appeared to survive on coffee alone. Sometimes his palate was surprised by a dish – such as *la petite marmite*, a slowly simmered concoction of beef and chicken gizzards – that he remembered from his youth and which, on a sudden whim, he had Céleste procure or even cook herself. In the last eight years of his life, she insists, the only solid foods she saw him touch, apart from *la petite marmite*, were mullet (once), whitebait (twice), eggs (also twice), and on a few occasions Russian salad or fried potatoes. Even allowing for Céleste's faulty memory at over fifty years' remove, it seems that by the time he relocated to the Rue

Hamelin Proust's was a diet of extreme asceticism, punctuated by episodes of childish luxury.

His body, meanwhile, was awash with drugs. After moving to the new apartment, he tried hard to reduce his use of the Legras powders. The combination of atropine and hyoscyamine, notes Ronald Hayman, relieved his asthma by dilating and drying the bronchial tree, but may well also have blurred Proust's vision, made him weak and giddy, and given him palpitations. As his energy waned, he had recourse to more caffeine to keep him awake and productive, though this too he tried to cut back, in favour, disastrously, of dosing himself with adrenalin: 'it will give you more stimulus than champagne,' he wrote to a friend. On one occasion, he forgot to dilute the liquid and burned his oesophagus so badly that he passed out from the pain. On another, having fallen over in his bedroom – Hayman conjectures that the Legras powders may have caused difficulty in walking – he took seven tablets of opium, and two other narcotics, and only narrowly avoided having his stomach pumped; it took him several weeks to recover from the overdose. Meanwhile he ignored the advice of his doctors, sending Céleste out to buy the medicines they prescribed but almost always having them thrown away unused. To relieve the congestion of his lungs, he was prescribed injections of camphorated oil, but had developed a horror of injections, and made Céleste promise, as the end approached, that she would allow no doctor to 'torture' him with a needle.

Proust knew that he was dying. His excursions into the outside world grew less frequent. One afternoon in the spring of 1922, he greeted Céleste with the news that in the small hours of the morning he had written the word *fin* at the end of his manuscript. There was still much work to be done correcting proofs, which in Proust's case was always an opportunity to add more material. 'Now I can die,' he told Céleste, who would hear nothing on the subject. By September he was suffering badly from influenza, and Dr Bize asked

Robert Proust to intervene and convince his brother to take better care of himself. But Marcel refused to leave his unheated room for the nearby clinic that Robert suggested. Pneumonia set in, and an abscess on the lung, followed inevitably by septicaemia. He coughed incessantly and scarcely used his voice, relying instead on scribbled notes to Céleste: 'I have just coughed more than three thousand times, my back and stomach are finished, everything.' He had her send out for iced beer, which was now the only thing that he would, or could, ingest. On the 17th of November, he declared to Céleste: 'tomorrow will be the ninth day of my attack. If I ever get over it, I shall show the doctors what I am made of. Ah! Céleste, I knew you were kind, but I would never have thought that you could be to such an extent.' He began to dictate additions to his manuscript, but at two o'clock in the morning was too exhausted to speak, so took up the pen and wrote himself until half past three. It was probably then – around the time Proust turned to her and said: 'Let's stop. I can't do any more. But don't go' – that, according to Robert Proust, the abscess on his brother's lung burst and his fate was sealed.

According to Céleste, Proust remained lucid until the last moment. He thanked her repeatedly for her kindness, and tried to please his brother by drinking a little coffee. Early in the morning, Céleste noticed that M. Proust was plucking at the sheet and gathering the papers on his bed towards him: she had heard people in her village say that the dying gather things around them at the last. He then spoke of a fat woman in black who stood at the end of his bed; Céleste promised to chase her away. Dr Bize arrived, and gave Proust an injection: the dying man reached out to pinch Céleste's wrist, admonishing her for breaking her promise. In the afternoon, Robert Proust came with oxygen cylinders, asked Céleste to fetch a Liberty eiderdown that Proust had never used because of the effect of the feathers on his asthma, and arranged his brother's pillows before giving him a little oxygen and asking: 'Is that a little

better, my little Marcel?' 'Yes, Robert.' 'I'm tiring you, my little
Marcel.' 'Yes . . . yes, Robert dear.' Around four o'clock, Robert
took Céleste aside in the passage outside the bedroom and asked
her to be brave, because there was nothing more to be done. They
went back into the room:

M. Proust never took his eyes off us. It was terrible.

We stayed like that for about five minutes, and then the professor suddenly moved forward, and bent gently over his brother, and closed his
eyes. They were still turned toward us.

I said: 'Is he dead?'

'Yes, Céleste. It is over.'

It was half-past four.

I couldn't stand upright for exhaustion and grief. But I couldn't believe
it – he had died so nobly, without a shudder, without a gasp, without the
life and the light of the soul even vanishing from the eyes looking on us to
the end. His last words had been the last two exchanges with his brother.
Despite what people have said – again for literature's sake, I suppose – he
didn't say 'Mother'.

8. Glenn Gould: Not of the World

'I simply feel that the artist should be granted, both for his sake
and for that of his public — and let me get on record right now that
I'm not at all happy with words like "public" and "artist" —
that he should be granted anonymity.'

Glenn Gould, 'Glenn Gould Interviews Glenn Gould
About Glenn Gould'

On Tuesday, the 8th of December 1959, Glenn Gould, who was
then aged twenty-seven, paid a visit to the Concert and Artist
Department at Steinway Hall, on West 57th Street in New York.
Since the release of his celebrated recording of Bach's *Goldberg Variations* almost four years earlier, he had been engaged in a gruelling
round of concert performances and recording sessions, and had
already expressed on several occasions his desire to give up the former in order to concentrate on the latter. It would be another five
years before he definitively abandoned his concert career and
retreated to the studio, weaving a technological cocoon that finally
satisfied his urge to separate himself physically from his public. His
retirement would also allow Gould to match on tape, in his own
time, his conception of the ideal performance: a delicate undertaking too often, he thought, upset by the variables of the concert hall,
the audience and the instrument. As regards this last, he had for
years now been taking full advantage of his status as a Steinway Artist
to press the venerable manufacturer to produce or modify a piano
to his exacting, idiosyncratic and often contradictory requirements.

Technicians at the company had already been driven to distraction by the young pianist's rejection of the lush, profound and stately Steinway sound, and his preference for a light, tight action that sounded, he said, 'a little like an emasculated harpsichord'. In January 1955, Gould had found what he considered the perfect Steinway, built in 1928 and designated CD 174, but two years later it was dropped in transit and had to be rebuilt; to Gould's ear it had been ruined. His preferred instrument now – the piano that he urged Steinway to emulate – was a Chickering, made in Boston in 1895, and considered by many who knew it to be a piece of trash.

Despite the near impossibility of their satisfying his technical demands, the staff at Steinway & Sons most likely welcomed Gould warmly at the end of 1959. It was in their interests, after all, to maintain cordial relations with the outstanding performer of his generation, a musician whose dishevelled good looks and curious tics at the keyboard had not only made him a global celebrity, but brought a brooding, modern species of glamour to his instrument and its most famous manufacturer. Besides, he was by no means a haughty or antisocial sort of artist: in person he was witty, playful and loquacious. If conversation with him frequently turned into an extended monologue on Gould's part, this was usually because he had somehow been rendered self-conscious, and was trying to overcome his native shyness and control the situation. Steinway's managers and technicians had grown adept in keeping Gould at his ease and warding off his more troubling quirks. When he turned up at their Manhattan premises this time, he must not have seemed too strange: his habit of wearing many layers of heavy clothing in all weathers, for example, would have been justified by the New York winter. And all employees had by this stage been well apprised of Gould's aversion to physical contact: he had warned the Steinway directors that an enthusiastic handshake might damage his fingers. So sensitive was the pianist on this point that he had lately taken to posting a typed notice on his dressing-room door; headed 'YOUR COOPERATION

WILL BE APPRECIATED', the text requested visitors to refrain from shaking his hand. Though this might seem discourteous, it read, the aim was 'simply to prevent any possibility of injury'. When they greeted Gould, the manager of the Concert and Artist Department, Frederick Steinway, and his assistant Winston Fizgerald, would have known to hold back as they welcomed him into the office.

Precisely what happened next is the subject of several competing accounts, though they really only differ on the crucial matter of the force applied to Gould's person rather than questions of intent, conspiracy or attendant circumstance. It seems that Gould was sitting with his back to the office door when William Hupfer, the department's chief concert technician, entered the room. The working-class son of German immigrants, Hupfer had first been employed by Steinway as a young man in 1917, and had risen steadily in the company as an itinerant tuner: for ten years he was Sergei Rachmaninoff's regular tuner, and in 1946 had been appointed to his current post in New York. He had worked often with Gould, and although he disagreed strongly with the prodigy's ideas concerning the proper tuning of a Steinway, he had not let his antipathy show in public. Gould, on the other hand, was wary of Hupfer: his handshake was alarmingly manly. A legendarily genial figure among musicians and technicians, Bill Hupfer was a burly and boisterous individual; as he walked into his manager's office, his large right hand may well have flexed, then relaxed as he reminded himself of the young man's fastidiousness. Nonetheless, he could not resist a friendly greeting, and as he passed by Gould he patted him, as he later recalled it, gently on the left shoulder. The pianist immediately recoiled and blurted out: 'Don't do that; I don't like to be touched.' An awkward silence filled the room as Gould slumped sulkily (as the two witnesses would later put it) into his chair. Hupfer, overcome with an unaccustomed embarrassment, quickly apologized, and within a few minutes Gould was again chatting amiably with Fitzgerald and Steinway. He remained in the office for at least another half an hour, and said no more about the incident.

Later that day, Gould, seemingly in good spirits, attended a film screening by the National Film Board at Canada House. He then left Manhattan for Syracuse, where he gave a recital, and was still apparently untroubled. Within weeks, however, he had begun to complain of various symptoms that he ascribed to 'the idiocy of one of Chez Steinway's senior employees'. On the 27th of January 1960, in a letter to Edith Boecker of the Philips record label, he detailed the consequences of Hupfer's laying a hand on his shoulder:

The initial injury was to the left shoulder and when x-rayed the shoulder blade was shown to have been pushed down about one-half an inch. That problem has basically been cleared up now but has caused a secondary reaction much more troubling. The nerve which controls the fourth and fifth fingers of my left hand has been compressed and inflamed or whatever with the result that any movement involving a division of the left hand, as a sudden leap to the left side of the keyboard, is, if not actually impossible, accomplished only by a considerable effort of will.

(The careless phrase 'or whatever' might alert us to the strange combination of intensity and ignorance that marks Gould's attitude to his body.) He was already considering, he told Boecker, 'some legal move'. Winston Fitzgerald seems to have had some difficulty taking the 'injury' seriously. Gould wrote to him:

I must say I was a little surprised at the tone of your letter in so far as you seem to express some bafflement about the nature of my malaise (or did I misread between the lines?) . . . At the moment it looks very grim – I am consulting with all kinds of orthopaedic people and others but they are all understandably reluctant to give positive answers as to when and how . . . If a miracle happens and the arm radically improves I will be in touch with you immediately on the subject of pianos.

He seemed intent on maintaining his professional relationship with Steinway, and dropped no hint to Fitzgerald at this stage that he was planning to take legal action.

In the meantime, Gould began to cancel concerts. Already in the habit of pulling out of an engagement at the last minute if he developed a cold or other mild affliction – this decidedly at odds with the attitude of most classical musicians and their audiences alike, for whom stamina in the face of illness was a matter of professional honour – he used this new injury to absolve himself of several forthcoming commitments. In June, he wrote to Abe Cohen of the Israel Philharmonic to say that the arm and shoulder were no better. It was a matter, he claimed, of endurance – rehearsals had to be kept to a bare minimum, and a full recital fatigued him terribly – and as a consequence he would not be coming to Tel Aviv. He had seen five doctors in the space of two months, all of whom, he claimed, had diagnosed the compression of a nerve by cervical vertebrae. (One of the five would later insist to Gould's friend and biographer Peter Ostwald that there had been no real injury at all.) His treatments culminated in six weeks in Philadelphia, four of which had been spent in a full body cast, with his left arm elevated, and two enduring rigorous physiotherapy, to little beneficial effect. A course of cortisone left him constantly nauseated but did not obviate the problem; nor did the 117 orthopaedic and chiropractic treatments he received in New York and his native Toronto between January and October. In the summer of 1961, to the dismay (though not the surprise) of his manager Walter Homburger, he was still cancelling concerts, including a lucrative tour of Europe. He did not, however, pull out of all engagements, and his insurance company refused a claim on the basis that he was still performing, albeit intermittently. There seemed no pattern or consistency to his choice of which bookings to honour.

Steinway & Sons, for their part, were at first bemused, then indignant: for a time, Gould was banned from entering Steinway Hall lest he antagonize staff or an employee inadvertently risk a repeat of the incident. On the 6th of December 1960, Gould filed a civil lawsuit against Hupfer and the company, claiming that the technician, approaching the unwary pianist from behind, 'wilfully or recklessly or negligently brought both his forearms down with considerable force on plaintiff's left shoulder and neck, driving plaintiff's left elbow against the arm of the chair in which he was sitting', thus causing an 'injury to the nerve roots in his neck and spinal discs in the neck region'. Facing a suit for $300,000, Steinway produced an internal report, entitled 'The Glenn Gould Case', which expressly stated, on the evidence of all three employees, that no pressure had been applied to Gould's back or shoulder at all. Gould seems genuinely to have believed that he had been injured and to have felt that Steinway ought to acknowledge the insult and his subsequent suffering. It was his sincerity, and his almost childish sense of grievance, that struck the company president Henry Z. Steinway when he and Gould were finally brought together to resolve the matter, in a sweltering New York hotel room, in August 1961. (Gould, habitually worried about catching a chill even in high summer, had turned off the air conditioning.) To Steinway's amazement and relief, the young man was willing to settle out of court for a mere $9,372.35, the precise figure of his medical and legal expenses; it left out all of his physiotherapy costs and his lost concert fees. Recalling the meeting thirty years later, Steinway wrote: 'In my opinion this settlement is entirely due to Glenn's lack of any trace of a vindictive nature, and perhaps some feeling for Steinway & Sons at least trying to satisfy his piano needs.' In a memo to all Steinway Hall staff in September 1961, he had directed that Gould was once again to be received with all the courtesy due a Steinway artist, but on no account, no matter the circumstances, was any physical contact to be risked: 'the reasons for this are self evident.'

*

By the mid 1950s, when he first became famous outside Canada, Glenn Gould's several strangenesses in performance and in private were already well known. Among the oddities that quickly composed the stock backdrop to any journalistic account of his musical career was his curious physical address to the piano. Gould sat a mere fourteen inches from the floor, on a folding chair that had been specially adapted by his father, and his piano was raised on wooden blocks. With his nose almost pressed to the keyboard, he looked, as many critics have noted, like a small boy in strained concentration on his instrument. Then there were the singing, clicking, mumbling and thrumming vocalizations that accompanied his playing, to the confusion or fury of listeners and colleagues, and which have been politely described for decades as 'humming'. The rituals that surrounded these performances were also public knowledge early on in his career: his immersing his arms in extremely hot water before playing, supposedly to relax the muscles; his hatred of draughty concert halls, which sometimes necessitated a phalanx of electric heaters directed at the pianist; his dressing in heavy sweaters, overcoat, cap, scarf and 'specially designed' gloves even in the heat of summer. (At least one colour photograph from the mid 1950s makes Gould's knitwear collection look rather boyish and bohemian; as he got older, it more closely resembled the wardrobe of a homeless person, and he was in fact occasionally mistaken for a tramp, especially after he took to carrying his belongings about in a plastic bag.) All of these eccentricities – they were not eccentricities, he insisted in interviews, but essential requirements of his delicate métier – combined to create a public persona that was in part guileless and sincere, in part a conscious elaboration of native quirks into useful legend.

Gould's hypochondria, of which the Steinway incident in 1959 is among the more dramatic examples, was certainly part of the mythology of the young genius, though it was perhaps precisely his youth that prevented his anxieties from being described in those terms at the time. Early in his career, he seemed artistically fastidious rather than obsessive or crankish. The main subjects of his fears were, however, already in place. When his future biographer, the young psychiatrist and violinist Peter Ostwald, met Gould backstage after a concert in California in 1957, he was struck immediately by the musician's recurring remarks on the subject of his health. As Ostwald stood in the overheated dressing room and expressed his admiration for the performance he had just heard, the pianist, apparently discomfited by his visitor's compliments, launched into an extended monologue on the physical toll taken by his current touring schedule:

Airplanes are a big problem for me because the cabins are never reliably heated and I'm extremely sensitive to temperature change. The air conditioning while waiting at an airport can be an ordeal; I have to be very careful to avoid draughts at all times. Large halls like this one make me very uncomfortable, as does the audience with its incessant coughing and sneezing. It is hard to protect myself from germs; I think I might actually be coming down with a fever, or a cold, as frequently happens. I'm not at all sure that I'll be able to play tomorrow night's concert.

Ostwald, taken aback by the seeming insecurity of the performer he had just witnessed giving one of the most electrifying (if strange) performances he had ever seen, tried to steer the conversation towards music, but in the course of the evening Gould reverted regularly to the state of his health.

The full extent of Gould's imagined symptoms was impressive even in his youth; later, their range would increase, and his ailments start to overlap with the real afflictions of middle age, some of which may have been caused or worsened by his hypochondria itself. As a small boy, he already worried about the safety of his fingers, and was loath to risk hurting them, for example, while playing games. He was extremely sensitive to bright colours – his father recalled his throwing a tantrum when presented with the gift of a red fire engine – and preferred for the rest of his life a palette of dull greys and browns in his clothes and surroundings. Gould's mother, it seems, was unusually solicitous about his health, warning him well into adolescence and even early adulthood to wrap up warm lest he catch cold, and expressing dire fears on his behalf of the germs that were spread easily in crowded places such as concert halls. A childhood friend, Bob Fulford, went so far as to say that 'if hypochondria could be inherited, we know who the villain was. His mother was constantly worried about his complexion. His complexion was too white, and his mother was worried about it, and it was "You must eat, you should eat more of this and you should do this and this, you should get out into the sun, why don't you and Robert go out and play."' Gould later surmised that his mother may have been worried in particular about polio, though this knowledge did not stop him expressing his own fear of infection in sometimes outlandish style: he was known to slam the phone down in panic if his interlocutor coughed or sneezed. At the age of ten, he suffered a very real injury to his back when he fell onto a rail his father used to transport a boat at the family's holiday home at Lake Simcoe; though he recovered fully, the accident appears to have made him especially anxious about his back and about musculoskeletal problems in general. It does not seem to have made him very curious about the actual workings of his body: throughout his life he maintained a deep and sometimes dangerous ignorance about human physiology.

By contrast, he had a truly encyclopaedic knowledge of pharmacology, combined with a reckless attitude to the use of prescription drugs. He seemed, noted more than one physician who treated him, to believe in a strictly reactive, mechanistic approach to the failings of the body: anyone who suggested a more preventive or holistic perspective, or risked the opinion that his mode of life might have something to do with his symptoms, was genially dismissed as a 'nature-boy type'. When Peter Ostwald found his way to his dressing room in 1957, Gould's coat pockets were already full of pills, and he talked casually of the barbiturates and other drugs he took to counter his pre-performance nerves and chronic insomnia. (Later in life, Gould would solve the problem of his not sleeping at night by the simple expedient of staying awake until dawn, then dozing as best he could until mid-afternoon.) Earlier in 1957, he had jokingly advised a pianist friend, Thomas McIntosh, on the uses of various drugs; the humorous tone of his letter does not hide his real enthusiasm for them. Giving his address as 'GOULD'S CLINIC FOR PSEUDO-PSEUMATIC THERAPY', he writes:

I am delighted to hear that Dr. Gould's prescriptions as usual proved efficacious. Due to my long experience with internal medicine practice I am unusually alert to the problems of neurotic artists. Whenever you are planning a trip up to Canada my nurse will be glad to arrange an appointment. The yellow sleeping pills are called Nebutal. The white sedatives are called Luminal. I believe that both will have to be obtained through your doctor. Luminal is perfectly harmless and can be taken generally three times a day: – one after the noon meal and two at bed time. I strongly advise however that you do not make a habit of Nebutol. It should definitely be reserved for the nights before special occasions and to break chronic sleeplessness.

There is no mention in his letter of the possible side effects of Luminal (a brand name for phenobarbital), which include ataxia, dizziness and nystagmus (abnormal eye movement).

Gould's apparent ignorance of how his body functioned, and what it might require to keep it healthy, extended to his attitude towards food. Many friends and colleagues reported never having seen him eat anything but arrowroot biscuits, which he nibbled during recording sessions and proffered by way of lunch to at least one guest at his apartment. (The biscuits were washed down with instant coffee made with water straight from the hot tap, Gould's kitchen serving no other useful purpose.) A constant supply of mineral water was part of his touring paraphernalia, along with the folding chair and the

piano-leg blocks, and he occasionally outraged a conductor by performing with a glass of water atop the piano. He was at best indifferent to food and at times frankly frustrated at the necessity to eat at all;
he once expressed amazement that other people could tell one food
from another by taste alone. His ambivalence was generally expressed
as impatience, as in his response in 1973 to a request for his favourite
recipe from the author of a forthcoming cookbook. He takes, he
regrets, an 'Anglo-Saxon' approach to food: 'My basic attitude . . . is
that it's a time-consuming nuisance . . . and I would be only too
delighted if one could effectively sustain oneself with all necessary
nutritional elements by the simple intake of X capsules per day. I
realize that this sounds forbiddingly ascetic, but it's a fair reflection of
my attitude toward the subject, and I beg to request exclusion from
your volume accordingly.' Earlier in his career, while still touring, he
had developed a specific fear of being seen eating in public. Gould's
attitude to food and eating suggests that he wanted to bypass the body
entirely, that he dreamed, even as his body gave itself away through
his manifold eccentricities, of becoming a pure conduit for musical
ideas, untethered from the messy and unpredictable physical world.
His anxieties and obsessions set him apart bodily from family, friends
and colleagues and also made sexual intimacy problematic (although,
against his asexual reputation, his biographers recount a number of
relationships with women).

*

As early as 1947, when he was only fifteen, a review had deplored
Gould's 'incipient mannerisms'. A decade later, after the *Goldberg
Variations* had made his name, critics could not decide whether his
bizarre performances were ludicrous, essential to his genius or the
product of a cynical desire to appear creatively strange. Reactions to
a concert in Detroit in 1956, for example, were instructively mixed.
The *Detroit Free Press* opined: 'it is his tragedy that his behaviour at
the piano produced laughter in his audience.' Another newspaper
thought the tics were a deliberate ploy: 'Gould's storm-tossed mane

of hair, his invertebrate posture at the keyboard and his habit of collapse at the end of each solo line was sheer show business.' On occasion he performed with his (fingerless) gloves on, or his shoes off, his
shirt tail out or his face so close to the keyboard that he appeared to
be playing, quipped one journalist, with his nose. Gould, for his
part, expressed (or affected) some surprise at the reactions his various habits provoked; as far as he was concerned they were 'simply
the occupational hazards of a highly subjective business'. A few years
after his first celebrity, he told an interviewer:

I had not regarded any of the things attendant upon my playing – my
eccentricities if you like – as being of any particular note at all. Then suddenly a number of well-meaning people in the arts said, 'My dear young
man, you must pull yourself together and stop this nonsense.' I had never
given any thought to their [sic] importance, at least to some people, of
visual image. When I suddenly was made aware of it in about 1956, I
became extremely self-conscious about everything I did. The whole
secret of what I had been doing was to concentrate exclusively on realizing a conception of the music, regardless of how it is physically achieved.
This new self-consciousness was very difficult.

However discomposed Gould may have felt by the attention his tics
elicited, he did not appreciably alter his appearance at the piano or
his bodily attitude in performance. Film of a recording session in the
late 1950s shows him alternately hunched over the keyboard and
leaning back perilously, his upper body swaying from side to side or
circling to describe an inverted cone whose point is the already rick-
ety folding chair. At times, his head falls back, eyes closed, in a sort
of austere ecstasy, and his mouth drops open as his vocal accompaniment ceases. Television footage from the same period records him
playing Bach at home while wearing a long overcoat – in a whimsical
edit, his dog Banquo is seen yawning at the performance. His half-
sung, half-spoken utterances sound like a sort of glossolalia, as

though Gould is channelling some unseen power, translating the music into his own private language, or that language into music. At one point (though the sequence may be a contrivance of the editor's) he breaks off as if impatiently from playing and stands at a window, where he carries on vocalizing, before returning to the piano. Filmed and televised performances of the mid 1960s and later – by which time he had given up live concerts – show his mannerisms almost unaltered: in middle age his back is a little more arched, his face (half hidden behind large owlish spectacles) perhaps a little closer to the keyboard, the tendency a touch exaggerated by which his left hand, whenever freed by the score, flutters upward into the gestures of a conductor. Descriptions of Gould humming along with his playing – and of the technical lengths to which engineers had to go to remove those sounds as far as possible from his records – do not do justice to the full range of his physical eccentricities: we might say instead that his whole body hummed.

For Gould, the meaning of this corporeal unity with the music was clear: without it he could not concentrate to the extreme degree needed to reproduce his conception of the score. He fretted over the music in the way – the suggestion is Peter Ostwald's – that his mother had perhaps fussed over him as he learned to play, by her side, as a small boy. Playing the piano, on this reading of his eccentricities at the keyboard, returned him to the maternal embrace, an interpretation that Gould knowingly courted when he described the experience of playing as 'womb-like'. But the accommodation between body and instrument is not as straightforward as that interpretation suggests – not least because Gould's relationship with his mother was never very affectionate, but more importantly because he was also known to accompany his playing, in rehearsal, with other sounds which he claimed helped him to concentrate. He had first discovered the trick, he said, when someone switched on a vacuum cleaner while he was practising: the noise, instead of distracting him, seemed to bring him closer to the music. In the same

way, the sound of a radio or television appeared to aid his concentration, and he sometimes played with both switched on in his
apartment or studio.

It is possible that Gould's humming, instead of tying him to the
music by the breath and resonance of his own body, actually functioned to distance him from the immediacy of performance and
shield him from the potentially shaming response of the audience, a
catastrophe that he always feared was imminent. His famous eccentricities were neither the inadvertent expression of a native oddness
(of a piece with old Romantic notions of the asocial genius) nor, in
his own avowed terms, part of the rigorously subjective process of
submerging himself in the music. Instead, his curious habits were a
means of keeping others at bay, an agitated buffer between himself
and the world, a way of being present and absent at the same time.
Until his final withdrawal from the concert stage, his physical
strangeness was the only means at his disposal – especially if we
include in his peculiarities the habit of pulling out of concerts
entirely – to maintain his overt separation from those around him.
Though it had the awkward effect of making him more conspicuous
as a performer, his eccentricity promised a retreat into an almost total artistic solitude. Reflecting on his retirement eight years later in
1972, he would write: 'I realize, of course, that for many people –
particularly those of the older generation – contact with an audience is an indispensable part of their performing craft. In my own
case, I confess it was never so; at best the presence of an audience
was a matter of indifference; at worst, impossible to reconcile with
the essentially private act of music-making.'

*

When Gould retired from live performance in 1964, it was in order
to perfect another way of being there and not-there, to become, in
effect, the ghost of himself. The proximity and realism afforded first
by the telephone and then by the microphone as a means of recording or broadcasting have had the paradoxical effect, increasingly in

the last half-century, of producing deliberately artificial and estrang-
ing works. Turning the mimetic power of recording technology to
unrealistic, even fantastical, ends has long been an essential element
of popular music: one thinks of the space-age echo of early
rock'n'roll records, the massed blare of voices in Phil Spector's
mid-1960s productions, the tape-splice experiments that the late
Beatles could not possibly have replicated in concert. At the time of
Gould's withdrawal from the stage, however, such electronic fan-
tasias had no place in recordings of the classical repertoire, where a
strict fidelity to the unique performance remained the rule. Of
course, as Gould himself was to point out some years later in a
radio documentary about the process of recording, there were substantial differences between recording techniques: notably, by the
1960s, between the (modern, American) replication of the rever-
beration of an intimate space such as the studio itself, and the (older,
European) fidelity to the sonic expanse of the traditional concert
hall. But what Gould discovered in the studio was something else:
the means to bypass 'live' performance entirely and produce a
montage of his best takes that existed only on tape.

What he feared most about the concert hall, he said, was the lack
of a second take: the judgement of the audience – 'a gallery of witnesses' – was immediate and final. The only way to counter the
inherent peremptoriness of the concert situation was to pretend that
the audience was not there. Swaddled in scarves and gloves, immured
in his own voice and body, he could create on-stage, he hoped, the
conditions he relished in the studio. Gould was familiar with the
studio from an unusually early age: he gave his first live radio performance in December 1950, aged eighteen. He quickly learned that
listening to recordings of his practice sessions was an efficient way of
improving his technique. He was one of the first musicians in
Toronto, he claimed, to use 'primitive tape recorders – strapping
the mikes to the sounding board of my piano, the better to emascu-
late Scarlatti sonatas, for example, and generally subjecting both

instruments to whichever imaginative indignities came to mind'. The tape recorder became for him 'the greatest of all teachers', and the studio the refuge where he could be alone with his teacher. In a radio broadcast of 1967, he said: 'I discovered that, in the privacy, the solitude and (if all Freudians will stand clear) the womb-like security of the studio, it was possible to make music in a direct, more personal manner than any concert hall would ever permit . . . I have not since then been able to think of the potential of music (or for that matter of my own potential as a musician) without some reference to the limitless possibilities of the broadcasting/recording medium.' Later, in middle age, his wealth allowed him to hire studios for as long as he liked and even to construct his own, filled with expensive recording equipment, in a hotel room at the Inn on the Park, a short walk from his apartment in Toronto. In a photograph taken there in the mid 1970s, Gould's assistant, Ray Roberts, sits at a cluttered desk against which, in the foreground, a tide of tape machines and mixing consoles is pressing. In the background, an amp or radio tuner sits atop a flickering television – like Elvis Presley and Andy Warhol, Gould hardly ever switched off his TV; his favourite programme was *The Mary Tyler Moore Show* – and the curtains are closed against the city outside. No doubt the windows were shut too, and the heating turned up to eighty degrees Fahrenheit so that it matched the constant temperature of his apartment.

The studio was not only an expression of his desire for solitude, nor simply the instrument, as assuredly as the piano itself, by which he arrived at a perfect technical expression of the sounds he heard in his head. It was also the place where, from the late 1960s onwards, he produced a set of works for radio, each comprising a complex narrative about the solitudes of others, which seem to allegorize his own withdrawal from the world. (In the wake of his retirement from the concert hall, the creative capacities of radio became, along with the artistic adventure of the recording studio, the main outlet for his intellectual and musical energies.) In what has come to be known as his 'Solitude Trilogy', Gould evolved a form he called 'contrapuntal radio': an aural montage of overlapping voices and environmental sounds that demand of the listener a constant creative shuttling between its separate strata. Instead of describing a linear narrative arc, the voices of his interviewees weave a thick texture of sound from which, during repeated listens, one may choose to unpick different threads, or allow oneself to be dazzled by the whole intricate pattern of the work. Whichever way one listens, it soon becomes clear that while the avowed subject of the three programmes is the separation of individuals or communities from the outside world, its real theme is the strict impossibility of such a total solitude. Complete isolation, it transpires, is a state of being that will eventually demand expression or narration to others, while remote communities turn out to be closer-knit, and more demanding of their members' social abilities, than the modern urban world they had thought to leave behind.

The first and most famous programme in the trilogy is *The Idea of North*, aired by the Canadian Broadcasting Corporation on the 28th of December 1967. The second, *The Latecomers*, produced in 1969, is about the pressure exerted on the remote communities of Newfoundland to modernize and urbanize themselves. The third, *The Quiet in the Land*, from 1977, reflects on the history of a Mennonite community near Winnipeg and its contemporary struggles with the ideal of detachment from contemporary society – its members being 'in the world but not of the world'. *The Idea of North* is concerned with a central motif of Canadian culture: the image of the Northern Territories as the nation's frontier and still, by virtue of its climate and topography, a remote and treacherous land that tests the physical and psychological mettle of those who visit and those who choose to live there. There are very few people, writes Gould in the liner notes to the CBC recording, 'who make contact with it and emerge entirely unscathed. Something really does happen to most people who go into the north – they become at least aware of

the creative opportunity which the physical fact of the country rep-
resents and – quite often, I think – come to measure their own
work and life against that rather staggering creative possibility: they
become, in effect, philosophers.' The five voices he marshalled to
essay a description of this challenging territory are eloquent and
insightful on the subject of their northern sequestration. In fact,
they sound not unlike Gould himself, though it is unclear whether
in this instance he scripted any of his speakers, as he was later in the
habit of doing for even the most casual exchange in his radio and
television documentaries. Gould's northern experts include a
nurse, a surveyor and an anthropologist, people who have experienced the territory intimately and with a certain scientific distance,
a circumspect eye trained on the place, their fellow 'northsmen'
and their own reactions. They concur with Gould – whose voice
introduces the hour-long programme, followed by the low rattle of
a train northwards from Winnipeg to Churchill – that the north pits
the individual 'up against himself . . . his own sad self'. It is something akin, says one of them, to the quiet room in which, according
to Blaise Pascal, one ought to remain philosophically still in order
to avoid doing harm in the world. But it is also, says another, a
paradoxical place where distance from civilization throws people
together; afraid of getting lost in the wilderness, they find themselves 'cooped in, in the wide open spaces', subject to all the alli-
ances and rivalries that tiny communities inevitably foster.

Gould himself was only fleetingly acquainted with the north. In
the opening narration to *The Idea of North* he says: 'I've long been
intrigued by that incredible tapestry of tundra and taiga which consti-
tutes the arctic and sub-arctic of our country. I've read about it, written about it, and even pulled up my parka once and gone there. Yet
like all but a very few Canadians I've had no real experience of the
North. I've remained, of necessity, an outsider. And the North has
remained for me a convenient place to dream about, spin tall tales
about and, in the end, avoid.' At first glance, the programme and its

two subsequent companion pieces might be said to embody a fantasy of the musician's: the image of a social and geographic withdrawal from the public life he was forced to lead in the first years of his fame. The mental space afforded by solitude; the application and self-denial needed to survive in an actual or self-described retreat; the rhythms of meditation and practice that such places and communities allow, or demand: all of this seems of a piece with Gould's stated aim to become an artistic hermit. But time and again the programmes in the trilogy complicate that desire by asserting the inevitability of human being-together. The kind of solitude Gould wants may not be possible – and besides, his real urge may not be to disappear from public view but to keep his audience at a distance, the better to anticipate and control their reactions to his work. The 'Solitude Trilogy', far from expressing Gould's ascetic distance from humanity, might best be read as broaching an ambiguous accord with his need for company, acknowledging to himself that he must balance solitude with regular reaching out to others. The trilogy is among his greatest works. (To this non-musician, for whom the *Goldberg Variations* are in technical terms a complete mystery, *The Idea of North* seems to demonstrate a mastery of narrative, tone and sonic nuance, even if it is not quite as formally or technologically audacious as its creator believed.) But it suggests too, in its tape-spliced heteroglossia, an artist who was unsure of the value of dialogue, whose own natural mode in conversation was to drown out the voices of others with his own (hence his scripting of his interlocutors in later broadcasts), to wall himself round with the sound of his own voice as assuredly as he had entrenched himself behind tape machines and mixing desks.

*

As Gould entered middle age, his monologic tendency, already familiar to friends and colleagues, became even more pronounced. When Peter Ostwald first met him, he had noted the young man's propensity for talking down his interlocutor. (Gould preferred one-to-one meetings, and grew uncomfortable when surrounded by unfamiliar groups of people.) Following their first encounter backstage, the pair ate a hurried dinner at a nearby coffee shop before going on to the apartment of a friend of Ostwald's, where Gould played into the small hours and then asked to be driven back to his hotel. All the while – except when discomfited at the apartment by the presence of others – he kept up his erudite, funny and sometimes bizarre monologue, evincing no interest in his new friend's opinions and having eventually to be coaxed out of Ostwald's car by the latter's protestations of exhaustion. Ostwald subsequently became used to Gould's unapologetic late-night phone calls. By the 1970s, he regularly worked until eleven o'clock, and then called friends until two in the morning. (Between four and seven in the morning, he typically ate his only meal of the day – scrambled eggs, salad, toast and tea – at a diner close to his apartment.) The telephone had become a way of keeping in touch with the world while also keeping it at a distance. Working regularly with the CBC, he was allowed to use the free phone line that linked the corporation's offices in Toronto, Ottawa and Montreal. He had a phone in his car, and his domestic bill regularly ran into four figures – in the nine months before his death in 1982, he spent a total of $13,000 on phone calls. Business calls during the day caused him great anxiety, and he always prepared notes beforehand. At night, he relaxed and read essays or whole books to bleary friends, rehearsed to impressively patient colleagues, expounded theories and opinions on music, radio, the future of recording, the careers or private lives of his professional rivals and, of course, the state of his own health.

In July 1975, Gould's mother was hospitalized after a stroke and died soon afterwards. Her son did not visit her – she had taught him to avoid places where germs might gather, so he greatly feared hospitals – but spoke to her by phone for hours each day. By this time, he was regularly consulting three physicians, keeping them secret from each other, as if engaged in a series of clandestine affairs with medical science. The closest of the three surgeries to his home in Toronto was that of Dr John A. Percival, who since 1971 had been dispensing reassurance and refraining from judging too harshly his patient's many eccentricities. Dr Percival later recalled: 'He'd talk for a while, we'd have a very nice visit, and he seemed to get up quite refreshed after.' Gould's chief complaint in recent years had been a light-headedness and loss of balance that Percival put down to labyrinthitis, a disorder of the inner ear usually caused by infection or allergy. (Labyrinthitis can cause tinnitus, which, despite his need for attendant noise, it seems Gould did not suffer from; it may also lead, perhaps more pertinently, to chronic anxiety.) Less than a year after his mother's death, Gould's blood pressure was consistently high, though not, thought Percival, high enough to warrant drug treatment. Gould disagreed, and consulted doctors at Toronto General Hospital and Mount Sinai, where he was prescribed a low dose of an anti-hypertensive drug called methyldopa. He began to measure his blood pressure daily, then hourly – compiling meticulous notes of the figures – using an American-made cuff and monitor. In case this apparatus should fail or prove inaccurate, he bought two more, one German and the other Japanese. It was not his first investment in medical technology: during his first conversation with Ostwald he spoke enthusiastically of the $500 ultrasound machine he was using to treat his aching or spastic muscles.

In addition to his blood pressure, he worried about his chest, fearing in particular the onset of pneumonia or cancer. He was concerned, as he got older, for the condition of his prostate. It does not seem to have occurred to him that the discomfort he felt in the vicinity of his genitals and anus might have been caused by the now ruinous state of his piano stool: the folding chair modified by his father was by this stage frayed and worn down to its wooden frame, and the bare slats pressed on his perineum when he sat down to play. Gould submitted to prostate examinations and barium enemas with the same exhaustiveness he brought to investigations into his liver, spleen and kidneys, or tests of his levels of potassium, cholesterol and uric acid. He made long lists of symptoms before each consultation – one such (partly illegible) inventory, from the 22nd of December 1977, gives some indication of his state of mind:

1. Blood pressure escalating – evening 140/100 even without activity.
2. Chills as indication of rise; on occasion absolutely uncontrollable shivering; most frequently mitigated by even small amounts of cold liquid but sometimes [word illegible] this assistance – alleviated by activity.
3. Nostrils – plugged after conversation, especially animated variety [illegible words] with difficulty in breathing . . .
4. Gastro-intestinal – hiatus hernia style symptoms for 1 *month or so* (!) give history – Barium meal test etc.
5. Sleep 3–4 hours segments for *4-5 months*; currently improved.

Gould's voluminous archives of his symptoms – his diary entries include page after page of blood-pressure statistics and pulse rates – are not without their moments of self-mockery. On the 12th of June 1980, he records the appearance of 'some odd spots . . . on my abdomen – right of the navel, and in the area where the hiatus hernia is often knotted up – and, indeed, has been so for the last couple of days'. At the end of that day's entry he appends an update – 'have taken a bath; spots have disappeared' – to the effect that they were caused by a leaking pen.

Alongside his archival impulse, he had developed an array of odd behaviours to do with writing. He practised his signature repeatedly, fearing that in its execution he described too many squiggles at the end of his first name; he took to signing autographs and other documents with only one 'n'. Cheques were a special source of anxiety for him: not only might he botch the signature and have to start again, but certain cheques – signed, for example, on an inauspicious date – could become unlucky, and would have to be redrawn. Writing notes to colleagues, he would sometimes start his opening sentence dozens of times before it satisfied him. Many of these abandoned drafts were saved and archived, as if he could not bear to relinquish control even of his mistakes.

Gould's diaries and papers also contain countless references to certain ill-defined 'syndromes' and 'phenomena' that seem – though we cannot judge with complete certainty – to denote perfectly ordinary and passing bodily sensations. He often suffered from flatulence, he noted, especially on rising; the various locations of trapped air, and the precise nuances of his awareness of it, are all recorded. He complained of 'back of head phenomenon', 'pressure-point awareness', 'pressure at left temple' and 'pockets of "ulcer-like" pain through to back' after consuming liquids. He discovered black marks on his tongue and experienced 'locked muscles' in his mouth. His urination was frequent and painful. Mostly, however, in a reversion to the weakening and disruption of coordination he suffered after the Steinway incident, he worried about his hands. He now spent hours analysing the movements of his fingers at the keyboard, the sensations he felt while playing – 'harp-like note-by-note sensation . . . crescent-like sensation' – and the resulting effects on the quality of his performances. He struggled to locate the part of his body from which all movements of his fingers, as he saw it, ought to originate or to be regulated: at times, it was a matter especially of controlling his thumbs, at others of conceiving of his neck as the crucial nexus, or of achieving the correct 'image' of the keyboard by sitting further forwards or backwards. Resorting (as he often did when describing his symptoms) to his own idiosyncratic terminology, he tried the 'fall-into-keyboard approach' and 'elevation through upper-arm foreshortening', but after a slight improvement found that he was troubled with 'enlarged veins on hands syndrome'. At one point he even claimed to have discovered a means of governing the movements of his fingers by tightening the muscles of his face: the 'frown (or wrinkled brow) syndrome' seemed to make his hands more responsive, and a wrinkle-free expression to cause them to revert once more to their awkward, intractable state.

Footage of Gould from this period – and there is a lot of it: he made numerous television programmes for the CBC and other broadcasters – shows a middle-aged man who has lost much of his hair but retained (probably without giving it any thought) the swept-back style of his youth, who has run slightly to fat but still seems gangly and adolescent of frame. Colleagues and friends report that by the late 1970s Gould had begun to look haggard and unwell, though he was still tireless in his working habits and enthusiastic about forthcoming projects. His skin looked increasingly grey; his hair (according to one acquaintance who had not seen him for some time) appeared brittle and 'dead-looking'; his movements had slowed and he had developed a tremor in his hands. This last is clearly to be seen in a film of the studio sessions for the new version of the *Goldberg Variations* that he recorded in 1981: he is pale, puffy and more tightly hunched over the keyboard than before.

Some aspects of his physical decline may well have been the results of decades of self-medication. In addition to his usual regimen of tranquillizers, he was now taking drugs for hypertension, headaches, gout and constipation; dosing himself (pointlessly) with antibiotics when colds or flu threatened, as well as with vast quantities of vitamin C; and keeping himself awake through the night with copious amounts of caffeine. Perhaps more ruinous to his health, however, had been his relative self-neglect, which was paradoxically of a piece with his hypochondria. His diet still remained that of a thoughtless teenager. He took no exercise apart from occasional walks with his dog at the Gould family's lakeside house. And of course he pursued a nocturnal existence that, like Proust's, left him chronologically adrift from those around him, so that on those occasions when he had to work during the day he must have seemed dazed and distant from fatigue.

Throughout the summer of 1982, as his fiftieth birthday approached, he complained of a nagging cold. He took Vicks cough syrup, Phenogram CV expectorant, codeine, antibiotics and Percodan, and his symptoms improved, but as autumn settled in he once again felt congested and sluggish. On the afternoon of the 27th of September, two

days after an uneventful birthday during which he spoke to several
friends by phone, he woke with a bad headache and a numb left leg.
Ray Roberts, his assistant, called Dr Percival, who did not consider
the symptoms very alarming until Roberts called back later in the
afternoon to say that Gould's speech was becoming unclear and his
discomfort getting worse. Roberts drove him to Toronto General
Hospital, where a CAT scan confirmed what had already become
obvious: he had suffered a severe stroke. By nightfall, though well
enough to receive visitors, he was confused and disoriented; a nurse
recalled that, shortly before he fell into a coma the following day, he
imagined he was in a recording studio. On the 30th, as fluid began
to collect in his chest and the pressure in his head showed no signs of
reduction, an electroencephalogram revealed that brain activity was
significantly reduced – there was now no chance of his recovering
without severe impairment. He lingered until Monday the 4th of
October, when at eleven in the morning the life-support machine
was switched off and he was pronounced dead. An autopsy, carried
out early that afternoon, discovered two blood clots, one in his
carotid artery, another in the right cavernous sinus; it was the
pressure of this latter that around the time of his birthday had felt
like the return of his summer cold. The autopsy, writes his friend
Peter Ostwald, showed some enlargement of the left side of the
heart, to be expected given his high blood pressure, and a mildly
fatty liver, which Ostwald attributes to his poor diet. The kidneys,
prostate, bones, joints and muscles – all of which he had worried
and complained about for years – were found to be quite healthy.

*

Gould's anxiety over his health, and the curious combination of
self-medication and self-neglect that it led him to maintain over
decades, no doubt contributed to his fragile physical condition in
the last few years of his life. But no matter how neat and tempting
the irony, it would be a gross exaggeration to say that he died
because he was a hypochondriac – we have no way of knowing how

far, if at all, his real organic disease was caused by his style of life, and he shared the predisposing factors for hypertension (and thus for stroke) with too many others for his physicians or biographers to make definitive pronouncements on the matter. What we can say with some certainty is that his hypochondria was ravelled up for most of his life with his prodigious talent – his physical inhibitions and ailments allowed him to sequester himself from the curiosity and judgement of his public, while his innate sense of the dramatic allowed him to announce his withdrawal with a sulky flourish.

Illness and art were the avowed pretexts for his preferred soli-tude, but his bodily wariness and waywardness constituted too a mode of being present to that public, almost a form of exhibition-ism: in his tics and tremors at the piano, and in the hermetic incan-tations with which he accompanied his playing, Gould performed his genius, his solitude, his strangeness, his very hypochondria itself. The great paradox of his performing life, and of his life in general, is the way he exported his presence far beyond the stated borders of his temperament and constitution, all the while claiming a jealous protectionism at the level of both making music and being in the world. For a hypochondriac who was apparently so keen to compose himself, to protect his physical integrity from assault, he did a remarkably thorough job of losing his composure and blurring the edges of his bodily being: first by his numerous and highly visi-ble eccentricities, and second by his replicating himself – his voice and his playing – in the studio. He may be said, without straining the metaphor too far, to have unravelled himself like a spool of tape, and edited this single strand into a kind of fractured psychic and corporeal montage, to have made a living artwork out of anxi-ety. In the process of securing his privacy and physical inviolability, he made public his vulnerability and his confusion, and allowed himself, in a sense peculiar to himself, to be touched.

9. Andy Warhol's Magic Disease

'I never fall apart because I never fall together.'

Andy Warhol, *The Philosophy of Andy Warhol: (From A to B and Back Again)*

Andy Warhol lies face down on a pale parquet floor, cushioned by a plastic or rubber mat covered with a dark towel. His silver wig obscures his face: an acrylic mop at the end of a spindle-thin and pallid body. He is naked but for a pair of white briefs and a corset that bisects his body like the hinged waist of a plastic doll; Warhol looks as though he might buckle or even snap in two if roughly handled. This grisly impression is especially irresistible because above the artist kneels a heavily muscled blond masseur, who grasps Andy's left foot firmly with both hands, as if intending to wrench off his leg. The younger man's face is also hidden by his thick hair, and he wears only a pair of tight-fitting jeans, making his body seem a cruelly attractive counter-image of the piteous, brittle form on the floor in front of him.

In this photograph, taken in 1983 by his assistant Christopher Makos and rarely reproduced since, Andy Warhol's body (as so often) is hard to look at. It is not just because, as he put it many times in his diaries, he had a 'bad body'. His already slight frame had been further weakened by childhood illness, and although he tried inter-mittently to improve his physique – he attended a gym in his youth and later engaged a personal trainer – he never attained anything remotely resembling the bodies of the male actors, models and hus-tlers who populate his films of the 1960s and his nude photographs of the early 1980s. He was shot and badly wounded in 1968, and was left with a hernia he never had corrected – hence the corset, which, he may have hoped, gave him a semblance of the inverted-triangle torso that had been the mainstream male ideal (both gay and straight) when he was a young man in the 1950s. In middle age, his weight fluctuated: he looked alternately emaciated and slightly flabby, with no healthy mean. His skin was pale and blotchy, with open pores and frequent pimples – a remnant again of his childhood afflictions, made worse, if anything, by adult recourse to crude cosmetic treatments. He had lost much of his hair in his twenties, and the succession of blond, grey, white and finally silver wigs he wore made him look scarcely human: a black-clad mannequin with a spectral aspect whom gossip columnists, towards the end of his life, delighted in calling 'Death's undertaker'. But it is not the manifold failings of the Warholian body, nor its famous (and false) 'asexuality', that make it so difficult to look at head on, even in this small black-and-white snapshot. It is rather the sense that what one is seeing is both strenuously artificial and oddly blurred at the same time: that in the countless photographs and miles of footage of him, Warhol is instantly recognizable and yet, beyond the props and prosthetics of his public image, surprisingly hard to describe.

Warhol tried to give himself a 'good body', or to contrive the appearance of a good body, and knew that both efforts only made him look odder, like more of a 'freak' – so in response he claimed to embrace his own peculiarity, turning his body problems into a provocation. But the ruse only worked up to a point: until his death in 1987, he remained genuinely preoccupied with the problem of his body, with the problem of having a body and what (or what not) to do with it, and with whom. He was tormented by beauty, but also by the threat of illness and its remembered reality. Warhol was a hypochondriac for whom health and aesthetics were inextricably linked, an artist who confronted the truth of the body as fearlessly as he did its fantasies, and yet remained quite unable, in private, to accommodate himself to the reality of his own physical decline and the illnesses (and deaths) of those closest to him. In his pathological investment in the ideas of beauty and ugliness, health and disease, and in his inability to tell those two continuums apart, he is our contemporary. Warhol's fears are our own, and we have to choose between the conflicting means he found to express and assuage them.

*

The origins of Warhol's hypochondria, as of the prodigious value he put on physical beauty, are superficially easy to discern. In his 1975 book *The Philosophy of Andy Warhol: (From A to B and Back Again)*, he claims to have had 'three nervous breakdowns when I was a child, spaced a year apart. One when I was eight, one at nine, and one at ten. The attacks – St. Vitus Dance – always started on the first day of summer vacation.' This is too neat a summation of his childhood career in illness, characteristically so – to a journalist, Warhol once quipped that he became unwell simply because 'I was weak and I ate too much candy.' According to his brother Paul Warhola, Andy had already been sickly for some years before the crisis that seems to have changed him for good. At the age of two, his eyes swelled up and had to be bathed with boric acid. At four, he broke his arm when he fell on some streetcar tracks near his home, but for two days he told nobody about his accident; when he did, his mother, Julia Warhola, assumed he had sustained only a minor injury. When she discovered the truth some months later, the bone had set in a curve and his arm had to be broken again and straightened. His secrecy on the subject certainly prefigures his later reactions to his own and others' illnesses, but it is perfectly explicable too in terms of a guilty child's conscience, pricked or not by prior parental warnings. He also had scarlet fever at six, and his tonsils out at seven. There is nothing singular about those episodes except the meanings he and his family attached to them in retrospect: they were part of the narrative of his physical and emotional enfeeblement.

The more serious illness, the affliction that altered Andy for the rest of his life, was rheumatic fever, which he came down with at the age of eight, in 1936. Up to 20 per cent of childhood and adolescent cases of rheumatic fever may develop into St Vitus's Dance, or Sydenham's chorea (named after the seventeenth-century English physician Thomas Sydenham), a disease of the nervous system that is characterized by involuntary movement, disturbed gait, grimacing and hypotonia or abnormally low muscle tone. According to his biographer Victor Bockris, in the wake of his first bout of fever Andy developed tremors and slurred speech, and had difficulty performing simple tasks such as writing his name or tying his shoelaces. He became nervous at school, where his tics and his physical weakness drew the attention of bullies. The Warhola family doctor recommended complete physical and mental rest, and Andy was confined to bed for a month.

He recalls this period, during which his mother lavished him with attention, in his *Philosophy*: 'My mother would read to me in her thick Czechoslovakian accent as best she could and I would always say, "Thanks Mom", after she finished with Dick Tracy, even if I hadn't understood a word. She'd give me a Hershey bar every time I finished a page in my colouring book.' After a month's rest he seemed to have recovered, but he baulked at returning to school. His father, Andrei, was away, and so the family's next-door neighbour, John Elachko, tried to take charge of the situation, grabbing the frightened child by the shoulder and shouting: 'You're going to school!' Andy promptly collapsed, and began to kick Elachko, who nonetheless insisted on dragging him to the nearby school. A relapse followed, and another protracted stay in bed. After he had finally recovered, he was left with reddish-brown blotches on his face, back, chest, arms and hands. He was left too with an abiding sense of his own frailty and difference. In the aftermath of his illness, according to friends and family, the young Andrew Warhola became even more timid, and more attached to his mother, than he had been before. While she indulged his delicate constitution and personality, his father was more distant and traditionally austere in his expectations of his three sons. Still, the whole family began to orient itself around the sensitivity of its youngest member, acknowledging his 'nervous' (also, by this time, artistic) temperament.

By the time Andy was in his early adolescence, his father had health problems of his own, suffering from recurring jaundice. The removal of his gall bladder seemed to clear up the problem, but before long his liver had begun to fail – according to Julia Warhola, Andrei and his workmates drank contaminated water while working at a West Virginia mine, and the doctors could do nothing for him. Whatever the cause of his illness, Warhol's father, in his early fifties, went into a rapid decline: he became housebound during 1939, when his youngest son was eleven years old. He died in 1942, having declared a few days earlier to his son John that he would not survive another stay in hospital. Paul Warhola recalled his brother Andy's reaction when their father's body was laid out in the family's Pittsburgh house: 'He just didn't wanna see Dad. When they brought the body into the house Andy was so scared he ran and hid under the bed. But we didn't push Andy too much when Dad died because we didn't want him to have a relapse. We were always fearful that his nervous condition might come back.' According to Victor Bockris, Andy was taken to the funeral, but such was his later unwillingness to face the reality of death that it may well have been the only funeral he ever attended.

Two years later, Julia, who for some time had been suffering from a debilitating case of haemorrhoids, was diagnosed with cancer of the colon and told that surgery offered her only hope of survival. It seems that Andy's Czech mother – whether due to confusion and distress or to the fact that she was still not (and never would be) fluent in English – failed to grasp the implications of the procedure to which she was about to consent. When she woke from the operation and discovered that she would have to use a colostomy bag for the rest of her life, she fell into a depression. Julia and her sons were later convinced that she had not had cancer at all, and that the devastating surgery had been totally unnecessary. (Julia would live for another twenty-eight years, much of that time spent living with Andy in New York.) Warhol was then aged sixteen, and according to his brothers had expected his mother to die. Henceforth, he felt a horror of the obscure power of hospital doctors to take control of the patient's body. Years later, in a diary entry dictated shortly after watching the 1978 television drama *Holocaust*, he would compare the relationship of doctor and patient to that of concentration-camp guard and inmate: 'They gassed the little girl. I was thinking everybody really is in their own little world. They tell you something, and you don't know what's going on, they're the ones who know, you're at their mercy . . . It's like when you go to a hospital – they take you and they do anything with you, because you don't know about their world.' The comparison is excessive, even hysterical, but it indicates where Warhol's adolescent horror of the hospital would eventually lead him. At the same time, he developed an equally sickening fear of what the body itself was capable of: it threatened, like his mother's body, to expose its inner workings in a livid and shameful way, confusing the categories of inside and outside, surface and depth, human and inhuman.

*

By the time Warhol had his first success as a fine artist in the early 1960s – he had spent the previous decade establishing himself as a commercial artist – he was tormented by ugliness rather than illness. Photographs of him before his attacks of chorea show an angelic blond child; even in adolescence, from the right angle, he could look handsome in a way soon to be popularized by James Dean. But already, as his complexion worsened, his brothers had taken to calling him Andy the Red-Nosed Warhola. As a young man trying to make his way as an illustrator in the New York fashion world, he presented an unprepossessing exterior. Tina Fredericks, editor of *Glamour* magazine, recalled her first meeting with 'a pale, blotchy boy, diffident almost to the point of disappearance but somehow immediately and immensely appealing. He seemed all one colour: pale chinos, pale wispy hair, pale eyes, a strange beige birthmark over the side of his face.' In the *Philosophy*, he tells an implausible anecdote to account for this eerie pallor:

I had another skin problem, too – I lost all my pigment when I was eight years old. Another name people used to call me was 'Spot'. This is how I think I lost my pigment: I saw a girl walking down the street and she was two-toned and I was so fascinated I kept following her. Within two months I was two-toned myself. And I hadn't even known the girl – she was just somebody I saw on the street. I asked a medical student if he thought I caught it just by looking at her. He didn't say anything.

We can readily grasp his ambiguous attitude to his own physiognomy in an earlier passage from the same book. Here is Warhol in dialogue with his friend and Factory associate Brigid Polk ('B'), describing his skincare routine, reading from his press clippings and somehow revelling in his own imperfections:

Okay, B, okay. So now the pimple's covered. But am I covered? I have to look in the mirror for more clues. Nothing is missing. It's all there. The affectless gaze. The diffracted grace . . . The bored languor, the wasted pallor . . . The chic freakiness, the basically passive astonishment, the enthralling secret knowledge . . . The chintzy joy, the revelatory tropisms, the chalky, puckish mask, the slightly Slavic look . . . The childlike, gum-chewing naïveté, the glamour rooted in despair, the self-admiring carelessness, the perfected otherness, the wispiness, the shadowy, voyeuristic, vaguely sinister aura, the pale, soft-spoken magical presence, the skin and bones . . . The albino-chalk skin. Parchmentlike. Reptilian. Almost blue . . . The knobby knees. The roadmap of scars. The long bony arms, so white they look bleached. The arresting hands. The pinhead eyes. The banana ears . . . The graying lips. The shaggy silver-white hair, soft and metallic. The cords of the neck standing out around the big Adam's apple. It's all there, B. Nothing is missing. I'm everything my scrapbook says I am.

Another friend (and probable lover), Carl Willer, recalled that in Warhol's mid twenties 'he had a lot of trouble with his skin and was forever having eruptions of pimples like a teenager. He was very conscious of that and he had a great deal of guilt about all this eating of sweet things because he thought that was making him fat and causing these skin eruptions. He was acutely self-conscious. He thought he was totally unattractive, too short, too pudgy. He thought he was grotesque.' It was Willer who persuaded Warhol to start wearing a wig, after he tired of seeing him in a cap with a snap-down brim, even at dinner parties. Andy bought a light-brown toupee, the first of several hundred he would order regularly from a Mr Bocchicchio in Queens; their colours gradually became paler. (He seems rarely, or never, to have thrown away the older wigs, preferring to archive them along with other ephemera in a succession of 'time capsules'.) Later, Warhol would rationalize his move towards a spectrally silver wig in terms of what was then a besetting problem of his middle years:

I decided to go gray so nobody would know how old I was and I would look younger to them than how old they thought I was. I would gain a lot by going gray: (1) I would have old problems, which were easier to take than young problems, (2) everyone would be impressed by how young I looked, and (3) I would be relieved of the responsibility of acting young – I could occasionally lapse into eccentricity or senility and no one would think anything of it because of my gray hair. When you've got gray hair, every move you make seems 'young' and 'spry', instead of just being normally active. It's like you're getting a new talent.

With the problem of his hair now partly solved – though it would be several years before he began to treat his wig as a trademark rather than simply a cosmetic prosthesis — there remained the matter of his complexion. In the autumn of 1956, Warhol's doctor recommended a procedure by which the unsightly red skin on his nose would be scraped away; he later referred to it as having his nose 'sanded'. The treatment was carried out at St Luke's Hospital in New York. The scars took two weeks to heal, after which time Andy was horrified to find that there had been no improvement whatsoever to the skin on his nose; in fact, he was convinced it looked even worse. Charles Lisanby, a friend with whom Andy had long been in love, recalled: 'He had very definitely the idea that if he had an operation on his nose then suddenly that would change his life. He thought he would become an Adonis, and that I and other people would suddenly think that he was as physically attractive as many of the people that he admired because of their attractiveness. And when that didn't happen, he became rather angry.' It was around this time that he first tried to improve his muscle tone by attending a gym and performing regular push-ups at home, but although acquaintances from the time recall some alteration to his physique, the regime had no long-term effect on his self-confidence. He would continue to live in one body and long for another.

*

Warhol, we might say, possessed two bodies — one real and one fantastical — and was possessed as an artist by the idea of such doubling. This is not a controversial thing to claim about his art or his character: repetition is an obvious and essential trait of his most famous paintings. His early renderings of such everyday icons as the Coca-Cola bottle and the Campbell's soup can only began to acquire their properly Warholian blank allure once he had hit upon the idea of repeating the images with minor differences, whether of painted texture (as in the increasing simplicity of the Coke bottles) or the objects' own appearance (the thirty-two varieties of soup, with their slightly different labels). And his singular insight into the mask-like nature of modern celebrity depends upon its endless replication in the silk-screened faces of Liz, Marilyn, Elvis, Mick and Mao. All of this repetition is familiar to the point of War-hol's ubiquity (and thus near-invisibility) in contemporary culture. The less well-known, and in some ways more acute, investigation of what it means to be embodied, and not merely to desire but to covet the body of another person, is to be found in Warhol's films of the mid 1960s, and to a lesser degree in his video works of the subsequent two decades. It is there that he attended most carefully and painfully to the beauty and the betrayals of the human body, and explored the agonies of being in proximity, real or imagined, to the kind of body he wished to own. Warhol, in other words, diagnosed on-screen his own strain or style of hypochondria: the films are his way of splitting himself in two and allowing his bad body to express its longing for the good.

Beyond frequent nudity and para-sexual content, Warhol's films are perhaps best known for being, in a special sense, boring. They are considered boring, usually, for one of two reasons: because of their scripted or improvised dialogue, which rarely advances beyond stilted bickering or seemingly opiated meander; or because – and this provokes the more interesting sort of boredom – so little actu-ally 'happens'. (In the most notorious instance, he took his camera to the forty-first floor of the Time-Life Building and pointed it at the Empire State Building for six hours and thirty-six minutes; *Empire* is unique among Warhol's films in being void of people, apart from a brief appearance by the artist's reflection at the begin-ning of the seventh reel.) But time and again his mute or almost mute subjects, or the 'characters' in more dialogue-heavy films such as *Chelsea Girls*, seem to compare each other's bodies or body images in ways that tell of the artist's own desires and anxieties. In his 1965 film *My Hustler*, for example, two men, both male prosti-tutes, played by the handsome blond Paul America and the older Joe Campbell, preen themselves in front of a mirror, the older man trying to coax the younger into admitting that he is a hustler. The evasive Mr America is perhaps Campbell's (and certainly Warhol's) projection of himself: a figure with the passive, laconic glamour of an Elvis or Marilyn painting. What is usually deprecated as Warhol's 'voyeurism' is actually a rapt concentration on the body of another person as a possible projection of one's own, or on the bodies of two (or more) who are engaged in the same act of projection or mirroring as Warhol himself.

The doubling is not restricted to those films in which there is more than one body on-screen at any one time. Warhol's first film, *Sleep*, made in 1963, is composed of fifty three-minute reels showing the naked, sleeping body of the poet John Giorno. It is certainly an erotic film – the artist and the poet had a frustrated relationship, and Warhol fragments Giorno's body in what might be considered a fetishistic manner – but also a film about the very fact of being embodied, and being at home in one's body in a way that Warhol himself, watching the slightly slowed-down frames of this five-hour film, could only dream about. *Sleep*, in other words, is a film as much concerned with the fantasies that may be projected onto the sleeping body as it is with Giorno's body itself. This sense of the single body or face on-screen being imaginatively doubled is there too in the 472 short, silent, black-and-white *Screen Tests* that Warhol made between 1964 and 1966. His sitters included Marcel Duchamp, John Ashbery, Dennis Hopper and Bob Dylan, as well as numerous regular faces from the Factory and the New York art-world, and society names. For three minutes, the subject sits in front of the camera – usually in tight close-up – and keeps, or loses, his or her composure. It is as if what is being tested is not, as we might suspect of Warhol, the subject's charisma, but his or her self-possession. The young critic Susan Sontag, for example, addresses the camera stiffly in the first of her seven *Screen Tests*, but then gradually assumes a degree of confidence that sees her leaning into the camera in an almost conspiratorial fashion. At one sitting, however, boredom seems to get the better of her, and she begins to leer and grin awkwardly at the camera, having abandoned her former sense of bodily propriety.

The films from this period that most rigorously examine Warhol's own doubled sense of his body, its failings, and the fantasy of having a 'good' body, are *Blow Job*, from 1964, and *Outer and Inner Space*, completed the following year. *Blow Job* lasts forty-one minutes, although like many of Warhol's films of this period it was shot at twenty-four frames per second and projected at sixteen – the action was over quicker than the film, which has a slightly dream-like pace. It shows the head of a young man, leaning against a rough brick wall and gradually, so it seems, giving himself up to the act that only the title of the film actually affirms. The man's face is frequently beatific, his head thrust back so that it becomes an abstract arrangement of shadows, his eyes, when they come into view again, glassy and introverted. Eventually, as he trembles and bites his lip, he seems to have reached orgasm, and even lights a cigarette in the final reel; the viewer, however, will never know if he has been acting or not. *Blow Job* is perhaps the most mysterious of Warhol's films: even the artist was subsequently unable to recall who the actor was, and it is left to the viewer to decide whether the person giving the blow job is male or female. But what is not ambiguous at all is the centrality to the film of physical abandon, and of a male ideal that Warhol wishes to share with the viewer.

The star of *Outer and Inner Space* is Edie Sedgwick, the young, rich, unstable and boyishly beautiful 'Superstar' who had recently become Warhol's constant social companion and bleached doppelgänger. *Outer and Inner Space* is projected on two screens, on each of which Edie appears; she was filmed twice during the same session. In both images, she sits in front of a video recording of her own face looking apprehensively upwards in profile. The film lasts just over half an hour, during which time Edie poses, fidgets, giggles, crosses her eyes at the camera, sneezes, jumps in surprise as her double sneezes on the screen behind her, and all the while addresses (though the soundtrack is mostly too muffled to hear what she says) an off-screen presence that can only be Warhol himself. At least one unobservant critic has commented of this film that it depicts a vacuous character, 'glassy-eyed' and frivolous; even attentive viewers seem to concur that Warhol here exposes the emptiness of his sitter as a two-dimensional product of the TV era. Although, to some degree, *Outer and Inner Space* may be said to punish its subject for her physical perfection – making her confront her own grainy, faltering image on the screen – what Warhol captures at the same time in the face and body of Edie Sedgwick is precisely her presence, and self-presence: a perfect fit – the fit he knew he did not possess – between thought and expression. She is entirely in control of every small, birdlike movement of her hands, of the merest twitch of her nose or flicker of an eye away from the artist and towards his camera. Later, in his *Philosophy*, he would claim to have been appalled, on the one occasion when they shared a bed, by Edie's constant drug- or anxiety-induced tics as she slept, but in *Inner and Outer Space* her incessant mobility is exactly what Warhol, shut up in the fragile, static image he had by then contrived for his bad body, must have envied most.

*

On Monday, the 3rd of June 1968, Warhol's 'bad body' suffered more violently than ever before the confusion of inside and outside, human and inhuman, living and dead. At about 4.15 p.m., Valerie Solanas, sole member of the Society for Cutting Up Men and a minor figure on the edges of his coterie, walked into the fifth-floor office at 33 Union Square West to which Warhol had relocated the Factory earlier in the year, and fired a handgun three times at him, missing twice but hitting him in the side with the third bullet. Thinking she had killed him, Solanas then turned on the others in the office, shooting the art critic and curator Mario Amaya in the hip before levelling her revolver at the head of Fred

Hughes, Warhol's business manager, who was by then kneeling and begging for his life. The gun jammed, the elevator door opened, and Solanas fled. Warhol, in agony, lay fighting for breath beneath his desk, the bullet (as Bockris recounts it) having 'entered his right side, passed through his lung and ricocheted through his oesophagus, gall bladder, liver, spleen, and intestines before exiting his left side, leaving a large gaping hole'. An ambulance took Warhol and Amaya to Columbus Hospital; en route, the driver announced that for an extra $15 he could turn on the siren. At the emergency room, the doctors had no idea who their patient was; as he drifted out of consciousness, Warhol heard voices muttering 'forget it' and 'no chance'. At 4.51 p.m. he was pronounced clinically dead; it was apparently only at the insistence of Amaya, who was being treated in the same room, that the head of the medical team, Dr Giuseppe Rossi, attempted to revive him, opening his chest and massaging the heart.

Warhol spent five and a half hours on the operating table. The surgeons removed his ruptured spleen and the bottom part of his punctured right lung, and repaired as far as possible the damage to his other vital organs. Having determined from his regular physician that the patient was allergic to penicillin, Dr Rossi administered a different antibiotic, sewed up Warhol's chest and abdomen, and wrote up his notes, which appear to suggest that the bullet came from the opposite direction to that posited in most biographical accounts:

This patient was brought to the emergency room via ambulance and at the time of admission was without blood pressure and heartbeat. He had a gunshot wound entering the left chest at the midaxillary line at the ninth interspace and exiting in the right chest, midaxillary line at the fourth interspace. He was in deep shock and there was profuse bleeding from the right chest wound . . . The patient was immediately intubated and via a venous cutdown a large amount of Ringer's lactate solution was injected with no visible effects on blood pressure and other vital signs. He was taken to the operating room and explorations of the right chest, left chest and abdomen were carried out with control of bleeding and evacuation of blood volume.

According to Paul Warhola, his brother's doctor had told him in the recovery room that Andy had perhaps 'a fifty-fifty chance of survival'. At six the next morning, the hospital announced that, having lived through the night, he would more than likely recover; New York newspapers proclaimed: 'ACTRESS SHOOTS ANDY WARHOL' and 'ANDY WARHOL FIGHTS FOR LIFE'. Later that day, as he lay in bed, his head swimming unpleasantly because of the painkilling medication, Warhol heard in the distance the voice of a television announcer: 'Kennedy . . . assassin . . . shot.' Media attention turned quickly away from the perforated body in a private room at Columbus Hospital.

In the aftermath of the shooting, Warhol fled more swiftly than ever from any reminder of physical fragility and death. When friends phoned him at the hospital, he recalled, they often cried until he could steer the conversation towards more 'gossipy' subject matter. His sole act of bravado was to have himself photographed by Richard Avedon with his shirt raised and his scars showing. The image suggests that he had come to terms with his injuries and wore the scars as a new addition to the freakish paraphernalia of his public image. But the more accurate record of Warhol's attitude to his body after he was shot is to be found in a portrait painted of him by Alice Neel in 1970. Here, he sits hunched and half naked on a bed; the same pattern of scars as appears in the Avedon photographs is there, but so too is a frailty that the former image does not capture: his shoulders are narrow, his legs skeletal and chest flabby, hands clasped between his knees, and eyes closed as if he cannot bear to look at his own ravaged body. The corset that keeps him intact, where his ruined abdominal muscles can do so no

longer, seems loose around his middle, as though it might not quite
hold him together.

*

There now began a pattern of preoccupation and avoidance that
would last the rest of Warhol's life, and which may in fact have
precipitated his early death at the age of fifty-eight. On the one
hand, he became increasingly disturbed – more than is usual, that
is, in middle age – by the proximity of illness and death: the diaries
he began to dictate (initially for the purpose of recording his daily
expenses) in the late 1970s express time and again his fear of specific illnesses and his horror of ageing. He had recourse to various
alternative remedies for his symptoms, and regularly entertained
new theories as to his optimum weight, how much exercise he
ought to take and which treatment or skincare regime might at last
rid him of his pimples. On the other hand, he tried to erase the
memory of his time in hospital, and to deny the reality of the gall
bladder problems that were first diagnosed three years afterwards.
Benjamin Liu, an assistant towards the end of Warhol's life, recalled
that he would cross the street rather than pass by Cabrini Hospital
when he went for a walk. For years, he had spoken of the recently
deceased as having 'gone to Bloomingdales', and Liu describes how,
in the 1980s, he would ritually announce, as they passed by the
store, that his mother was inside, shopping. (Julia Warhola had
died in 1972, her son having sent her back to his family in Pittsburgh when she became ill; although her death sent him into a deep
depression, many of his friends and associates in New York did not
even know she had died.) He thus contrived to ignore the most
obvious of his own ailments and the illnesses, and even the deaths,
of those who were, or had been, close to him. When he was told
that Edie Sedgwick had died (of a barbiturate overdose) in November 1971, he is said to have inquired how she died and then, apparently unperturbed, to have asked who would inherit her money.

Warhol's diary begins in 1976, and quickly establishes the

structure of his anxieties: seemingly serious health scares are frequently inseparable in his mind from minor problems and from the illnesses of those around him that he fears, against any tangible evidence, he is likely to catch. In June 1977, on the advice of his regular physician Denton Cox, he had a biopsy on a worrisome lump on his neck. A month earlier, he had heard of a couple in his social circle both suffering from the same cancer, and fretted to the diary: 'I guess you *can* catch it from other people.' Now, even having received a negative result of his own biopsy (he went to church soon after to thank God for the all-clear), Warhol was extremely unsettled by the sight of other patients when he went to have his stitches removed at the hospital: 'Cabbed to Sloan-Kettering ($2.50) and the waiting room there freaked me out. People with noses cut off. It was so shocking.' In the months that followed, he worried that the medicine he was taking to clear up his acne was making him ill, that a slight fever was failing to respond to prescription drugs, that an outbreak of legionnaires' disease in the neighbourhood might reach the Factory, that on vacation in Colorado he suffered chest pains at altitude and that too many people were coughing in his presence. 'I bought some garlic pills,' he recorded on the 8th of April 1980, 'because I just read a book that said garlic is against sickness, and I believe that, it seems right. Forgot to say that at a cocktail party the other night a woman came over and kissed me on the lips and then said, "I'm so sick, I'm dying." Why do people do that? Are they trying to pass their disease on to somebody so *they* won't have it anymore?'

A year later, claiming to the diary that he had been diagnosed with pneumonia, he traced the illness to his having drunk 'a really cold daiquiri. I can feel it, it pierced me . . . And what I forgot to say is the other night I had a blackout like I used to when I was little. At first I thought it was because of flash bulbs, but there were no flash bulbs really right there, and it got me so scared that I'm having a brain tumour or that I'm getting the *Dark Victory* disease.' This last

reference is to the 1939 film, starring Bette Davis as Judith Tra-
herne, a carefree, athletic and hard-drinking debutante who after a
series of falls in her early twenties is diagnosed with a brain tumour.
Her physician, a pioneer in brain surgery, operates and discovers
that the disease is incurable, but will present no more symptoms
until just before her death, when she will suddenly go blind and
expire painlessly within hours. Judith returns to her former life,
falls in love with her increasingly tormented doctor, but discovers
the diagnosis among his papers just as they are to be married – it is
then her turn to conceal the truth, some months later, when the
darkness starts to encroach as he is about to travel to a medical con-
ference. Davis's character dies peacefully and heroically, alone in
her bed, the screen fading to black at the last. The melodramatic
plot is almost stereotypically suited to Warhol's camp tastes (as a
sickly child, he had pored obsessively over Hollywood magazines
while in his mother's care), but it is surely of a piece too with his
actual, convoluted attitudes to illness and death: the anxious bal-
ancing act, poised between knowledge and ignorance, secrecy and
bravado, which he sustained in the last decades of his life. Conjec-
turing almost daily about the state of his own health and the hale or
failing bodies with which he came into contact, he seemed alternately ready to believe anything, and to doubt everything.

This state of devious confusion extended, throughout the late
1970s, to the way Warhol conceived of his own physical appearance. In January 1979, he informs the diary that he has had the
unsightly veins on his nose removed: 'It doesn't last, but for a while
it looks great. For about three months, then you have it done again
. . . The doctor who sandpapered my nose twenty years ago had
done a bad job, gone too deep.' He compares himself to friends
such as Truman Capote, then recovering from a facelift, and Diana
Vreeland, whom he observes anxiously, perhaps superstitiously,
exerting herself to look youthful and vigorous in front of Cecil Bea-
ton, who had recently suffered a stroke. He comments time and

again on the weight of various friends and associates – he seems
especially to relish the moments when 'beauties' such as Liz Taylor,
Bianca Jagger or Jerry Hall (whose pregnancy does not allow her to
escape his judgement) are seen to have let themselves go. Throughout the diaries, he regularly retreats in the hours before a social
engagement to 'glue myself together'; he is referring specifically to
his wig, but the phrase suggests a more generalized fear that he
might come apart in public if he is not vigilant enough, that his
sense of his physical self is still precarious and provisional. He
exhibits a strange admixture of middle-aged ennui about his appearance and a still youthful, callow apprehension: 'Every single thing I
do looks strange. I have such a strange walk and a strange look. If I
could only have been a peculiar comic in the movies, I would have
looked like a puppet. But it's too late. What's wrong with me?'

While he fretted about his appearance and about the numerous
medical threats to his person, Warhol effectively ignored the one
dangerous illness from which he was actually suffering. In the early
1970s, Denton Cox had already informed him that he needed gall
bladder surgery, but such was his patient's fear of hospitals that he
simply refused to countenance an operation. Over the next decade
and a half, he endeavoured to manage his symptoms by regulating
his diet – an almost impossible discipline for Warhol, who was just
as addicted in adulthood to cakes and candy as he had been as a cosseted child – and by recourse to a variety of medicines, among them
prescription painkillers, tranquillizers (he worried in June 1981
that he was becoming addicted to Valium) and a new drug, as yet
unapproved in the United States, that he had specially imported
from Japan. In July 1981, Brigid Polk, one of the few denizens of
the bohemian Factory of the 1960s who had made the transition to
Warhol's more commercial studio operation of the subsequent
decades, phoned him to say that 'she'd just gotten out of the hospital. She has gallstones the size of grapenuts. She said they want to
operate. I told her they *always* want to operate, that it's like doing

portraits, you don't care who you do as long as you have someone
to do. Because that's how they make their bucks.' He had begun the
1980s much as he started the 1970s: convinced that he must never
set foot in a hospital again, no matter how elaborate his anxieties,
no matter how acute his symptoms. In the years that followed, as a
new and more terrifying threat appeared, his fears were only to
become more involuted and isolating.

*

On the 3rd of July 1981, the *New York Times* published a short
article by Lawrence K. Altman on the mysterious appearance of forty-
one cases of Kaposi's sarcoma in New York and California. This
rare cancer, sometimes diagnosed after a slow onset of up to ten
years, usually befell elderly men, announcing itself by red or purple
bruise-like patches on the skin (especially the skin of the legs) that
gradually turned brown. (Altman noted, in what now seems an
ominous aside, that while there were about two cases for every
3 million people in the United States, Kaposi's sarcoma accounted
for up to 9 per cent of all cancers in a belt across equatorial Africa,
where it commonly affected children and young adults.) The novel
and often rapidly fatal form of the disease appeared not only to
strike young men, but young homosexual men – especially those,
wrote Altman, who had had many sexual encounters and multiple
partners. A geographical pattern was conjectured too: several of
the patients in California had been recent or frequent visitors to
New York. The illness seemed to progress at a startling rate, the
characteristic lesions appearing simultaneously on several parts of
the body. As yet, no cause could be found for the alarming and
unprecedented outbreak, though the reporting doctors noted that
their patients had often also been treated for such viral infections as
herpes and hepatitis B, and were not infrequently drug users. A
viral origin was indicated, though it was to be three years before it
was definitively isolated and named. In the meantime, a chaos of
ignorance, anxiety, distrust and frank intolerance surrounded the

new 'gay cancer' and the young gay men who were its most statisti-
cally visible victims.

Warhol's response to the unfolding AIDS crisis of the 1980s was
predictably confused. He feared what he did not know, partly
because, at first, nobody knew anything about the cause of the epidemic, its potential amplitude or duration, the transmission of the
virus or the precautions and treatments that might slow its advance.
As the facts slowly emerged, and the devastation the disease had
wrought became clear, Warhol publicly supported New York AIDS
charities by his presence at fundraising events and by the sale of
donated paintings. His private attitudes, however – while by no
means peculiar to him – are considerably more complex. His fear
of AIDS in the early to mid eighties was such that it made him wary
of the young gay and artistic crowd with which he had once more
begun to associate after spending much of the 1970s in more
moneyed or mainstream company. It made him shun older friends
and associates who were among the first to succumb to the disease.
And shortly before his death in 1987, it made him react to the death
of an ex-lover with a cowardice, or callousness, that would be
straightforwardly shameful if we did not know so much about the
roots of his medical fears and emotional aversions.

In the published version of his diary, the first mention of the
disease appears in the entry for the 6th of February 1982: 'I went to
Jan Cowles's place at 810 Fifth Avenue where she was having a
party for her son Charlie. Gave Charlie a Dollar Sign painting and
Leo was there. Joe MacDonald was there, but I didn't want to be
near him and talk to him because he just had gay cancer. I talked to
his brother's wife.' (Joe MacDonald was a model; in June 1983,
New York magazine's cover story on 'AIDS Anxiety' began with a
description of his last photo shoot in the winter of 1982, and he
died in the spring.) Three months later, he worries that 'a boy but-
ler' has handled the food at a Park Avenue dinner party, and six
days after that reads the second *New York Times* article about the

disease: 'The *New York Times* had a big article about gay cancer, and
how they don't know what to do with it. That it's epidemic pro-
portions and they say that these kids who have sex all the time have
it in their semen and they've already had every kind of disease there
is – hepatitis one, two and three, and mononucleosis, and I'm worried that I could get it by drinking out of the same glass or just being
around these kids who go to the Baths.' Private anxiety and public
avoidance continue to alternate in the months that follow: on the
18th of September, Warhol's intermittent boyfriend Jon Gould
leaves for 'a gay cancer funeral' in Los Angeles and Andy frets:
'And I mean, I get so nervous, I don't even *do* anything and I could
get it.' The following day, in a typical shift of register from the peril
of AIDS to his own minor ailments, he notes of Robert Hayes, picture editor of his magazine *Interview*:

I'd seen Robert Hayes's boyfriend Cisco going down the street with
someone else the other day, and I saw Robert crying, and so I thought
they'd broken up, and I asked Mac Balet and he told me that Cisco had
just found out he had gay cancer but that it was a secret. But then later
that day Robert told me anyway. They told him he got it three years ago
and it takes three years for it to show up, but I don't know how they
would know that, since they don't know anything about it or even what
it is. Robert says he's been checked and he doesn't have it. But he's been
going to [Warhol's beautician] Janet Sartin and he was there at the same
time I was, and I just know she used the same needle on me, and I don't
know if she sterilizes it. I only like it when you use the needle once and
throw it away. And I'm not going to go to her anymore, anyway, because
I'm just covered with pimples, I don't know what good it's done.

When Robert Hayes was diagnosed with AIDS in 1984 – Warhol
had begun referring to the 'gay cancer' by its new name early in
1983 – he confided to his diary that he simply couldn't face calling
him: 'It's too abstract. I just can't do it. And I was never really

friends with him too much anyway.' On the 28th of June, shortly before Hayes died, Warhol's diary records: 'Brigid made me write a letter to Robert Hayes. A note. So I copied down what she wrote and she sent it off to him. He's going home to Canada to die.' When the news of his death came a month later, Warhol simply 'didn't want to think about it'.

*

In the mid 1980s, as his reputation in the art world improved and his artistic output became more novel and varied again – he had spent much of the 1970s delivering commissioned portraits to wealthy clients whose tastes often ran no further than a slightly slicker version of his 1960s silk-screen paintings – Warhol's renewed public image concealed a worsening hypochondria. He worried that he might catch something from his dogs, which slept on his bed, or from the dog shit that he trod in on the street. He began to employ a personal trainer, but became concerned every time he experienced pain while exercising. At Denton Cox's surgery, he fretted that the thermometer had been used on other patients, and was unsettled by the fact that Cox's nurse refused, at the height of AIDS anxiety, to take blood samples from new patients. On the 29th of September 1983 he dictated to the diary: 'Cabbed uptown ($5) to the chic new supermarket at Park Avenue and 18th Street, the Food Emporium, but a gay guy there made my sandwiches and so I couldn't eat them.' At the same time, he submitted to new and varied treatments for his familiar cosmetic problems. Having lost weight in order to look younger, he now had sunken cheeks – they are especially noticeable in photographs from the early part of the decade – and so began to have regular, and painful, collagen injections to flatten out his features again. He wanted to appear smoothed and integrated with himself, buffed and buffered against the world.

Among the methods Warhol canvassed to ward off illness and ageing was the increasingly modish 'crystal healing', a relic of the 1960s faith in transformative substances, and the alternative spiritualities of the 1970s, that had migrated from California to New York in recent years. In his diary entry for the 1st of August 1984, he writes:

I went to the crystal doctor [a Dr Bernsohn] and it takes fifteen minutes and the three people in the waiting room I knew, even. It cost $75 and he told me my pancreas was the only thing still giving me pimples. It was fascinating. Really fascinating. He and the secretaries wear crystals around their necks. He said his was very special because it was programmed by the head person of the crystal place.

Regular appointments followed. The next session, said Warhol, was 'like an exorcism . . . I really do believe that all this hokum-pokum helps. It's positive thinking.' During one visit, in December of the same year, he was surprised to discover the star of *Blow Job* sitting in the waiting room: 'I never did know his name. He goes to Bernsohn too.' The crystal doctor began to seem suspect: 'It's like a – what's the word? – a "scam". But then you do feel energy, so it's working. And the healing people do have such hot hands. There must be something to it.' Despite his doubts, he continued to see Bernsohn, who had by this time begun to diversify in terms of his diagnostic conjectures, and to intimate that Warhol's body had been 'walked into' by somebody else when he was young. The mechanism by which this doubling or usurping of the body took place was unclear – 'I still don't get it,' Warhol complained to the diary – but the notion that he had somehow been colonized by an alien body is wholly of a piece with his life and art.

He continued to worry about AIDS, which he had now taken, in his diary, to calling 'the magic disease', perhaps because of its still mysterious origin, or because of the frequency with which it now made members of his circle disappear from public view almost over-night. (In a sense, for Warhol, all disease was magical: it struck with no warning, while being veiled at the same time, to his mind, in

arcane knowledge, rumour and superstition of which he was privately terrified.) He still avoided acquaintances whom he knew to
have been diagnosed with the disease. On the 3rd of May 1984 he
had dinner with Jean-Michel Basquiat, the young and celebrated
painter with whom he had recently been collaborating: 'Robert
Mapplethorpe was there and something's wrong with the way he
looks now. He's either lost his looks or he's sick.' Warhol and Mapplethorpe had much in common: they had both been associated, in
the 1960s and 1970s respectively, with New York's hip, gay underground, and in many ways the photographer was heir to Warhol's
former reputation as chronicler of a modern demi-monde, especially in the way he combined sometimes scandalous subject matter
with a heightened sense of glamour and commercial visibility. They
had each made portraits of the other, and Mapplethorpe's photographs had appeared regularly in Warhol's *Interview*. But Warhol had
long been wary of the younger man, and now could not bring himself to acknowledge his visibly sickly presence. A few months before
his own death, he attended an art-world dinner and confided to his
diary: 'Bruno wanted to sit with Robert Mapplethorpe but I didn't
want to. He's sick. I sat at another place.' Mapplethorpe had been
diagnosed with full-blown AIDS the previous year; he died in 1989.

Perhaps the most instructive example of Warhol's inability to
escape from his fear and its corollaries of physical and emotional
isolation came with the illness and death of his ex-boyfriend Jon
Gould. Warhol had been introduced to Gould, a film producer at
Paramount, by Christopher Makos in the summer of 1981, and had
immediately fallen in love with the tall, handsome thirty-year-old.
Gould often claimed to be exclusively straight. While this was
untrue, he seems not to have been sexually attracted to Warhol,
and friends later said that they had never been physically intimate.
(Warhol had several such relationships with men who did not want
to sleep with him, or with whom, out of his native physical unease,
he was himself disinclined to have sex.) They nonetheless became a

couple of sorts, Warhol showering Gould with expensive presents and the younger man moving into Warhol's house on East 66th Street two years later. Gould appears to have taken knowingly cruel advantage of Warhol's adoration of him, and Andy even suspected him, during a skiing holiday, of having deliberately engineered an accident that left Warhol bruised and humiliated. Early in 1984 Gould became ill with pneumonia; Warhol instructed his house-keepers that their clothes and dishes were to be washed separately in future. Later that year Gould was diagnosed with AIDS, though he denied it even to close friends; early in 1985 he was hospitalized again for several weeks. Warhol visited him daily, but after he was discharged it became clear that their relationship had deteriorated, and Gould left for Los Angeles. Mutual friends knew that Gould sometimes returned to New York, but he did not contact Warhol, who henceforth affected to have forgotten him. When word of his death came in September 1986, Dr Bernsohn, who broke the news, recalled that his reaction was 'quite neutral'. To his diary, he simply said: 'And the Diary can write itself on the other news from LA, which I don't want to talk about.'

By the time of Gould's death, Warhol's own health had got much worse. He was plagued by pains that he persisted in attributing to obscure sources other than his gall bladder. His various therapists, trainers and healers fuelled his fantasies, telling him that he was allergic to potatoes, or to certain types of tea, and that a course of vitamins, or more strenuous exercise, was required. In late 1986 he exhibited his most recent self-portraits at the Anthony d'Offay Gallery in London; the writer Philip Hoare, who was present on the opening night, recalls being introduced to 'quite possibly the most sickly looking individual I'd seen who wasn't actually sick'.

In fact, unknown to his admirers, Warhol's condition was rapidly worsening. Early in 1987, during a trip to Milan for the opening of another exhibition, the pain, which he passed off as flu, became so bad that he could scarcely get out of bed, or even sit still on the flight back to New York. The symptoms abated on his arrival, but returned in the middle of February. Once more he sought out eccentric remedies, and instead of Denton Cox consulted his dermatologist, Karen Burke, who prescribed painkillers, and his chiropractor, whose attentions only made the pain more severe. On the 16th he was scheduled to accompany Miles Davis on the catwalk at a fashion show; photographs of the event show him emaciated and in obvious pain as he strains to perform for the crowd. The following day, Karen Burke persuaded him to see Dr Cox, who gave him the news he must already have known: his gall bladder was badly infected, and needed to be removed immediately. Warhol simply refused, telling Cox: 'I'm not afraid of death. But I will not go to the hospital. You must help me. You're the only one who can – the only one I trust. I will do anything else you say.' Cox, in exasperation, prescribed powerful antibiotics and persuaded Warhol to see a colleague, Bjorn Thorbjarnarson, whose diagnosis was the same: an infected and enlarged gall bladder, in imminent danger of rupture and requiring immediate surgery. Warhol insisted that he needed more time to decide, and returned home with his medication.

Despite his perilous condition, the operation to which Warhol was about to submit was routine and without much risk, even for a patient with a history of abdominal trauma and major surgery. The exact nature of the surgery, we must assume, was not really what troubled him; rather, as he finally gave in on the 20th of February and agreed to check in to New York Hospital, it was the accumulated burden of meaning and fear, accrued over years of anxiety in his youth and during the days after his shooting, swelled by the excessive value he placed on physical perfection, and nursed during the AIDS crisis that had devastated his intimate circle, that weighed on him now and made him frantically gather as many of his possessions as he could into the safe at his house. He was perhaps not so much convinced that he was going to die as that he would never, in the euphemistic formulation that his father had given of his predicament just over forty-five years earlier, come out of the hospital again. He had now, however, no choice in the matter, and arrived at the hospital at eleven in the morning. (The receptionist who admitted him later recalled that he was the only patient she had ever met who had known his health-insurance number by heart.) The surgery was successful: Thorbjarnarson, who carried out the operation, noted immediately that the gall bladder was gangrenous, and would soon have ruptured, leading to peritonitis and a swift death. Having removed it, he repaired Warhol's hernia, so that he would no longer have to wear the corset that held him together. In the hours that followed, the patient's vital signs were encouraging, and he chatted amiably, if weakly, with his surgeons, assuring them that he would soon be back for a facelift. Between eight and ten that evening he slept, then was woken and encouraged to attempt some breathing exercises. He briefly telephoned his housekeepers and told his nurse, Min Cho, that he was comfortable and did not require any pain medication. From two o'clock, he slept. According to Min Cho's account of the night's events, at around half past four she first noticed that he looked pale. His pulse had weakened and she called for help. The 'code team' spent an hour trying to revive him; his heartbeat flickered back to life several times before fading again, and at half past six he was pronounced dead. The precise cause of his death was heart failure, perhaps the result of a surge of adrenalin as he slept. Its origin may never be known, nor can we definitively say, in what would undoubtedly be too neat a symmetry, that he died of fear itself; but it is clear that having placed himself at the mercy of a hospital for the second time in his life, and relinquished at the last the fragile control he had hoped to have over his body, Andy Warhol died of exactly what he feared the most.

*

Warhol himself had pointed to another event as his greatest fear, this one painfully and humiliatingly realized while he was all too conscious. Fourteen months before he died, on the 30th of October

1985, he had dictated to his diary: 'Okay, let's get it over with. Wednesday. The day my biggest nightmare came true.' He had recently published a book, *America*, and been invited to sign copies at the Rizzoli bookshop in SoHo, where he was installed behind a table on the store's balcony. 'I'd been signing *America* books for an hour or so when this girl in line handed me hers to sign and then she – did what she did.' What she did was pull Warhol's silver wig from his head and throw it to a young man who was waiting below the balcony: 'I don't know what held me back from pushing her over the balcony. She was so pretty and well-dressed. I guess I called her a bitch or something and asked how she could do it.' Cameras flashed among the bystanders. The Rizzoli staff asked him if he'd like to stop, but Warhol said no: pulling the hood of his Calvin Klein coat over his head, he simply went back to signing books for the waiting crowd. He also declined to press charges against the woman.

The experience, he said, was akin to being shot again: 'It was so shocking. It hurt. Physically. And it hurt because nobody had warned me.' To Warhol, the attack was of a violence that we can only understand if we recall how essential the wig was to his sense of self. Not even Jon Gould had seen Warhol without his wig: it is still precariously in place in photographs of him being stretchered to the ambulance in 1968, and he was to wear it again on the operating table in 1987. It was the element in his public persona – more so than the sunglasses and leather jackets he wore in the 1960s or the fey laconism of his interview style – that glued him together and set him apart, that ostensibly made him look younger and more normal but at the same time amplified his freakish nature, made him seem the alien or robotic double of himself. To have that futuristic prosthesis torn from his body, to be revealed as merely a scrawny, pale and bald man of fifty-seven, was to feel himself almost literally disintegrate.

Warhol's efforts to keep himself whole and integral seem to fuse or condense certain essential strands in the history of hypochondria. Fearing illness and medicine in equal measure, he imagined that physical well-being consisted in remaining inviolate from both and thought that a healthy body was a body that was unified, self-same, wholly itself and itself alone; this was why he so admired beauties who were mostly blank. His own efforts to seem all of a piece with himself were doomed: his blankness was always offset by some graceless or uncanny detail – his pallor, his nose, his birth-marks, his tendency to look not healthily slim but skeletal – that made the whole seem sinisterly false. The hypochondriac's histori-cal mistake is to imagine a condition of bodily being that is physi-cally and psychically null or neutral, a state of simultaneous (therefore impossible) vigour and inertia. According to this fantasy, nothing happens inside the body and yet it continues to function, becoming in fact more energetic, more efficient, even as it aspires to desiccation and stasis. It does not occur to the hypochondriac that the state he or she describes is a kind of living death.

Warhol both knew and did not know this. His art attests to a keen awareness of the contradictions inherent in his dreams of health and beauty, of having a good body. In this sense, as is true of several other individuals discussed in this book, his hypochondria was an essential aspect of his art. His private life and his diary sug-gest, however, that he could not abandon the fantasy of a neutral and autonomous body, just as he could not be persuaded to treat his real disease instead of the fearful company of phantom ailments that followed him from adolescence to middle age. In the *Philosophy*, he writes that instead of dying, and being remembered, he would like to vanish completely; this, he considers, would be 'the best Ameri-can invention – to be able to disappear'.

It is this desire to be physically fully present and vital, paradoxi-cally wedded to an urge to make the body disappear, which makes Warhol's hypochondria seem so contemporary. His art was once thought to be solely about fame; it is now clear that it is also funda-mentally an exploration of what it means to have a body and to be painfully aware both of that body's frailty and of its potential for perfection. In his superstitions regarding cancer and other endemic diseases of the modern world, in his panic and denial in the face of a global epidemic, in his embrace of medical treatment for the cosmetic signs of natural human ageing, in his desire to have a good body, his squeamishness and denial in the face of the facts of illness and death, his credulousness and faddishness with respect to alternative or spiritual therapies and his passive-aggressive distrust of the medical profession, Warhol is our hypochondriac precursor. Almost every historical period has felt itself to be an era of heightened hypochondriacal anxieties: the disorder remains current, but its specific manifestations shift and alter and overlap from one century, or even one decade, to another. We live now at a time when Warhol's fears are emphatically our own – weight, complexion, age, aesthetics, the virulence of new diseases and the efficacy of the cures for the old ones – but they also ought to remind us of the fears of the seventeenth, eighteenth and nineteenth centuries. Our bodies are not alone, but trailed by the sickened and the dying, and by those who merely thought they were sick or dying, that have gone before us. Hurrying to escape them, we project ourselves into an ambiguous future; like Burton's melancholic, we hover anxiously, 'tormented hope and fear betwixt'. Our bodies, which at our most confident we imagine to be wholly our own, are doubled and shadowed, like Warhol's, by the temptation towards beauty and the certainty of decay.

Note on Sources

Three categories of books have informed my overall thinking about hypochondria: classic treatises, recent medical or cultural studies and a less easily described subset that has more oblique things to say on the subject. In the first category, Robert Burton's *The Anatomy of Melancholy* (New York: NYRB, 2001) sometimes seems as though it encompasses all subsequent studies; Burton's short section on hypochondriacal melancholy is essential, but so too is his general interest in and sympathy for psychic suffering. Jennifer Radden's *The Nature of Melancholy: From Aristotle to Kristeva* (New York: Oxford University Press, 2000) contains key texts on the adjacent disorder of hypochondria, while Stanley W. Jackson's *Melancholia and Depression: From Hippocrates to Modern Times* (New Haven: Yale University Press, 1986) is a classic account of the history of mental pain of many varieties.

A number of studies of hypochondria and related disorders have been invaluable, among them Susan Baur's *Hypochondria: Woeful Imaginings* (Berkeley: University of California Press, 1988); Carla Cantor and Brian A. Fallon's *Phantom Illness: Shattering the Myth of Hypochondria* (New York: Houghton Mifflin, 1996); Marina Van Zuylen's *Monomania: The Flight from Everyday Life in Literature and Art* (Ithaca, NY: Cornell University Press, 2005), and Darian Leader and David Corfield's *Why Do People Get Ill?* (London: Hamish Hamilton, 2007). The essays collected in Don R. Lipsitt and Vladan Starcevic (eds.), *Hypochondriasis: Modern Perspectives on an Ancient Malady* (New York: Oxford University Press, 2001) and Gordon J. G. Asmundsen, et al. (eds.), *Health Anxiety: Clinical and Research Perspectives on Hypochondriasis and Related Conditions* (Chichester: Wiley,

2001) have formed the basis for my understanding of current thinking about the subject from a clinical point of view. Tim Boon and Ian Jones's *Treat Yourself: Health Consumers in a Medical Age* (London: Science Museum & The Wellcome Trust, 2003) suggested useful connections between historical anxieties and contemporary fears.

The third category is more diffuse, and includes books that either state or imply a good deal about how we experience our bodies and how we may come to fear them. These include John Donne's 'Meditations', excerpted in *Selected Prose* (Harmondsworth: Penguin, 1987), and Michel de Montaigne's essay 'On the Power of the Imagination', in *The Complete Essays*, trans. M. A. Screech (Harmondsworth: Penguin, 1991). Roland Barthes's *The Neutral*, trans. Denis Hollier and Rosalind Kraus (New York: Columbia University Press, 2005), outlines a certain fantasy of retreat and modesty, while Georges Didi-Huberman's *Invention of Hysteria: Charcot and the Photographic Iconography of the Salpêtrière*, trans. Alisa Hartz (Cambridge, Mass.: MIT Press, 2003), recounts a crucial stage in the dramatizing of the sick body.

1. James Boswell's English Malady

A good deal of Boswell's own account of his time in Holland, and the hypochondriac crisis he experienced there, has been lost to posterity. The notes, journals and letters that remain nonetheless afford an intimate account of his breakdown; they are collected in *Boswell in Holland 1763–1764*, ed. Frederick A. Pottle (London: William Heinemann, 1952). Pottle also edited Boswell's essential *London Journal* (London: Book Club Associates, 1974), which describes his earlier attacks of the English malady.

His life and his ailments are authoritatively recounted in Peter Martin's *A Life of James Boswell* (London: Weidenfeld & Nicolson, 1999) and Allan Ingram's *Boswell's Creative Gloom* (London: Macmillan,

1982). Boswell's own *Life of Samuel Johnson* (London: J. M. Dent, 1946) treats of Johnson's hypochondria at various points, and records his advice to his young friend on the subject. The periodical essays that Boswell published in the guise of 'The Hypochondriack' were edited and introduced by Margery Bailey as *The Hypochondriack* (Stanford, Calif.: Stanford University Press, 1928).

George Cheyne's *The English Malady* was edited by Roy Porter (London: Routledge, 1991). Immanuel Kant's *The Conflict of the Faculties*, trans. Mary J. Gregor (Lincoln: University of Nebraska Press, 1979), claims a more rigorous attitude than Boswell could muster to the malaise of the eighteenth century.

2. *Charlotte Brontë: A Little Nervous Subject*

The most suggestive of Charlotte Brontë's reflections on her own hypochondria are to be found in her novels: *The Professor* (Harmondsworth: Penguin, 1989); *Villette* (Harmondsworth: Penguin, 1985); *Jane Eyre* (Harmondsworth: Penguin, 1985) and *Shirley* (Harmondsworth: Penguin, 1985).

The classic biographies of Brontë are Rebecca Fraser, *Charlotte Brontë* (London: Methuen, 1988), Winifred Gérin, *Charlotte Brontë* (Oxford: Oxford University Press, 1967) and, of course, Elizabeth Gaskell, *The Life of Charlotte Brontë* (Oxford: Oxford University Press, 2002). Her letters are collected in *The Letters of Charlotte Brontë*, ed. Margaret Smith (Oxford: Clarendon Press, 2003). The Brontë family's guide to health and medicine, from which Charlotte may have gleaned her conception of hypochondria, was Thomas John Graham's *Modern Domestic Medicine: A Popular Treatise* (London: Simpkin and Marshall, 1835).

Other relevant mid-nineteenth-century portraits of the hypochondriac appear in Benjamin Rush, *Medical Inquiries and Observations Upon the Diseases of the Mind* (Philadelphia, Penn.: Grigg and

Elliott, 1835) and Forbes Winslow, *Obscure Diseases of the Brain and Mind* (Philadelphia, Penn.: Henry C. Lea, 1866). Edgar Allan Poe's 'The Fall of the House of Usher' presents an especially acute case; see *Selected Writings* (Harmondsworth: Penguin, 1977).

3. On the Expression of Emotion: Charles Darwin

Darwin's brief autobiographical writings are collected in *Autobiographies*, ed. Michael Neve and Sharon Messenger (London: Penguin, 2002), his theory of gesture and expression in *The Expression of the Emotions in Man and Animals* (London: HarperCollins, 1998). The most extensive recent biography is that of Janet Brown, *Charles Darwin* (London: Pimlico, 2003). Several books have been devoted to Darwin's illnesses; among them, Ralph Colp, *To Be an Invalid: The Illness of Charles Darwin* (Chicago, Ill.: University of Chicago Press, 1977) and John H. Winslow, *Darwin's Victorian Malady* (Philadelphia, Penn.: American Philosophical Society, 1971). The chapter on Darwin in George Pickering's *Creative Malady* (London: George Allen & Unwin, 1974) remains a clear and sympathetic account of his sufferings.

On the water cure, James Manby Gully's *The Water-Cure in Chronic Disease* (New York: Samuel R. Wells, 1873) sets out the theory and practice at the time of Darwin's first taking the waters at Malvern. E. S. Turner's *Taking the Cure* (London: Michael Joseph, 1967) recounts the history of hydrotherapy and the spa towns, while Tim Binding's *On Ilkley Moor: The Story of an English Town* (London: Picador, 2001) includes a detailed and fascinating account of the regimen to which Darwin submitted. His life at Down House is detailed in *Charles Darwin at Down House* (London: English Heritage, 1998).

4. Florence Nightingale and the Privilege of Discontent

For Florence Nightingale's *Cassandra*, I have relied on the edition edited by Myra Stark (New York: Feminist Press, 1979). The most recent, and the most ambitious, biography of Nightingale is Mark Bostridge's *Florence Nightingale: The Woman and Her Legend* (London: Viking, 2008). Among the countless other published lives, the notable biographies are Sir Edward Cook, *The Life of Florence Nightingale* (London: Macmillan, 1925); Cecil Woodham-Smith, *Florence Nightingale: 1820–1910* (London: Constable, 1950) and Hugh Small, *Florence Nightingale: Avenging Angel* (London: Constable, 1998). The chapter on Nightingale in Lytton Strachey's *Eminent Victorians* (Harmondsworth: Penguin, 1986) is of course something more than a mere biography.

The theory of Nightingale's suffering from brucellosis was first broached authoritatively by D. A. B. Young in 'Florence Nightingale's Fever', *BMJ* 311 (23 December 1995): 1697–1700. The miasmatic Great Stink that overcame London in 1858 is described in Steven Johnson's *The Ghost Map: A Street, an Epidemic and the Two Men who Battled to Save Victorian London* (London: Allen Lane, 2006). Other perspectives on illness and withdrawal appear in Herman Melville's *Bartleby the Scrivener* (London: Hesperus, 2007), Joris-Karl Huysmans's *Against Nature*, trans. Robert Baldick (Harmondsworth: Penguin, 1959) and Virginia Woolf's *On Being Ill* (Ashfield, Mass.: Paris Press, 2002).

5. The Exaltation of Alice James

Alice James's extraordinary wit and self-possession in the face of her many ailments and eventual mortal illness are recorded in *The Death and Letters of Alice James*, ed. Ruth Bernard Yeazell (Boston, Mass.: Exact Change, 1997) and *The Diary of Alice James*, ed. Leon Edel (Boston, Mass.: Northeastern University Press, 1999). Jean Strouse's

Alice James: A Biography (Harvard, Mass.: Harvard University Press, 1980) provides a detailed context for the letters and diary.

William James's 'The Hidden Self' was first published in *Scribner's Magazine* 7: 3 (March 1890): 361–2. Charles Fayette Taylor propounded his remedy for neurasthenia in *Theory and Practice of the Movement Cure* (Philadelphia, Penn.: Lindsay & Blakiston, 1864).

6. *The Delusions of Daniel Paul Schreber*

Schreber's own account of his illness and incarceration is to be found in *Memoirs of My Nervous Illness*, trans. and ed. Ida Macalpine and Richard A. Hunter (New York: NYRB, 2000), and Freud's reading of it in *The Schreber Case*, trans. Andrew Webber (London: Penguin, 2002). Elias Canetti's *Crowds and Power*, trans. Carol Stewart (London: Victor Gollancz, 1962), essays a sociological interpretation of Schreber's delusions, a reading further elaborated in Eric L. Santner's *My Own Private Germany: Daniel Paul Schreber's Secret History of Modernity* (Princeton, NJ: Princeton University Press, 1996). Zvi Lothane examines the place of the *Memoirs* in the history of psychiatry in *In Defense of Schreber: Soul Murder and Psychiatry* (Hillsdale, NJ: Analytic Press, 1992).

Cervantes' 'The Glass Graduate' is collected in *Exemplary Stories*, trans. C. A. Jones (London: Penguin, 1972). Gill Speak provides a comprehensive history of the glass delusion in 'An Odd Kind of Melancholy: Reflections on the Glass Delusion in Europe (1440–1680)', *History of Psychiatry* 1 (1990): 191–206.

7. *Marcel Proust and Common Sense*

The most intimate account of Proust's daily life, and thus of his health, appears in Céleste Albaret's memoir, *Monsieur Proust*, trans.

Barbara Bray (New York: NYRB, 2003). Diana Fuss's *The Sense of an Interior* (London: Routledge, 2004) describes his household arrangements in fascinating detail. Walter Benjamin derives the most profound insights into Proust's fiction from those domestic circumstances in his essay 'The Image of Proust', collected in *Selected Writings, Volume 2: 1927–34*, trans. Rodney Livingstone, et al. (Harvard, Mass.: Belknap Press, 1999).

In my references to *À la recherche du temps perdu*, I have relied on *Remembrance of Things Past*, trans. C. K. Scott Moncrieff and Terence Kilmartin (Harmondsworth: Penguin, 1989), and for Proust's correspondence on *Letters*, trans. Mina Curtiss (New York: Helen Marx Books, 2006). The major biographies all have a good deal to say about Proust's illness and the uses to which he put it: Jean-Yves Tadié, *Marcel Proust: A Life*, trans. Euan Cameron (London: Penguin, 2001); Ronald Hayman, *Proust: A Biography* (London: Heinemann, 1990); George Painter, *Marcel Proust: A Biography* (Harmondsworth: Penguin, 1983); and Edmund White, *Proust* (London: Weidenfeld & Nicolson, 1999).

Mark Jackson's *Allergy: The History of a Modern Malady* (London: Reaktion, 2006) rigorously reconstructs the medical and cultural history of (among other ailments) Proust's disease, while Daniel Heller-Roazen's *The Inner Touch: Archaeology of a Sensation* (New York: Zone Books, 2007), in its investigation of the suppressed 'common sense', reveals a field of medical knowledge familiar to Proust but lost to his later readers.

8. Glenn Gould: Not of the World

Gould's *Selected Letters*, ed. John P. L. Roberts and Ghyslaine Guertin (Toronto: Oxford University Press, 1992), is a rich source for understanding his many anxieties. His eccentricities are recounted in detail in Peter F. Ostwald's *Glenn Gould: The Ecstasy and Tragedy of Genius* (New York: Norton, 1998) and Kevin Bazzana's *Wondrous Strange:*

The Life and Art of Glenn Gould (Toronto: McClelland & Stewart, 2003). Habits related to his pianos, and his search for the ideal instrument, are outlined in Katie Hofner's *A Romance on Three Legs: Glenn Gould's Obsessive Quest for the Perfect Piano* (New York: Bloomsbury, 2008). Gould discusses his quest for artistic solitude, and his retirement from the concert hall to the studio, in *Conversations with Glenn Gould*, ed. J. Cott (Chicago, Ill.: Chicago University Press, 2005) and *The Glenn Gould Reader*, ed. Tim Page (New York: Vintage, 1993). Steven Connor's essay 'Beside Himself: Glenn Gould and the Prospects of Performance' is among the most astute interpretations of his life and character: http://www.bbk.ac.uk/english/skc/gould.htm, accessed 28 November 2008.

9. *Andy Warhol's Magic Disease*

By far the most intimate, instructive and entertaining evidence for Warhol's hypochondria is to be found in *The Andy Warhol Diaries*, ed. Pat Hackett (New York: Warner Books, 1991). Among his other writings, *POPism: The Warhol Sixties* (London: Penguin, 2007) and *The Philosophy of Andy Warhol: (From A to B and Back Again)* (London: Penguin, 2007) are also rich sources of biographical detail and for Warhol's telling reinventions.

A number of biographies allow us to tell image from reality in his life; in order of their merit they are: Victor Bockris, *The Life and Death of Andy Warhol* (London: Fourth Estate, 1998); Wayne Koestenbaum, *Andy Warhol* (London: Weidenfeld & Nicolson, 2001); Fred Lawrence Guiles, *Loner at the Ball: The Life of Andy Warhol* (London: Bantam Press, 1989); and Paul Alexander, *Death and Disaster: The Rise of the Warhol Empire and the Race for Andy's Millions* (London: Warner Books, 1996).

Among the numerous studies of Warhol's art and milieu, the most useful for my purposes have been David Bourdon, *Warhol*

(New York: Abrams, 1989); Callie Angell, *Andy Warhol Screen Tests* (New York: Abrams, 2006); Roy Grundmann, *Andy Warhol's 'Blow Job'* (Philadelphia, Penn.: Temple University Press, 2003); and the catalogue of the 2008–9 Warhol exhibition at the Hayward Gallery, London: Eva Meyer-Hermann, *Andy Warhol: A Guide to 706 Items in 2 Hours 56 Minutes* (Rotterdam: NAi Publishers, 2008).

Acknowledgements

My editors, Brendan Barrington at Penguin Ireland and Eric Chinski at Farrar, Straus and Giroux, guided the book into being with diligence and flair. Thanks too to their colleagues in Dublin, London and New York.

Thanks to my agent, Peter Straus, and to Melanie Jackson.

Michael Bracewell's enthusiasm for the project, and his constant encouragement, have been invaluable. Tony McGuinness solved an initial problem of conception and structure at a single, imaginative stroke. Toby Litt alerted me to a grievous omission; I hope I have done his suggestion justice. Marina Van Zuylen read the early chapters with all the care and enthusiasm she brings to her own scholarship.

Parts of this book have been tested in essays, reviews and lectures written or delivered during its composition. I would like to thank *Cabinet* magazine and the Slought Foundation, organizers of a symposium on 'Sloth' at the Cooper Union, New York, in December 2007. *Cabinet* also published my thoughts on the history of hypochondria and on the Victorian craze for hydrotherapy; thanks to all the editors who worked on those essays. Thanks also to Elena Filipovic and Adam Szymczyk, the curators of the Berlin Biennial 2008, for including my 'Notes on Hypochondria' in their extraordinary catalogue. The editors of the *London Review of Books*, Caroline Walsh at the *Irish Times* and Sam Leith of the *Daily Telegraph* cheerfully kept me supplied with new volumes about sickness, pain, depression and death.

Numerous friends and colleagues have contributed to the content and form of the book, among them Tom Boncza-Tomaszewski, Julia

Borossa, Steven Connor, Marie Darrieussecq, Rod Edmond, David Ellis, Rosalind Furness, Maria Fusco, Martin Herbert, David Herd, Philip Hoare, Lorraine McColgan, Robert Macfarlane, Jeremy Millar, Sina Najafi, Caroline Rooney, Colm Tóibín, Elizabeth Wainwright, Victoria Walsh, Sarah Wood.

Any errors of fact, thought or style that remain are my own.

As ever, Felicity Dunworth sustained the book, and its author, through various crises and remissions – it could not have been written without her love and support.